Oracle SOA Suite 11*g* Developer's Cookbook

Over 65 high-level recipes for extending your Oracle SOA applications and enhancing your skills with expert tips and tricks for developers

Antony Reynolds

Matt Wright

BIRMINGHAM - MUMBAI

Oracle SOA Suite 11g Developer's Cookbook

First published: December 2012

Production Reference: 1191212

Published by Packt Publishing Ltd.
Livery Place
35 Livery Street
Birmingham B3 2PB, UK.

ISBN 978-1-84968-388-3

www.packtpub.com

Cover Image by Artie Ng (artherng@yahoo.com.au)

Credits

Authors

Antony Reynolds

Matt Wright

Contributors

James Goddard

Adrian Lewis

Brett Lomas

ShuXuan Nie

Geoff Trench

Reviewers

Edwin Biemond

Phil McLaughlin

Acquisition Editor

Stephanie Moss

Lead Technical Editor

Susmita Panda

Technical Editors

Veronica Fernandes

Worrell Lewis

Copy Editors

Insiya Morbiwala

Brandt D'Mello

Alfida Paiva

Project Coordinator

Leena Purkait

Proofreader

Linda Morris

Indexer

Hemangini Bari

Graphics

Aditi Gajjar

Production Coordinator

Nilesh R. Mohite

Cover Work

Nilesh R. Mohite

About the Authors

Antony Reynolds has worked in the IT industry for more than 25 years, first getting a job to maintain yield calculations for a zinc smelter while still an undergraduate. After graduating from the University of Bristol with a degree in Mathematics and Computer Science, he worked first for a software house, IPL in Bath, England, before joining the travel reservations system Galileo as a development team lead. Galileo gave him the opportunity to work in Colorado and Illinois where he developed a love for the Rockies and Chicago style deep pan pizza.

Since joining Oracle in 1998, he has worked in sales consulting and support. He currently works as a Sales Consultant helping customers across North America realize the benefits of standards based integration and SOA. While at Oracle he has co-authored *Oracle SOA Suite Developer's Guide, Packt Publishing* and *Oracle SOA Suite 11g R1 Developer's Guide, Packt Publishing*.

Antony lives in Colorado with his wife and four children who make sure that he is gainfully employed playing games, watching movies, and acting as an auxiliary taxi service. He is a slow but steady runner and can often be seen jogging up and down the trails in the shadow of the Rocky Mountains.

I would like to thank my wife Rowan, and my four very patient children, who have put up with my staying at home on family trips and working late nights in my basement office as I completed this book. My managers Ed Lee and Troy Hewitt were very supportive and many of my colleagues contributed knowingly or unknowingly to the recipes.

I am appreciative of Michael Weingartner and his team for their continued enhancement and development of the SOA Suite which has enabled Matt and myself to write this book. The reviewers provided valuable guidance and corrections and any errors still remaining are entirely mine. Finally, the team at Packt Publishing constantly nagged and cajoled Matt and myself to keep some sort of schedule. Without them this book would still be on the drawing board.

Matt Wright is a director at Rubicon Red, an independent consulting firm helping customers enable enterprise agility and operational excellence through the adoption of technologies such as Service-Oriented Architecture (SOA), Business Process Management (BPM), and Cloud Computing.

With over 20 years of experience in building enterprise scale distributed systems, Matt first became involved with SOA shortly after the initial submission of SOAP 1.1 to the W3C in 2000, and has worked with some of the early adopters of BPEL since its initial release in 2002. Since then, he has been engaged in some of the earliest SOA-based implementations across EMEA and APAC.

Prior to Rubicon Red, he held various senior roles within Oracle, most recently as Director of Product Management for Oracle Fusion Middleware in APAC, where he was responsible for working with organizations to educate and enable them in realizing the full business benefits of SOA in solving complex business problems.

As a recognized authority on SOA, he is a regular speaker and instructor at private and public events. He also enjoys writing and publishes his own blog (`http://blogs.bpel-people.com`). He holds a B.Sc. (Eng) in Computer Science from Imperial College, University of London.

He has worked on *Oracle SOA Suite Developer's Guide, Packt Publishing* and *Oracle SOA Suite 11g R1 Developer's Guide, Packt Publishing*.

I would like to express my deep appreciation to everyone who has reviewed this book. Their invaluable feedback and advice not only helped to validate the overall accuracy of the content, but more importantly ensure its clarity and readability.

A book like this doesn't make it into print without a lot of work from the publisher. I would like to thank the team at Packt Publishing for all their support; especially Stephanie Moss, Leena Purkait, and Susmita Panda.

A special mention must go to John Deeb for his continual encouragement, input, and above all support in ensuring that I found time to write the book; I couldn't ask for a more supportive friend and business partner.

Finally, I would like to say a very, very special thank you to my wife Natasha and my children Elliot and Kimberley, who have been incredibly patient and supportive in allowing me to spend far too many evenings and weekends stuck away in my office writing this book.

Contributors

The creation of the content for this book has been very much a team effort, with many contributions from the great team at Rubicon Red. In particular I would like to thank James Goddard, Adrian Lewis, Brett Lomas, ShuXuan Nie, and Geoff Trench, each one of whom contributed ideas and recipes to the book.

James Goddard is a software developer with 10 years of experience in IT, initially within the telecommunication and utility industries in Melbourne, Australia. He specialised in system integration design and development using Oracle Middleware before joining Rubicon Red as a Consulting Architect in 2010. As a member of an energetic and innovative team of Oracle experts, James was able to advise and contribute to SOA initiatives at a variety of organisations around Australia.

He currently holds a position within Amazon Kindle, building highly scalable web services for Amazon's digital product offerings in Seattle, WA.

Adrian Lewis is an SOA & Integration Solution Architect for Rubicon Red in Australia. He is currently responsible for delivering a BPM and SOA solution for a Victorian state government office using an implementation of Rubicon Red's FMW reference architecture. Adrian spent the previous 5 years working as a Principal Consultant for Red Rock, delivering SOA, Human Workflow, and integration solutions in Victoria and Queensland. Adrian holds a BEng(Hons) in Cybernetics and Control Engineering from the University of Reading in England.

Brett Lomas has been working in the IT industry for over 10 years in an ever varying capacity. He is known for his passion for IT and how it can transform businesses when used effectively. In his spare time he likes to use his pilot's license to explore Australia.

Brett has recently worked for Oracle in the capacity of a Solution Architect , helping partners gain the most value out of Oracle's Middleware stack. Most recently Brett is employed as an SOA and BPM practitioner for Rubicon Red working with key customers throughout Australia and New Zealand.

ShuXuan Nie has more than 10 years of experience in the IT industry that includes SOA technologies such as BPEL, ESB, SOAP, XML, and Enterprise Java technologies, Eclipse plug-ins, and other areas such as C++ cross-platform development.

Since 2010, she has been working in Rubicon Red and helping customers resolve integration issues. Prior to Rubicon Red, she has worked for Oracle Global Customer Support team, IBM China Software Development Lab, and the Australia Bureau of Meteorology Research Center where she was responsible for the implementation of an Automated Thunderstorm Interactive Forecast System for Aviation and Defence. ShuXuan holds an MS in Computer Science from Beijing University of Aeronautics and Astronautics.

Geoff Trench has been playing with computers since the days of the Atari 800XL, and working with them professionally for over 15 years, building solutions for a wide range of industries with too many languages and tools to count.

About the Reviewer

Edwin Biemond is an Oracle ACE and Solution Architect at Amis, specializing in messaging with Oracle SOA Suite and Oracle Service Bus, and an expert in ADF development, WebLogic, High Availability and Security. His Oracle career began in 1997 where he was developing an ERP, CRM system with Oracle tools. Since 2001 he changed his focus to integration, security, and Java development. He was awarded with the Java Developer of the year 2009 by Oracle Magazine. In 2010, he won the EMEA Oracle Partner Community Award. He is the co-author of the *Oracle Service Bus 11g Development Cookbook, Packt Publishing,* has contributed to the *Oracle SOA Handbook, Packt Publishing,* is an international speaker at Oracle OpenWorld & ODTUG, and has a popular blog called *Java / Oracle SOA blog* (http://biemond.blogspot.com).

www.PacktPub.com

Support files, eBooks, discount offers and more

You might want to visit www.PacktPub.com for support files and downloads related to your book.

Did you know that Packt offers eBook versions of every book published, with PDF and ePub files available? You can upgrade to the eBook version at www.PacktPub.com and as a print book customer, you are entitled to a discount on the eBook copy. Get in touch with us at service@packtpub.com for more details.

At www.PacktPub.com, you can also read a collection of free technical articles, sign up for a range of free newsletters and receive exclusive discounts and offers on Packt books and eBooks.

http://PacktLib.PacktPub.com

Do you need instant solutions to your IT questions? PacktLib is Packt's online digital book library. Here, you can access, read and search across Packt's entire library of books.

Why Subscribe?

- ▶ Fully searchable across every book published by Packt
- ▶ Copy and paste, print and bookmark content
- ▶ On demand and accessible via web browser

Free Access for Packt account holders

If you have an account with Packt at www.PacktPub.com, you can use this to access PacktLib today and view nine entirely free books. Simply use your login credentials for immediate access.

Instant Updates on New Packt Books

Get notified! Find out when new books are published by following @PacktEnterprise on Twitter, or the *Packt Enterprise* Facebook page.

Table of Contents

Preface

Service Oriented Architecture (**SOA**) provides the architectural framework needed to integrate diverse systems together and create new composite applications. Oracle SOA Suite 11gR1 provides the tools needed to turn an SOA architecture into a working solution. SOA Suite provides the developer with several high level components such as:

- **Oracle Service Bus** (**OSB**), an enterprise strength service bus for full support of service bus patterns including validation, enrichment, transformation, and routing (the VETRO pattern)
- **Service Component Architecture** (**SCA**) that hosts a number of components
- **Business Activity Monitoring** (**BAM**) that provides real-time reporting on SOA Suite activities

SCA components include:

- Mediator for light weight transformation and routing
- Rules for abstraction of business rules
- BPEL for orchestrating long running or complex integrations
- **Human workflow** (**HWF**) for allowing human interaction with long running processes
- Spring for integrating Java Spring components

This book looks at many common problems that are encountered when integrating systems and provides solutions to them in the form of more than 67 cookbook recipes. The solutions explain the problem to be solved alongside clear step by step instructions to implement a solution using SOA Suite components. Each recipe also includes a discussion of how it works and what additional problems may be tackled by the solution presented.

What this book covers

Chapter 1, Building an SOA Suite Cluster, explains how to prepare the environment to follow Oracle's Enterprise Deployment Guide. The Enterprise Deployment Guide is Oracle's blueprint for building a highly available SOA Suite cluster. The chapter includes key questions to ask the network storage team, the networking team, and the Database Administrators before the actual SOA Suite installation and deployment begins.

Chapter 2, Using the Metadata Service to Share XML Artifacts, explains how we can use MDS to share XML artifacts, such as XML schemas, WSDL's fault policies, XSLT Transformations, EDLs for event EDN event definitions and Schematrons between multiple composites.

Chapter 3, Working with Transactions, looks at the different ways to use transactions within SOA Suite. This includes enrolling a BPEL process in an existing transaction, forcibly committing or aborting a transaction within BPEL and catching faults that have caused the transaction to be rolled back. It also covers how to apply reversing transactions when a system does not support transaction functionality in its public interface.

Chapter 4, Mapping Data, covers how to copy and transform data using the SCA container. It includes how to deal with missing XML elements and how to control the mapping of Java objects to XML including dealing with abstract Java classes. It also covers how to process arrays of data in both BPEL and XML stylesheet transforms (XSLT).

Chapter 5, Composite Messaging Patterns, explores some of the more complex but relatively common message interaction patterns used in a typical SOA deployment. It includes recipes for implementing patterns around message aggregation, singletons, and the dynamic scheduling of BPEL processes and services.

Chapter 6, OSB Messaging Patterns, explores some common message processing design patterns for delegation of execution to downstream services and provides recipes for implementing them using Oracle Service Bus. It includes recipes for dynamic binding to services, splitting out messages, as well as dynamic Split-Joins.

Chapter 7, Integrating OSB with JSON, covers how we can use the Service Bus to integrate with RESTful web services that exchange data using JavaScript Object Notation (JSON) instead of XML. It also looks at how to expose OSB Services as RESTful JSON web services.

Chapter 8, Compressed File Adapter Patterns, explains how to use the file/FTP adapter to compress/uncompress the contents of exchanged files. This is particularly common in Business-to-Business scenarios, where network bandwidth is more of a constraint.

Chapter 9, Integrating Java with SOA Suite, explains different ways to integrate Java code into SOA Suite. This is demonstrated through creating a custom XPath function for use in SCA and OSB, as well as re-using EJBs and Spring Beans in SOA Suite. It also shows how to access the SOA runtime environment from within a BPEL process.

Chapter 10, Securing Composites and Calling Secure Web Services, shows the developer how to restrict access to a composite by applying a security policy, as well as showing how to create a new security policy. It also explains how to make a call to a security protected service and how to manage security stores.

Chapter 11, Configuring the Identity Service, details how to configure the Oracle Platform Security Services (OPSS) to use various LDAP providers for authentication and authorization within the Oracle SOA Suite. It covers configuration for Active Directory, Oracle Internet Directory, Sun iPlanet, and Oracle Virtual Directory.

Chapter 12, Configuring OSB to use Foreign JMS Queues, covers how to configure the Service Bus to read/write messages from various JMS providers, including OC4J, JBoss, and across WebLogic domains.

Chapter 13, Monitoring and Management, includes recipes to monitor the completion status of SOA composites through the EM dashboard, measuring their message throughput in real time. It also covers setting up the SOA environment to use the SOA Suite provided Monitor Express reports to take advantage of pre-built BAM dashboards.

What you need for this book

This book was written using Oracle SOA Suite 11.1.1.6 and Oracle JDeveloper 11.1.1.6 with the SOA Suite design extensions. The contents are relevant for all SOA Suite 11gR1 releases, although some features may not be available in revisions before 11.1.1.6 and some screenshots may vary between revisions.

Who this book is for

This book will benefit SOA Suite developers, designers, and architects who want to get the most value out of their SOA Suite investments.

Conventions

In this book, you will find a number of styles of text that distinguish between different kinds of information. Here are some examples of these styles, and an explanation of their meaning.

Code words in text are shown as follows: "Run the `leasing.ddl` script as the leasing user."

A block of code is set as follows:

```
Operation getTotalPrice( book_list ):
  totalPrice := 0
  for each order in book_list
  loop
    total_price := total_price +
```

```
       Book.priceCheck(order.isbn ) * order.qty
end loop
return total_price
```

When we wish to draw your attention to a particular part of a code block, the relevant lines or items are set in bold:

```
Operation getTotalPrice( book_list ):
  totalPrice := 0
  for each order in book_list
  loop
    total_price := total_price +
      Book.priceCheck(order.isbn ) * order.qty
  end loop
  return total_price
```

New terms and **important words** are shown in bold. Words that you see on the screen, in menus or dialog boxes for example, appear in the text like this: "Open your proxy service and select the **Message Flow** tab."

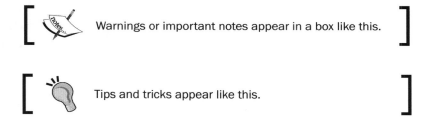

Warnings or important notes appear in a box like this.

Tips and tricks appear like this.

Reader feedback

Feedback from our readers is always welcome. Let us know what you think about this book— what you liked or may have disliked. Reader feedback is important for us to develop titles that you really get the most out of.

To send us general feedback, simply send an e-mail to feedback@packtpub.com, and mention the book title via the subject of your message.

If there is a topic that you have expertise in and you are interested in either writing or contributing to a book, see our author guide on www.packtpub.com/authors.

Customer support

Now that you are the proud owner of a Packt book, we have a number of things to help you to get the most from your purchase.

Downloading the example code

You can download the example code files for all Packt books you have purchased from your account at `http://www.PacktPub.com`. If you purchased this book elsewhere, you can visit `http://www.PacktPub.com/support` and register to have the files e-mailed directly to you.

Errata

Although we have taken every care to ensure the accuracy of our content, mistakes do happen. If you find a mistake in one of our books—maybe a mistake in the text or the code—we would be grateful if you would report this to us. By doing so, you can save other readers from frustration and help us improve subsequent versions of this book. If you find any errata, please report them by visiting `http://www.packtpub.com/support`, selecting your book, clicking on the **errata submission form** link, and entering the details of your errata. Once your errata are verified, your submission will be accepted and the errata will be uploaded on our website, or added to any list of existing errata, under the Errata section of that title. Any existing errata can be viewed by selecting your title from `http://www.packtpub.com/support`.

Piracy

Piracy of copyright material on the Internet is an ongoing problem across all media. At Packt, we take the protection of our copyright and licenses very seriously. If you come across any illegal copies of our works, in any form, on the Internet, please provide us with the location address or website name immediately so that we can pursue a remedy.

Please contact us at `copyright@packtpub.com` with a link to the suspected pirated material.

We appreciate your help in protecting our authors, and our ability to bring you valuable content.

Questions

You can contact us at `questions@packtpub.com` if you are having a problem with any aspect of the book, and we will do our best to address it.

1
Building an SOA Suite Cluster

In this chapter, we will cover recipes to simplify the configuration of an SOA Suite cluster:

- ▸ Gathering configuration information
- ▸ Preparing the operating system
- ▸ Preparing the database
- ▸ Preparing the network

Introduction

An SOA Suite cluster can process more composite instances by spreading the load across multiple machines, providing greater capacity. It also provides resiliency by allowing composites to continue to execute on remaining machines in the cluster in the event of a machine failing.

Using a cluster provides the following benefits:

- ▸ Greater capacity
- ▸ Greater resiliency

Oracle provides a comprehensive guide to creating an SOA Suite cluster called the **Enterprise Deployment Guide** (**EDG**). Rather than duplicating the guide, this chapter will provide recipes that enhance the guide and elaborate on the steps required.

Terms used

SOA Suite is normally deployed on a WebLogic application server and in this chapter we will use WebLogic nomenclature to describe SOA Suite entities:

- **Machine:** A physical computer that hosts SOA Suite components
- **Server:** A WebLogic instance executing in a Java Virtual Machine
- **Admin server:** A WebLogic server that is used to manage the cluster
- **Managed server:** A WebLogic server that is dedicated to running applications such as SOA Suite

Target solution

The following figure shows the target SOA Suite deployment architecture for a three-machine SOA Suite cluster:

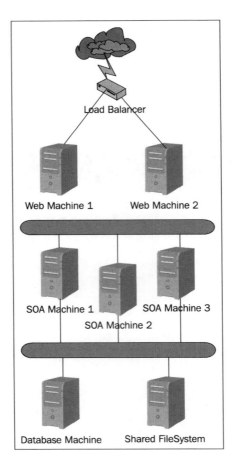

At the heart of the cluster are three physical machines running SOA Suite. They make use of a highly available database and a shared filesystem. HTTP access to the machines is provided through two web server machines which run HTTP servers. Finally, a load balancer is used to distribute the load across the web servers. See the *Preparing the network* recipe for more details on the load balancer.

This architecture may be scaled by adding additional SOA machines. For most environments, the two web servers are only required for resilience. They can generally handle all but the highest client loads. Each web server machine will distribute requests to all machines in the SOA Suite cluster; there is no affinity between a particular HTTP machine and a particular SOA machine.

Note that each set of machines forms a layer that may be separated by using firewalls to improve security. If this is not required then the web servers may run on the SOA machines, removing the need for the web machines.

The database is required by SOA Suite to store composite instance state and configuration information. The shared filesystem is required by WebLogic to store shared configuration files, transaction logs, and queues. A highly available database, such as **Oracle Real Application Clusters (RAC)**, is recommended.

Cluster details

An SOA Suite cluster is typically made up of several WebLogic clusters; a Web Services Manager cluster, an SOA cluster, and a BAM cluster. These clusters may share hardware, as shown in the following figure:

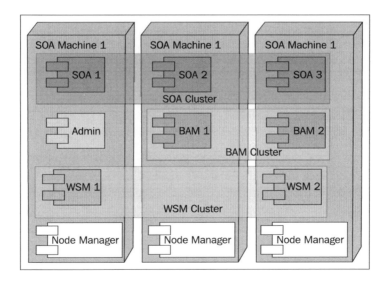

An SOA Suite Cluster contains not just the core SOA Suite functionality of BPEL, Mediator, Rules, and Human Workflow but also Web Services Manager and BAM. The Web Services Manager and BAM have their own WebLogic clusters which run alongside the core SOA cluster. Hence, the SOA Suite cluster has within it three WebLogic clusters, one of which, the SOA cluster, has the core SOA Suite functionality.

In our three-machine cluster we have chosen to have an SOA Cluster with three managed servers, a BAM cluster with two managed servers, and a WSM cluster with two managed servers. We can adjust the number of managed servers in a cluster to accommodate different numbers of physical machines. Note that in our example each machine hosts at least two servers, but the machines may host more or fewer servers depending on their capacity (CPU, memory, and network).

The Node Manager is responsible for monitoring the state of the managed servers and restarting them in the event of failure, either on the original machine if possible, or in the event of machine failure on another machine in the cluster.

Gathering configuration information

Before starting to build an SOA Suite cluster it is important to ensure that you have all the required configuration information and the environment is prepared correctly. Time spent doing this properly will save a lot of heartache and delay later.

Getting ready

Make sure you know how big a cluster you wish to build in terms of number of managed servers.

How to do it...

1. Create a drawing of the topology.

   Before starting, make sure you understand the topology of the cluster you wish to build and draw a picture of it either on a whiteboard or using a drawing tool such as Visio.

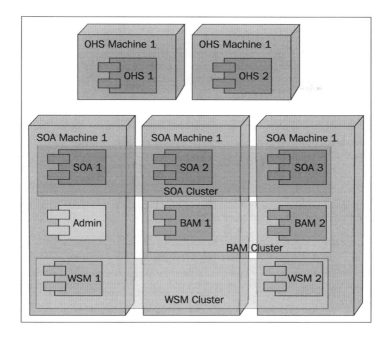

2. Identify physical machines for web servers.

   Get the names of the physical servers that will be running the web servers and fill them in on a list similar to the one shown as follows. Also identify the port number that the web server will be running on and the protocol that it will be using.

Web server machine	Web server port number	Protocol
WebMachine1	7777	HTTP
WebMachine2	7777	HTTP

3. Identify physical machines for WebLogic servers.

   Get the names of the physical servers that will be running SOA Suite and fill them in on a worksheet similar to the one shown as follows. Use the WebLogic Servers column to identify which servers will normally run on the physical machine, ignore fail over for now.

WebLogic server machine	WebLogic servers
SOAMachine1	Admin server WLS_SOA1 WLS_WSM1
SOAMachine2	WLS_SOA2 WLS_BAM1
SOAMachine3	WLS_SOA3 WLS_WSM2 WLS_BAM2

4. Identify port numbers for WebLogic servers.

   Create a table identifying the port number to be used for each type of server in your cluster similar to the one as follows:

Server type	Port number
Admin server	7001
WSM server	7010
SOA server	8001
BAM server	9001

   The previous table shows the suggested values from the EDG.

5. Identify floating IP addresses for WebLogic servers.

   Create a table identifying the virtual, or floating, IP addresses to be used for each server that requires whole server migration similar to the one shown as follows:

WebLogic server	Virtual hostname	Virtual/Floating IP
Admin server	AdminServerVHN	10.1.1.30
WLS_SOA1	SOA1VHN	10.1.1.31
WLS_SOA2	SOA2VHN	10.1.1.32
WLS_SOA3	SOA3VHN	10.1.1.33
WLS_BAM1	SOA1VHN	10.1.1.40

How it works...

The topology drawing and the list of physical machines for WebLogic and web servers will help the team provisioning the hardware to understand what physical or virtual machines must be provided and how they are connected.

The list of web server machine names, WebLogic server machine names, and port numbers can be provided to the network team who will use it in conjunction with the topology diagram to configure the firewall. They will also use it to create server pools in the load balancer for each protocol type and then add the web servers to the newly created pools.

The list of WebLogic server floating IP addresses can be used by the network team to allocate suitable IP addresses and, when coupled with the port numbers for WebLogic servers can be used to identify ports that must be opened in any firewalls between the web servers, and the WebLogic servers.

When running the domain wizard, the names of the managed servers and their associated floating IP addresses and port numbers will be required.

The Admin server is treated differently from managed servers because the Admin server does not share its shared filesystem with other WebLogic instances. A failover script can be used to unmount and mount shared storage for the Admin server as part of the failover task.

There's more...

If the web servers will be running multiple protocols then you can use multiple lines for a single web server machine.

Web server machine	Web server port number	Protocol
WebMachine1	7777	HTTP
WebMachine1	4443	HTTPS
WebMachine2	7777	HTTP
WebMachine2	4443	HTTPS

Downloading the example code

You can download the example code files for all Packt books you have purchased from your account at http://www. packtpub. com. If you purchased this book elsewhere, you can visit http:// www.packtpub.com/support and register to have the files e-mailed directly to you. The code package for the book includes an Excel workbook SOA-Cookbook-Cluster-Workbook.xls with worksheets containing templates for the tables used in this recipe.

See also

▶   The *Preparing the network* recipe in this chapter

Preparing the operating system

This recipe will identify the steps required to prepare the operating system for installation and configuration of an SOA Suite cluster. This recipe uses Linux as the operating system, the actual commands required vary between operating systems. These steps are required because SOA Suite high availability makes use of whole server migration.

Getting ready

Certain tasks mentioned in this recipe must be performed by a system administrator. As the installer of the SOA Suite does not necessarily have system administrator privileges for the operating system, it is a good idea to get all the tasks that require administrator privileges completed before starting the installation and configuration of the SOA Suite.

How to do it...

1. Grant sudo privileges to the Oracle user.

   As root on each machine that will be hosting WebLogic servers, run the `visudo` command and add the following lines to the end of the file:

   ```
   # Node Manager Grants
   oracle ALL=NOPASSWD: /sbin/ifconfig,/sbin/arping
   ```

   `oracle` should be replaced with the user you will be running SOA Suite under.

2. Set up a shared mount point for use by the domain.

3. Write a file to the mount point from each machine and ensure that the files are readable and writable from all the other machines.

4. Set up a shared mount point for use by the Admin server.

5. Write a file to the Admin server mount point from each machine that will run the Admin server and ensure that the files are readable and writable from all the other machines that can run the Admin server.

6. Capture the mount points that will be used by the Admin server and by all other managed servers in a worksheet similar to the one as shown next:

Servers	Mount point
Admin server	`/share/aserver`
Managed servers	`/share/cluster`

How it works...

The granting of sudo privileges is used to allow the non-root user executing the WebLogic NodeManager to execute a limited subset of commands. These commands are used by the node manager to assign and register the virtual IP addresses used by the SOA managed servers and the BAM server. These commands are also used to unregister and release the virtual IP addresses.

Floating or virtual IP addresses are used by the SOA, Admin, and BAM servers to allow these servers to have the same IP address when they migrate from one machine to another.

When we run the configuration wizard to create our cluster, we will need to have a shared file location in which to create the domain. The Admin server shared file location is used to hold the domain configuration for the Admin server. The domain wide shared mount point is used to hold managed server domain directories as well as configuration plans. The EDG currently recommends using a shared filesystem for both server transaction logs (TLogs) and for JMS Queue storage. When migrating an Admin server, the shared storage for the Admin Server can be unmounted from the original machine and mounted on the new machine hosting the Admin server.

The shared filesystem may use a number of technologies, including SMB, NFS, NAS, and SAN technologies. The key is that the filesystem supports shared access.

There's more...

It is possible to place the SOA Suite software onto shared storage. When doing this, Oracle recommends having at least two copies of the installed software to make it easier to patch and to reduce the risk of corruption.

Shared software installations

Certain shared storage configurations can cause very slow startup when the software is placed in shared storage because the classloader reads just a small amount from the disk for each class loaded. When the software disk is shared, it may not be able to cache reads and so classloading can introduce a lot of latency into the startup process. This can more than double the startup time for WebLogic servers. Once started and in the *RUNNING* state then they will not suffer a performance impact from having shared software storage.

Instead of using shared storage for TLogs and Queue stores, it is possible to place these in the database. This imposes a small performance overhead but simplifies fail over to a DR site because all the transaction logs and queues are replicated as part of the database replication to the DR site.

See also

▶ The Enterprise Deployment Guide, *Chapter 14, Configuring Server Migration for an Enterprise Deployment, Section 14.6, Setting Environment and Superuser Privileges for the wlsifconfig.sh script* (http://docs.oracle.com/cd/E23943_01/ core.1111/e12036/server_migration.htm)

▶ The Enterprise Deployment Guide, *Chapter 4, Preparing the File System for an Enterprise Deployment , Section 4.3, About Recommended Locations for the Different Directorie*s (http://docs.oracle.com/cd/E23943_01/core.1111/ e12036/file_sys.htm)

Preparing the database

An SOA Suite cluster requires specific configuration which is covered in this section.

Getting ready

The database preparation requires SYSDBA privileges. As the installer of the SOA Suite does not necessarily have SYSDBA privileges for the database, it is wise to get all the tasks that require SYSDBA privileges completed before starting the installation and configuration of the SOA Suite.

How to do it...

1. Check the character set requirements.

   Have DBA verify that the database character set is AL32UTF8.

   ```
   SQL> select value from nls_database_parameters where
        PARAMETER='NLS_CHARACTERSET';
   ```

   If it is not AL32UTF8 then the DBA needs to change the character set (easy if the current character set is a strict subset of AL32UTF8, hard if it is not) or create a new database with the correct character set.

2. Check process requirements are satisfied.

   Have the DBA verify that there are sufficient processes, at least 300 for SOA and 400 if using BAM with SOA.

   ```
   SQL> show parameter PROCESSES
   ```

   If necessary, increase the number of processes and restart the database.

   ```
   SQL> Alter system set PROCESSES=400 scope=spfile;
   ```

   If the database is an RAC database, have the DBA create database services for the SOA components. Additional services can be created for WSM and BAM if desired.

3. Create database services for SOA and WSM.

   ```
   SQL> execute DBMS_SERVICE.CREATE_SERVICE(SERVICE_NAME =>
        'soacluster.cookbook', NETWORK_NAME =>
        'soacluster.cookbook');
   ```

   Where 'soacluster.cookbook' is the name of the service you want to create.

4. Register the service with database instances in the RAC cluster.

   ```
   > srvctl add service -d orcl -s soacluster -r orcl1,orcl2
   ```

   Where `orcl` is your database name and `orcl1` and `orcl2` are instances in your RAC cluster.

5. Start the service.

   ```
   > srvctl start service -d orcl -s soacluster
   ```

6. Create the SOA repository.

   Have the DBA run the **Repository Creation Utility** (**RCU**), it requires SYSDBA privileges. After completion, verify that you can connect to the `<prefix>_soainfra` schema.

   ```
   SQL> connect dev_soainfra/welcome1
   ```

7. Configure SOA schema for transaction manager recovery.

   With SYSDBA privileges, grant visibility on pending transactions to the `soainfra` schema:

   ```
   SQL> grant select on sys.dba_pending_transactions to
     dev_soainfra;
   ```

8. Grant ability to commit or rollback in doubt transactions to `soainfra` schema:

   ```
   SQL> grant force any transaction to dev_soainfra;
   ```

9. With SYSDBA privileges, create a leasing tablespace:

   ```
   SQL> create tablespace leasing logging datafile
     '/home/oracle/app/oracle/oradata/orcl/leasing.dbf' size
     32m autoextend on next 32m maxsize 2048m extent management
   local;
   ```

   Where `/home/oracle/app/oracle/oradata/orcl` is the location of the database data files (`<ORACLE_BASE>/oradata/<DB_NAME>`).

10. Create a leasing user with privileges to create tables and connect to the database:

    ```
    SQL> grant create table, create session to leasing
      identified by welcome1;
    ```

    Where `welcome1` is a password of your choosing.

11. Set the leasing user to use the leasing tablespace and allow him/her unlimited size in the tablespace:

```
SQL> alter user leasing default tablespace leasing;
SQL> alter user leasing quota unlimited on leasing;
```

12. Get a copy of the `leasing.ddl` script found in "`<WL_HOME>/server/db/oracle/920`" where `<WL_HOME>` is the location of the WebLogic server directory. This may have to wait until you have installed the WebLogic server software.

13. Run the `leasing.ddl` script as the leasing user:

```
SQL> connect leasing/welcome1
SQL> @leasing.ddl
```

This assumes that you are running SQL*Plus from the directory where `leasing.ddl` is located. Note that if you get errors about unknown commands and an error about table or view does not exist, these can be safely ignored.

```
SQL> @leasing.ddl
SP2-0734: unknown command beginning "WebLogic S..." -
  rest of line ignored.
SP2-0734: unknown command beginning "Copyright ..." -
  rest of line ignored.
DROP TABLE ACTIVE
            *
ERROR at line 1:
ORA-00942: table or view does not exist
```

How it works...

Setting the database to `AL32UTF` character set is important if you will be processing non-Latin characters through the SOA Suite. Failure to set this character set can result in mis-representation of non-Latin character sets such as Chinese, Arabic, and Korean.

The leasing table is used by WebLogic to track which machines are running which migratable managed servers. A migratable managed server is configured to be able to migrate from one machine to another in the event of machine or other failure. The SOA servers and the BAM servers should be configured to do this.

Preparing the network

There are a number of tasks that require network configuration to be completed. As the installer of the SOA Suite does not necessarily have network administrator privileges, it is a good idea to get all the tasks that require administrator privileges completed before starting the installation and configuration of the SOA Suite.

Getting ready

The following figure shows the hostnames associated with our cluster. Note that hostnames associated with floating IP addresses (may migrate between machines) are given in italics and all the names on the load balancer refer to virtual IP addresses.

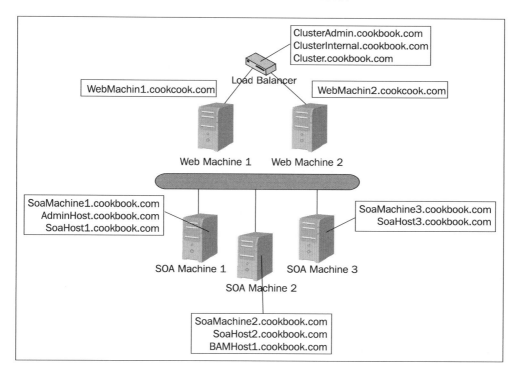

How to do it...

1. Collect managed server hostnames and IP addresses.

   The Admin server, each SOA managed server, and one of the BAM managed servers will require a unique hostname and IP address that must be routable across the cluster. These IP addresses are separate from the IP addresses of the machines hosting the managed servers. Enter the server type (Admin, SOA, or BAM) and WebLogic server name in a worksheet similar to the one shown next. The server name is the name used within WebLogic to refer to this server. Then have the network administrator complete the table by allocating hostnames and IP addresses for the servers. These hostname/IP address pairs should be put into an internal DNS.

Server type	Server name	Hostname	IP address
Admin	AdminServer	AdminHost	10.2.0.121
SOA	WLS_SOA1	SOAHost1	10.2.0.131
SOA	WLS_SOA2	SOAHost2	10.2.0.132
SOA	WLS_SOA3	SOAHost3	10.2.0.133
BAM	WLS_BAM1	BAMHost1	10.2.0.141

2. Get frontend details for the load balancer.

   The SOA Suite cluster will have at least one, and usually two or three, virtual hostnames for use by the load balancer. Create a table listing those requirements and get the network administrator to complete the hostname, port number, and protocol details.

Role	Virtual hostname	Port	Protocol
Admin access	ClusterAdmin.cookbook.com	443	HTTPS
Internal access	ClusterInternal.cookbook.com	80	HTTP
External access	Cluster.cookbook.com	443	HTTPS

3. Configure the load balancer to listen on all the virtual hostnames and ports identified in step 2 and load balance across all the web server hostnames and ports identified in the *Gathering configuration information* recipe.

How it works...

The load balancer is used to distribute requests across the two web servers. The web servers form a routing pool (or multiple routing pools if listening on multiple protocols). The load balancer presents a single address to SOA Suite clients to access the cluster via HTTP and HTTPS.

The web servers will be configured by the EDG to load balance across the WSM cluster using the hostnames of the physical servers running OWSM. They will distribute the load across the BAM cluster using the name of the physical servers running the BAM web interfaces and the virtual hostname of the BAM server itself. The web servers use the virtual hostnames of the SOA servers to distribute the load across the cluster. Finally, the virtual hostname of the Admin server is used to route requests to whichever physical machine is hosting the Admin server at the time of the request.

Using virtual hostnames for the SOA managed servers, the BAM server and the Admin server allows these managed servers to move across physical machines without requiring reconfiguration of the load balancers.

The node managers are dedicated to physical machines and so, like the WSM managed servers, they are able to use the physical hostname of the server on which they run.

There's more...

Note that although the SOA cluster may not receive SOAP requests, the load balancer may still be required to support access to web-based portions of the SOA Suite such as human workflow, the B2B console, and the SOA composer application. If the only HTTP access to the SOA environment is to the consoles for management purposes, then it may be possible to remove the load balancer and web servers from the installation. In case that no load balancer or web servers are used, EJB clients may access the managed servers directly using a T3 protocol which supports load balancing. Similarly, adapters do not require the load balancer.

The three frontend addresses mentioned are recommended in the EDG, but it is possible to collapse the internal and external access into a single role. It is recommended to keep a separate Admin access role to reduce exposure to hacking.

Although we have shown only a single network interface for both the SOA layer and web layer machines, it is good practice to have two physical network adapters in these layers to provide physical isolation of the networks to increase security. Multiple adapters can also be used to reduce the risk of network outages impacting on the cluster.

See also

> ▶ The Enterprise Deployment Guide, *Chapter 3, Preparing the Network for an Enterprise Deployment, Section 3.4, About IPs and Virtual IPs* (`http://docs.oracle.com/cd/E23943_01/core.1111/e12036/net.htm`)

2

Using the Metadata Service to Share XML Artifacts

In this chapter we will cover:

- ▶ Creating a file-based MDS repository for JDeveloper
- ▶ Creating Mediator using a WSDL in MDS
- ▶ Creating Mediator that subscribes to EDL in MDS
- ▶ Creating an external reference using a WSDL in MDS
- ▶ Referencing Schematron in MDS for validation
- ▶ Referencing a fault policy deployed to MDS
- ▶ Deploying MDS artifacts to the SOA infrastructure
- ▶ Exporting an MDS partition to the filesystem
- ▶ Deleting XML artifacts from SOA infra MDS

Introduction

The WSDL of a web service is made up of the following XML artifacts:

- ▶ **WSDL Definition**: It defines the various operations that constitute a service, their input and output parameters, and the protocols (bindings) they support.

- ▶ **XML Schema Definition** (**XSD**): It is either embedded within the WSDL definition or referenced as a standalone component; this defines the XML elements and types that constitute the input and output parameters.

To better facilitate the exchange of data between services, as well as achieve better interoperability and re-usability, it is good practice to define a common set of XML Schemas, often referred to as the *canonical data model*, which can be referenced by multiple services (or WSDL Definitions).

This means, we will need to share the same XML schema across multiple composites. While typically a service (or WSDL) will only be implemented by a single composite, it will often be invoked by multiple composites; so the corresponding WSDL will be shared across multiple composites.

Within JDeveloper, the default behavior, when referencing a predefined schema or WSDL, is for it to add a copy of the file to our SOA project.

However, if we have several composites, each referencing their own local copy of the same WSDL or XML schema, then every time that we need to change either the schema or WSDL, we will be required to update every copy.

This can be a time-consuming and error-prone approach; a better approach is to have a single copy of each WSDL and schema that is referenced by all composites.

The SOA infrastructure incorporates a **Metadata Service** (**MDS**), which allows us to create a library of XML artifacts that we can share across SOA composites. MDS supports two types of repositories:

> ▸ **File-based repository**: This is quicker and easier to set up, and so is typically used as the design-time MDS by JDeveloper.
> ▸ **Database repository**: It is installed as part of the SOA infrastructure. This is used at runtime by the SOA infrastructure.

As you move projects from one environment to another (for example, from test to production), you must typically modify several environment-specific values embedded within your composites, such as the location of a schema or the endpoint of a referenced web service. By placing all this information within the XML artifacts deployed to MDS, you can make your composites completely agnostic of the environment they are to be deployed to.

The other advantage of placing all your referenced artifacts in MDS is that it removes any direct dependencies between composites, which means that they can be deployed and started in any order (once you have deployed the artifacts to MDS).

In addition, an SOA composite leverages many other XML artifacts, such as fault policies, XSLT Transformations, EDLs for event EDN event definitions, and Schematrons for validation, each of which may need to be shared across multiple composites. These can also be shared between composites by placing them in MDS.

Defining a project structure

Before placing all our XML artifacts into MDS, we need to define a standard file structure for our XML library. This allows us to ensure that if any XML artifact within our XML library needs to reference another XML artifact (for example a WSDL importing a schema), it can do so via a relative reference; in other words, the XML artifact doesn't include any reference to MDS and is portable. This has a number of benefits, including:

- ▶ OSB compatibility; the same schemas and WSDLs can be deployed to the Oracle Service Bus without modification

- ▶ Third-party tool compatibility; often we will use a variety of tools that have no knowledge of MDS to create/edit XML schemas, WSDLs, and so on (for example XML Spy, Oxygen)

In this chapter, we will assume that we have defined the following directory structure under our <src> directory.

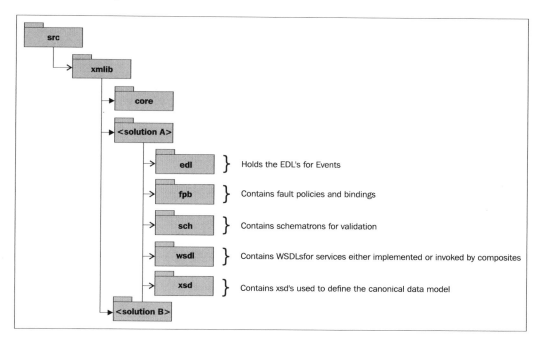

Under the xmllib folder, we have defined multiple <solution> directories, where a solution (or project) is made up of one or more related composite applications. This allows each solution to maintain its XML artifacts independently.

However, it is also likely that there will be a number of XML artifacts that need to be shared between different solutions (for example, the canonical data model for the organization), which in this example would go under <core>.

Where we have XML artifacts shared between multiple solutions, appropriate governance is required to manage the changes to these artifacts.

 For the purpose of this chapter, the directory structure is over simplified. In reality, a more comprehensive structure should be defined as part of the naming and deployment standards for your SOA Reference Architecture.

The other consideration here is versioning; over time it is likely that multiple versions of the same schema, WSDL and so on, will require to be deployed side by side. To support this, we typically recommend appending the version number to the filename.

We would also recommend that you place this under some form of version control, as it makes it far simpler to ensure that everyone is using an up-to-date version of the XML library. For the purpose of this chapter, we will assume that you are using Subversion.

Creating a file-based MDS repository for JDeveloper

Before we can reference this with JDeveloper, we need to define a connection to the file-based MDS.

Getting ready

By default, a file-based repository is installed with JDeveloper and sits under the directory structure:

```
<JDeveloper Home>/jdeveloper/integration/seed
```

This already contains the subdirectory soa, which is reserved for, and contains, artifacts used by the SOA infrastructure.

For artifacts that we wish to share across our applications in JDeveloper, we should create the subdirectory apps (under the seed directory); this is *critical*, as when we deploy the artifacts to the SOA infrastructure, they will be placed in the apps namespace.

We need to ensure that the content of the apps directory always contains the latest version of our XML library; as these are stored under Subversion, we simply need to check out the right portion of the Subversion project structure.

How to do it...

1. First, we need to create and populate our file-based repository. Navigate to the `seed` directory, and right-click and select **SVN Checkout...**, this will launch the Subversion **Checkout** window.

   ❑ For **URL of repository**, ensure that you specify the path to the `apps` subdirectory.

   ❑ For **Checkout directory**, specify the full pathname of the `seed` directory and append `/apps` at the end. Leave the other default values, as shown in the following screenshot, and then click on **OK**:

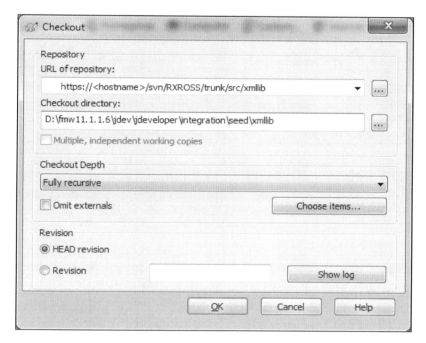

Subversion will check out a working copy of the `apps` subfolder within Subversion into the `seed` directory.

2. Before we can reference our XML library with JDeveloper, we need to define a connection to the file-based MDS.

   Within JDeveloper, from the **File** menu select **New** to launch the **Gallery**, and under **Categories** select **General | Connections | SOA-MDS Connection** from the **Items** list.

   This will launch the **MDS Connection Wizard**.

3. Enter `File Based MDS` for **Connection Name** and select a **Connection Type** of **File Based MDS**.

We then need to specify the MDS root folder on our local filesystem; this will be the directory that contains the `apps` directory, namely:

```
<JDeveloper Home>\jdeveloper\integration\seed
```

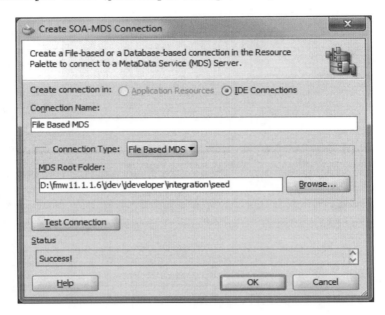

Click on **Test Connection**; the **Status** box should be updated to **Success!**. Click on **OK**. This will create a file-based MDS connection in JDeveloper.

4. Browse the **File Based MDS** connection in JDeveloper.

Within JDeveloper, open the **Resource Palette** and expand **SOA-MDS**. This should contain the **File Based MDS** connection that we just created.

5. Expand all the nodes down to the **xsd** directory, as shown in the following screenshot:

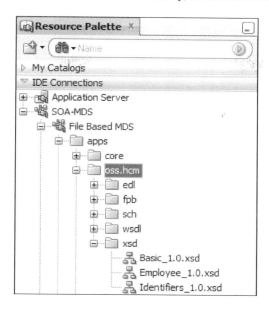

If you double-click on one of the schema files, it will open in JDeveloper (in read-only mode).

There's more...

Once the `apps` directory has been checked out, it will contain a snapshot of the MDS artifacts at the point in time that you created the checkpoint. Over time, the artifacts in MDS will be modified or new ones will be created. It is important that you ensure that your local version of MDS is updated with the current version.

To do this, navigate to the `seed` directory, right-click on **apps**, and select **SVN Update**.

Creating Mediator using a WSDL in MDS

In this recipe, we will show how we can create Mediator using an interface definition from a WSDL held in MDS. This approach enables us to separate the implementation of a service (a composite) from the definition of its contract (WSDL).

Getting ready

Make sure you have created a file-based MDS repository for JDeveloper, as described in the first recipe. Create an SOA application with a project containing an empty composite.

How to do it...

1. Drag Mediator from **SOA Component Palette** onto your composite. This will launch the **Create Mediator** wizard; specify an appropriate name (**EmployeeOnBoarding** in the following example), and for the **Template** select **Interface Definition from WSDL**.

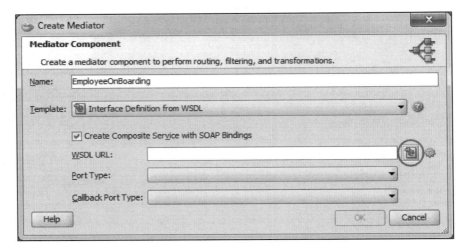

2. Click on the **Find Existing WSDLs** icon (circled in the previous screenshot); this will launch the **SOA Resource Browser**. Select **Resource Palette** from the drop-down list (circled in the following screenshot).

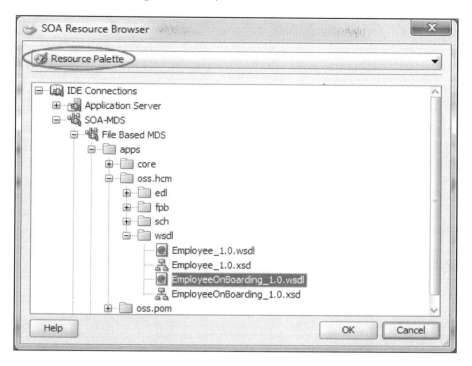

3. Select the WSDL that you wish to import and click on **OK**. This will return you to the **Create Mediator** wizard window; ensure that the **Port Type** is populated and click on **OK**.

    This will create Mediator based on the specified WSDL within our composite.

How it works...

When we import the WSDL in this fashion, JDeveloper doesn't actually make a copy of the schema; rather within the **componentType** file, it sets the **wsdlLocation** attribute to reference the location of the WSDL in MDS (as highlighted in the following screenshot).

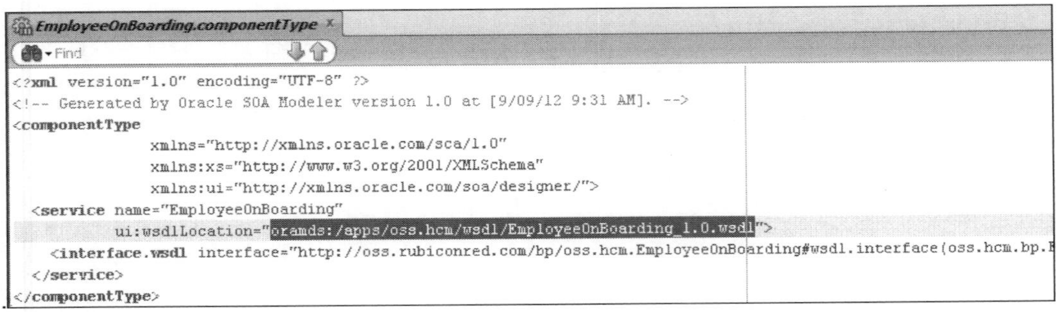

```
EmployeeOnBoarding.componentType

Find

<?xml version="1.0" encoding="UTF-8" ?>
<!-- Generated by Oracle SOA Modeler version 1.0 at [9/09/12 9:31 AM]. -->
<componentType
            xmlns="http://xmlns.oracle.com/sca/1.0"
            xmlns:xs="http://www.w3.org/2001/XMLSchema"
            xmlns:ui="http://xmlns.oracle.com/soa/designer/">
  <service name="EmployeeOnBoarding"
           ui:wsdlLocation="oramds:/apps/oss/hcm/wsdl/EmployeeOnBoarding_1.0.wsdl">
    <interface.wsdl interface="http://oss.rubiconred.com/bp/oss.hcm.EmployeeOnBoarding#wsdl.interface(oss.hcm.bp.E
  </service>
</componentType>
```

For WSDLs in MDS, the `wsdlLocation` attribute uses the following format:

```
oramds:/apps/<wsdl name>
```

Where `oramds` indicates that it is located in MDS, `apps` indicates that it is in the application namespace and `<wsdl name>` is the full pathname of the WSDL in MDS.

The `wsdlLocation` doesn't specify the physical location of the WSDL; rather it is relative to MDS, which is specific to the environment in which the composite is deployed.

This means that when the composite is open in JDeveloper, it will reference the WSDL in the file-based MDS, and when deployed to the SOA infrastructure, it will reference the WSDL deployed to the MDS database repository, which is installed as part of the SOA infrastructure.

There's more...

This method can be used equally well to create a BPEL process based on the WSDL from within the **Create BPEL Process** wizard; for **Template** select **Base on a WSDL** and follow the same steps.

This approach works well with **Contract First Design** as it enables the contract for a composite to be designed first, and when ready for implementation, be checked into Subversion.

The SOA developer can then perform a Subversion update on their file-based MDS repository, and then use the WSDL to implement the composite.

Creating Mediator that subscribes to EDL in MDS

In this recipe, we will show how we can create Mediator that subscribes to an EDN event whose EDL is defined in MDS. This approach enables us to separate the definition of an event from the implementation of a composite that either subscribes to, or publishes, the event.

Getting ready

Make sure you have created a file-based MDS repository for JDeveloper, as described in the initial recipe.

Create an SOA application with a project containing an empty composite.

How to do it...

1. Drag Mediator from **SOA Component Palette** onto your composite. This will launch the **Create Mediator** wizard; specify an appropriate name for it (**UserRegistration** in the following example), and for the **Template** select **Subscribe to Events**.

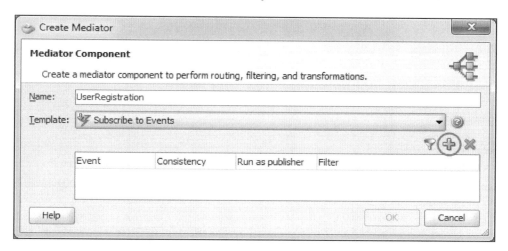

2. Click on the **Subscribe to new event** icon (circled in the previous screenshot); this will launch the **Event Chooser** window.

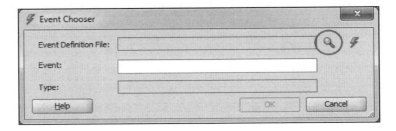

3. Click on the **Browse for Event Definition (edl) files** icon (circled in the previous screenshot); this will launch **SOA Resource Browser**. Select **Resource Palette** from the drop-down list.

4. Select the EDL that you wish to import and click on **OK**. This will return you to the **Event Chooser** window; ensure that the required event is selected and click on **OK**.

   This will return you to the **Create Mediator** window; ensure that the required event is configured as needed, and click on **OK**.

   This will create an event subscription based on the EDL specified within our composite.

How it works...

When we reference an EDL in MDS, JDeveloper doesn't actually make a copy of the EDL; rather within the `composite.xml` file, it creates an import statement to reference the location of the EDL in MDS.

There's more...

This approach can be used equally well to subscribe to an event within a BPEL process or publish an event using either Mediator or BPEL.

Creating an external reference using a WSDL in MDS

In this recipe, we will show how we can create an external reference using an interface definition from a WSDL held in MDS.

Getting ready

Make sure you have created a file-based MDS repository for JDeveloper, as described in the initial recipe. Then open the SOA project in which you want to create the external reference.

How to do it...

1. Drag a **Web Service** from the **Service Adapters** section of the **SOA Component Palette** onto your composite. This will launch the **Create Web Service** wizard; specify an appropriate name for it (**Employee** in the following example), and for **Template** select **Interface Definition from WSDL**.

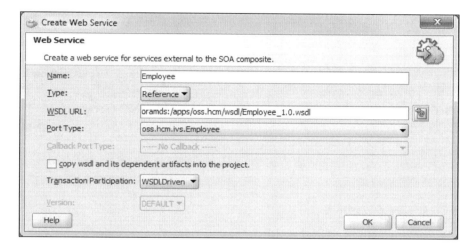

2. Click on the **Find Existing WSDLs** icon (as we did in the previous recipe); this will launch **SOA Resource Browser**. Select **Resource Palette** from the drop-down list.

3. Select the WSDL that you wish to import and click on **OK**. This will return you to the **Create Web Service Wizard** window; ensure that the **Port Type** is populated and click on **OK**.

This will create an external reference based on the specified WSDL within our composite.

How it works...

When we import a WSDL in this fashion, JDeveloper doesn't actually make a copy of the schema; rather within the `composite.xml` file, it sets the `wsdlLocation` attribute for the external service reference to point to the location of the WSDL in MDS.

There's more...

As you move composites from one environment to another (for example, from test to pre-prod to prod), you typically need to modify the WSDL to any external web service, to point it to the correct endpoint.

This should be done using a configuration plan; however using this approach enables all your endpoints to be configured separately in MDS, enabling your composites to be completely agnostic of the environment in which they are deployed.

 If your composite makes use of adapters, such as the file or database adapter, then it will still contain environment specific values. This can be avoided by using only the adapters within Oracle Service Bus.

Referencing Schematron in MDS for validation

In this recipe, we will show you how to reference Schematron defined in MDS to validate an incoming message within Mediator. This approach enables us to separate the validation rules for the actual composite, allowing us to change our validation rules without having to redeploy a composite.

Getting ready

Make sure you have created a file-based MDS repository for JDeveloper, as described at the start of this chapter, and that it contains a valid Schematron file.

Create an SOA application with a project containing Mediator (see the *Create a Mediator using a WSDL in MDS* recipe in this chapter).

How to do it...

1. Schematron validation of incoming messages within Mediator is specified at the routing rule level for an operation. Within JDeveloper, open the Mediator that you wish to apply the validation to. Click on the Schematron icon, circled in the following screenshot:

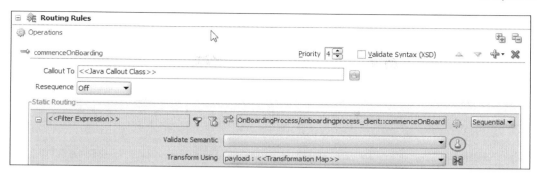

This will bring up the **Validations** window where you can specify one or more Schematron files for the routing rule.

2. To add Schematron, click on the plus sign; this will bring up the **Add Validation** window shown here:

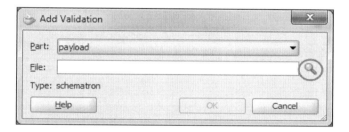

For **Part**, select the part of the SOAP message to which you want to apply the validation.

3. Next click ,on the search icon (circled in the previous screenshot). This will launch the standard **SOA Resource Browser** window; select **Resource Palette** from the drop-down list.

4. Select the Schematron that you wish to use and click on **OK**. This will return you to the **Add Validation** window.

5. Click on **OK**; this will return you to the **Validation** window, which will now list our newly created validation. Click on **OK**, and this will return you to the Mediator editor.

How it works...

When we reference Schematron in this way, JDeveloper doesn't add a copy of Schematron to the composite; rather within the Mediator plan, it sets the `schematron` element to reference the location of Schematron in MDS.

At runtime, when the composite references Schematron, it will use the one deployed to the SOA infrastructure, MDS Database repository.

There's more...

This has a number of distinct advantages. Firstly, you can ensure that all your composites use the same version of a particular Schematron.

Secondly, if you need to modify your validation rules, you simply need to update a single copy of your Schematron and redeploy it to MDS. Any composite that references that Schematron will automatically pick up the modified version, without the need to be re-deployed.

Referencing a fault policy deployed to MDS

Rather than creating the `fault-policies.xml` and `fault-binding.xml` files in your composite project, which then get deployed with the composite into the runtime environment, you can actually reference the fault policies deployed to MDS.

Getting ready

Make sure you have created a file-based MDS repository for JDeveloper, as described at the start of this chapter, and that it contains valid `fault-policies.xml` and `fault-binding.xml` files.

Then, open the SOA project in which you want to reference the external fault policy.

How to do it...

1. To reference the policies deployed on MDS, we need to add the properties `oracle.composite.faultPolicyFile` and `oracle.composite.faultBindingFile` to the `composite.xml` file.

2. These should be added *directly* following the `service` elements and reference the location of your policy and binding files in MDS, as shown in the following code screenshot:

```
<service name="EmployeeOnBoarding_ep">
</service>
<property name="oracle.composite.faultPolicyFile">
   oramds:/apps/oss.hcm/fpb/fault-policies.xml
</property>
<property name="oracle.composite.faultBindingFile">
   oramds:/apps/oss.hcm/fpb/fault-bindings.xml
</property>
```

How it works...

By default, at runtime the SOA infrastructure will look in the same directory, as `composite.xml` for the `fault-policies.xml` and `fault-binding.xml` files.

Specifying these properties overrides this default behavior, causing the SOA infrastructure to reference the specified location within MDS.

There's more...

This has a number of distinct advantages. Firstly, you can share fault policies across multiple composites. Secondly, if you need to modify your fault policies, you simply need to update a single copy of your fault policy and re-deploy it to MDS.

 When deploying an updated version of the fault policy, it will *not* be automatically picked up by any composite that uses it. Rather, you need to either re-deploy the composite or restart the server.

Deploying MDS artifacts to the SOA infrastructure

Before we can deploy a composite that references the artifacts held in MDS, we must deploy those artifacts to MDS on the SOA infrastructure. To do this, we need to create a JAR file containing the shared artifacts and then deploy it as part of an SOA bundle.

In this recipe, we will show you how to do this via JDeveloper, though in practice we would recommend the use of deployment scripts used in conjunction with tools, such as Maven and Hudson.

Getting ready

Make sure you have created an XML library containing your XML artifacts (as described at the beginning of this chapter).

How to do it...

1. Within JDeveloper, create a **Generic Application** (for example, `mdslib`), and when prompted to, create a project and give it an appropriate name (for example, `xmllib`). In the application navigator, right-click on the `xmllib` project and select **Project Properties**.

    This will launch the **Project Properties** window; select **Deployment** from the navigational tree, as shown in the following screenshot:

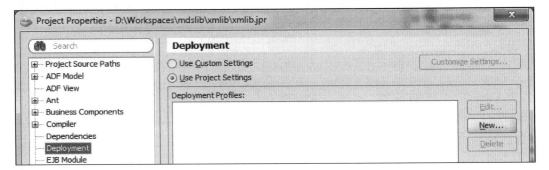

2. Click on **New**; this will launch the **Create Deployment Profile** dialog. Specify an archive type of **JAR File** and specify an appropriate name for it (for example, `xmllib`), and click on **OK**. This will launch the **Edit JAR Deployment Profile Properties** window where we can specify what goes in the JAR file.

3. Even though we are creating a JAR file, it's basically a ZIP file and not a real JAR file, so we need to remove the JAR file specific content; so deselect **Include Manifest File**.

Then select **File Groups | Project Output | Contributors** from the navigational tree and deselect **Project Output Directory** and **Project Dependencies**.

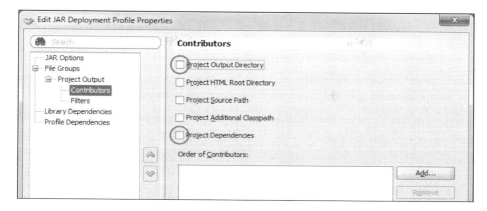

4. Next, specify the actual XML artifacts that we wish to add to the JAR file. Click on **Add**; this will launch the **Add Contributor** window.

5. Click on the magnifying glass and browse to the **apps** directory for your XML artifacts (this should be the one in your source repository — see the method to create the XML library given at the start of this chapter), and click on **OK**.

6. Next, select **File Groups | Project Output | Filters** and check that only the files we want are included within the JAR file.

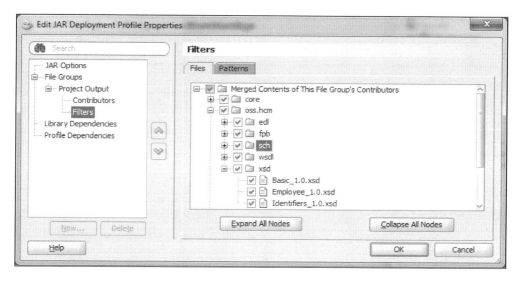

7. Click on **OK** to confirm the content of the JAR file, and then click on **OK** one more time to complete the deployment profile; finally, from the main menu select **Save All**.

8. The next step is to create an SOA bundle. From **Application Menu**, select **Application Properties**. This will launch the **Application Properties** window; from the navigational tree, select **Deployment** and then click on **New**. This will launch the **Create Deployment Profile** window, as shown in the following screenshot:

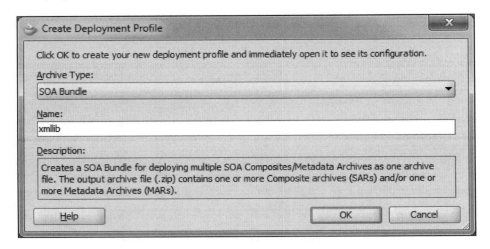

9. Specify an archive type and appropriate name for the SOA bundle, and click on **OK**. This will launch the **SOA Bundle Deployment Profile Properties** window, creating the XML library.

10. Select **Dependencies** from the navigational tree and ensure that **xmllib** is selected.

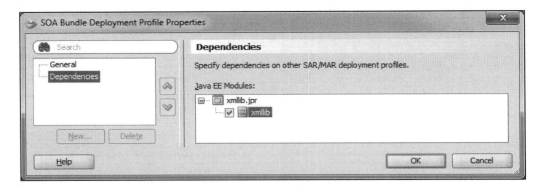

11. Click on **OK** twice and then select **Save All** from the toolbar.

12. We are now ready to deploy our XML schemas to the metadata repository. To do this, in **Application Menu** select **Deploy | SOA Bundle Name**; this will launch the **Deployment Action** dialog. Select **Deploy to Application Server** and follow the standard steps to deploy it to your target SOA infrastructure server(s).

How it works...

In order to deploy our JAR file to the metadata repository, we need to place it within an SOA bundle and deploy that to our SOA infrastructure.

The schemas will then be made available to the SOA composites deployed on the *same* SOA infrastructure.

There's more...

When you deploy an SOA bundle to MDS, it's a cumulative operation, in that new artifacts are added to MDS and artifacts that already exist in MDS are replaced by a new version. But if I don't deploy an artifact, then the previous one remains.

For example, if I deploy an SOA bundle containing A.xsd and B.xsd to MDS, and then deploy a new version of the SOA bundle containing A.xsd (an updated version) and C.xsd to MDS, I will have A.xsd (new version), B.xsd, and C.xsd deployed to MDS.

Exporting an MDS partition to the filesystem

Occasionally, we may want to validate the current content of all the XML artifacts deployed to the MDS repository on our SOA infrastructure. In this recipe, we will show how to export the content of MDS to the filesystem.

Getting ready

Make sure you have deployed some XML artifacts to the MDS repository running on the SOA infrastructure.

How to do it...

1. Log in to Enterprise Manager, and with the navigation tree expand the SOA node and right-click on **soa-infra**. Select **Administration | MDS Configuration**, as shown in the following screenshot:

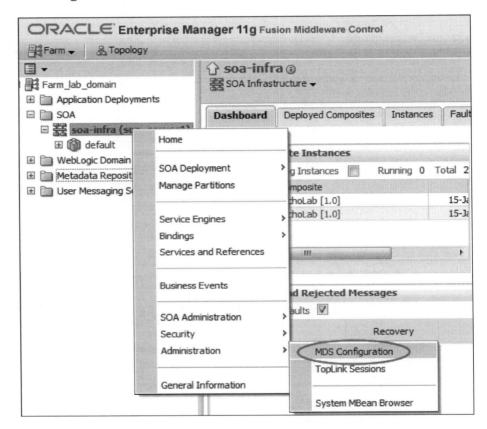

2. This will open the **MDS Configuration** page in Enterprise Manager, as shown in the following screenshot:

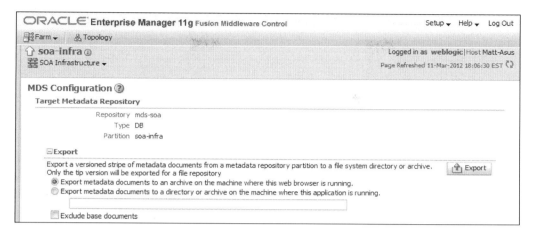

3. Select **Export metadata documents to an archive on the machine where this web browser is running.** and click on the **Export** button.

4. In the browser pop-up window, choose the path and filename and then click on the **Save** button.

This will download the current content of the MDS repository in a ZIP file to your local filesystem.

There's more...

The content of the MDS repository can also be exported using the WSLT command `exportMetadata`. This gives you more fine-grained control over what is exported, for example the following command:

```
wls:/lab_domain/serverConfig> exportMetadata(application='soa-
infra',server='soa_server1',toLocation='D:/MDSExport', docs='/apps/
core/**')
```

This will export just the content of the MDS repository under `/apps/core`.

Deleting XML artifacts from SOA infra MDS

When we deploy XML artifacts to MDS, it's a cumulative operation, in that new artifacts are added to MDS and artifacts that already exist in MDS are replaced by a new version. But, if I don't deploy an artifact, then the previous one remains.

For example, if I deploy an SOA bundle containing A.xsd and B.xsd to MDS, and then deploy a new version of the SOA bundle containing A.xsd (an updated version) and C.xsd to MDS, I will have A.xsd (new version), B.xsd, and C.xsd deployed to MDS.

In addition, every time we deploy a new SOA bundle, MDS retains the previous version of the SOA bundle.

Because of this, we often need to clean up and remove unnecessary and unwanted files from the MDS repository.

Getting ready

Make sure you have deployed some XML artifacts to the MDS repository running on the SOA infrastructure.

How to do it...

1. To do this we need to launch the WebLogic Server Administration Scripting Shell; go to the directory MIDDLEWARE_HOME/Oracle_SOA1/common/bin.

2. On Windows run the command wlst.cmd, and on Unix run the command wslt.sh.

   This will open the **WebLogic Server Administration Scripting Shell** (**WLST**) in offline mode, as shown in the following screenshot:

3. On the WLST command prompt, execute the following code:

```
connect('adminuser', 'adminpassword', 't3://hostname:port')
```

For example:

```
connect('weblogic', 'welcome1', 't3://localhost:7001')
```

The WLST should confirm that you have connected successfully with the text, similar to:

```
Connecting to t3://localhost:7001 with userid weblogic ...
Successfully connected to Admin Server 'AdminServer' that belongs
to domain 'soa_domain'.

Warning: An insecure protocol was used to connect to the
server. To ensure on-the-wire security, the SSL port or
Admin port should be used instead.
```

4. Use the `deleteMetadata` command to remove the XML artifacts from MDS, for example:

```
deleteMetadata(application='soa-infra',server='soa_
server1',docs='/apps/core/**')
```

This will delete all the content under the `/apps/core` location in MDS.

There's more...

The WLST command `purgeMetadata` can be used to remove all but the latest version (referred to as tip) of all the artifacts deployed to MDS.

3
Working with Transactions

In this chapter we will cover:

- Modifying a BPEL process to use the callers transaction context
- Committing a transaction
- Aborting transaction
- Catching rollback faults
- Applying a reversing or compensating transaction

Introduction

In this chapter we will examine recipes that allow us to control the transactional behavior of composites.

Transactions defined

A transaction may be thought of as a set of changes to the state of a system. All the changes must be applied together or none of the changes must be applied. For example, a transfer between two bank accounts involves two operations, debiting the payer's account and crediting the payee's account. In this case, if the credit operation fails we don't want to debit the payer's account because the money was not deposited in the payee's account.

We may have more than two changes in a transaction. For example, in addition to transferring the funds in our example, which requires two operations, we may also wish to notify the payer and payee that the transfer has occurred. Again, we want this to be part of the transaction because we do not want to send a notification unless the transfer of funds has also occurred, so we have now extended our transaction to four operations.

Transaction managers

A transaction manager is responsible for coordinating the operations in a transaction. If all the operations are in the same resource, such as the same database, then the resource may manage the transaction itself. If the transaction is spread across multiple resources, such as the database and message queue, then an XA transaction manager is required to co-ordinate the operations across different resources.

SOA Suite by default will use the XA transaction manager in the application server to co-ordinate its transactions. When a message arrives in SOA Suite, an XA transaction is started.

Compensating transactions

Not all transactions are managed by a transaction manager. Sometimes we want the benefits of a transaction but the services we are using are non-transactional, for example basic SOAP over HTTP services. In this case, we need to manage the transactional behavior within our composites.

In our example, if the two accounts are held at two separate banking institutions, things could become more complicated. This does not change the transaction requirements; it just makes implementing a transaction more complicated. We must now provide explicit reversing transactions to undo unwanted work when we are unable to complete all the operations in our transaction. These are called compensating transactions.

Within SOA Suite, the BPEL engine has built-in support for compensating transactions that allow us to register and invoke reversing operations (compensating transactions).

Hints on working with SOA Suite transactions

Always have a clear plan of where you want transaction boundaries to occur. Determine if you want BPEL processes to be part of existing transactions or if you want to execute them within their own transaction. Transactions can be committed by using a dehydrate statement or by calling a non-idempotent service. It is often helpful to create a diagram showing transaction boundaries within your composite.

Modifying a BPEL process to use the callers transaction context

We often want to include a BPEL process in the calling transaction, and this recipe shows how to modify the BPEL process to do this.

Getting ready

In JDeveloper, open the project that has the BPEL process that we want to make part of the calling transaction.

How to do it...

1. Switch to Source View.

    In JDevelper, open `composite.xml` that contains the BPEL process and click on the **Source** tab at the bottom of the diagram:

2. Add a Transaction Required property.

    Find the component that corresponds to the BPEL process in Source View; the component name attribute will be the same as the name of the BPEL process. Add a property called `bpel.config.transaction` with the value `required` to the component, as shown in the following code:

```
<component name="TransactionIDProcess" version="1.1">
  <implementation.bpel src="TransactionIDProcess.bpel"/>
  <property name="bpel.config.transaction"
            many="false"
            type="xs:string">required</property>
</component>
```

The BPEL process will now participate in the same transaction as the caller of the process.

How it works...

When creating a BPEL process with `sync` delivery in SOA Suite 11.1.1.6 and higher, we can specify the transaction attributes of the BPEL process as `required` or `requiresNew`. This sets the `bpel.config.transaction` property.

The `bpel.config.transaction` property has two values:

► `required`: This makes the BPEL process execute as part of the calling transaction. If no calling transaction exists, it will create a new one.

► `requiresNew`: This is the default value and makes the BPEL process execute as a separate transaction. Any existing transaction will be suspended.

These properties define the transaction semantics of the BPEL process to which they are applied. Any JCA adapters, such as a database or JMS adapter, can also be executed in the same transaction context as the BPEL process.

There's more...

When executing, the BPEL engine keeps track of which activities have occurred by updating the state in the dehydration database. This updating of the process state is done in the same transaction context in which the BPEL process is being executed. This keeps the state of the BPEL process in sync with the state of the resources used by the BPEL process. These updates are only committed when the process is dehydrated or a `RequiresNew` process is completed. One way in which this can occur is following a call to a non-idempotent partner link.

The BPEL engine uses a separate transaction context to keep a record of which steps were attempted; this is used to update the database with logging information and means that even if the BPEL process transaction rolls back, it will be possible to see what activities were executed before the rollback. This aids in debugging a failing BPEL process.

See also

► The *Aborting a transaction* recipe in this chapter.

Committing a transaction

We may wish to explicitly commit a transaction in our BPEL process. This recipe describes how to achieve this.

Getting ready

In JDeveloper, open the project containing the BPEL process that you wish to explicitly commit a transaction to.

How to do it...

1. Add a **Dehydrate** activity to the process.
2. Open the BPEL process that needs to explicitly commit the transaction.
3. From the **Component Palette** expand the **Oracle Extensions** section; drag a **Dehydrate** activity onto the BPEL process:

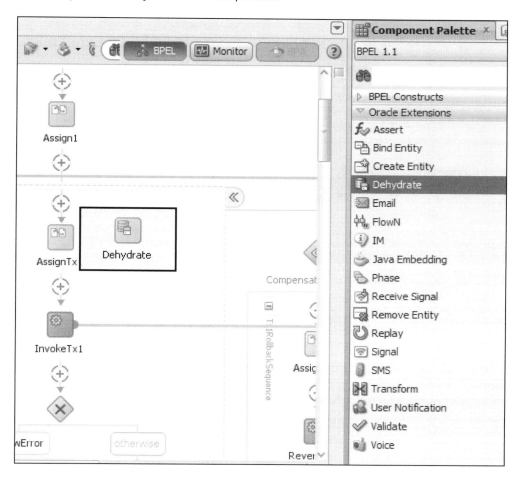

When executed, this will cause the current transaction to be committed and a new transaction to be started.

How it works...

The **Dehydrate** activity causes the current state of the BPEL process to be saved in the dehydration database. This also causes the current transaction context to be committed. Because the BPEL process is still active, a new transaction context is immediately created.

There's more...

A **Dehydrate** activity can be very useful in an asynchronous process, but should be avoided in a synchronous process unless the BPEL process's `bpel.config.transaction` property is not set or set to `requiresNew`.

> Synchronous BPEL processes that have the required transaction attribute should always leave the committing of the transaction to the caller; they should never force the committing of a transaction.

See also

▶ The *Catching rollback faults* recipe in this chapter.

Aborting a transaction

If an error occurs while we are in a transaction, we may wish to abort the transaction, thus rolling back any work that has already been done. This recipe shows how to rollback the currently executing transaction.

Getting ready

In JDeveloper, open the project containing the BPEL process, which may encounter errors, requiring the transaction to be rolled back.

How to do it...

1. Open the BPEL process that needs to cause the transaction to be rolled back.

2. From the **Component Palette**, drag a **Throw** activity onto the BPEL process:

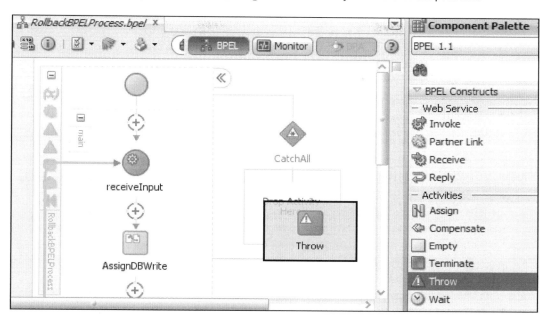

3. Double-click on the **Throw** activity that was created in the previous step.

4. Click on the 🔍 icon in the **Fault QName** section of the dialog to launch the **Fault Chooser** dialog:

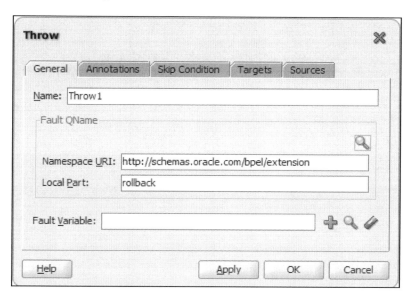

5. Select the **rollback** fault and click on **OK**:

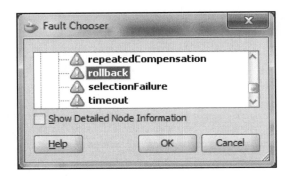

6. Click on **OK** to apply the changes to the **Throw** activity.

This activity will cause the current BPEL process transaction to be rolled back when executed.

How it works...

The `rollback` fault has a special meaning to the BPEL engine and causes the current transaction to be rolled back. The BPEL process will be restored to the state that it was in before the current transaction was started. A `rollback` fault can't be caught by a BPEL process in the same transaction context.

See also

> ► The *Catching rollback faults* recipe in this chapter

Catching rollback faults

A BPEL process may want to catch a rollback fault thrown by another BPEL process. This recipe shows how to do that.

Getting ready

Open the composites containing the caller BPEL process and the callee BPEL process.

How to do it...

1. Open `composite.xml` containing the callee BPEL process (the BPEL process that throws a `rollback` fault) and switch to the **Source View** tab.

2. Locate the `component` element corresponding to the callee BPEL process and verify that either:

   There is no `bpel.config.transaction` property:

   ```
   <component name="BPELProcess1" version="1.1">
     <implementation.bpel src="BPELProcess1.bpel"/>
     <!—No bpel.config.transaction property -->
   </component>
   ```

   Or the `bpel.config.transaction` property is set to `requiresNew`:

   ```
   <component name="BPELProcess2" version="1.1">
     <implementation.bpel src="BPELProcess2.bpel"/>
     <property name="bpel.config.transaction"
               many="false"
               type="xs:string">requiresNew</property>
   </component>
   ```

3. Open the caller BPEL process and add a catch block by selecting the triangular (⚠) icon on a scope containing the `invoke` activity to the callee BPEL process:

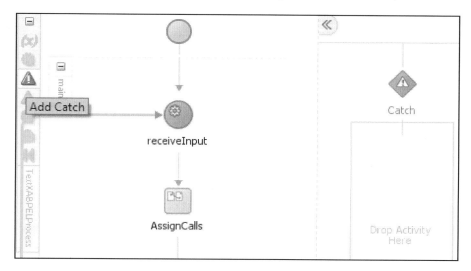

4. Double click on the **Catch** to bring up the **Catch** dialog.

5. Click on the 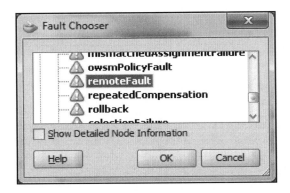 icon in the **Fault Name** section of the dialog to launch the **Fault Chooser** dialog:

6. Select the **remoteFault** fault and click on **OK**:

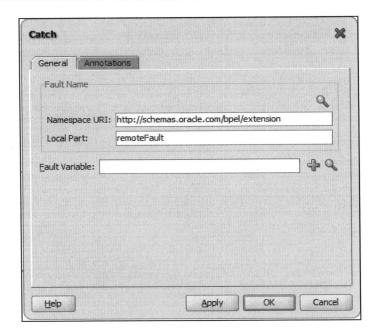

7. Click on **OK** to apply the changes to the catch.

How it works...

The catch block is to be executed when a rollback fault is thrown in the callee BPEL process.

When a BPEL process throws a `rollback` fault, it cannot be caught in the current transaction context. When the fault leaves the current transaction context, it is converted to a `remoteFault` that can be caught in the caller BPEL process. It is necessary to make sure that the caller and callee are in separate transaction contexts; hence the need to check the value of the `bpel.config.transaction` property is not set to `required`.

When a BPEL process throws any fault that is not caught in the current transaction context, it causes the current transaction to be rolled back. If instead of throwing a fault a BPEL process returns a fault through a `reply` activity, then the current transaction is not rolled back.

Applying reversing or compensating transactions

If operations occur that are not part of a transaction, then reversing operations must be applied to undo the changes. The reversing operations are performed to reverse the effects of the unwanted operations. This recipe shows how to do that.

Getting ready

Open the BPEL process that performs operations that cannot be rolled back as part of a transaction, and instead requires reversing operations to be applied in the case of a processing failure.

How to do it...

1. For each operation (usually an `invoke` activity) that has a corresponding reversing operation, wrap it in a `scope` activity by dragging a scope from the **Component Palette** and dropping it just after the operation that requires reversing:

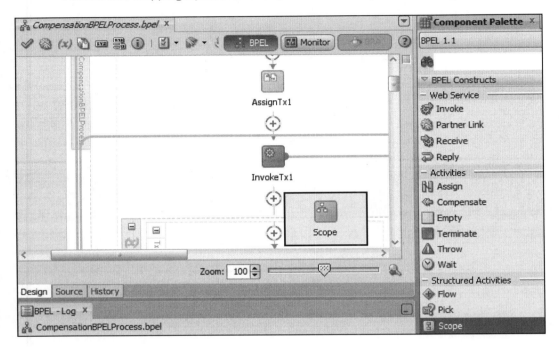

2. Move the activity or activities that require reversing into the scope by dragging-and-dropping them into the scope:

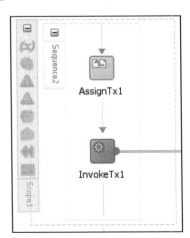

3. Click on the **Add Compensation Handler** icon ◀◀ in the scope to add a compensation handler:

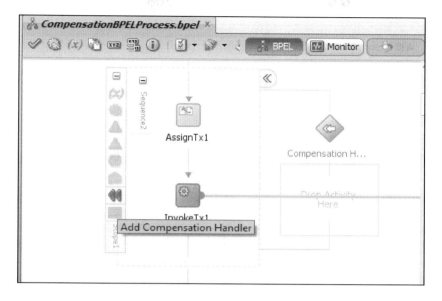

4. Drag appropriate activities (usually an `assign` and an `invoke`) into the compensation handler to reverse the operations in the corresponding scope:

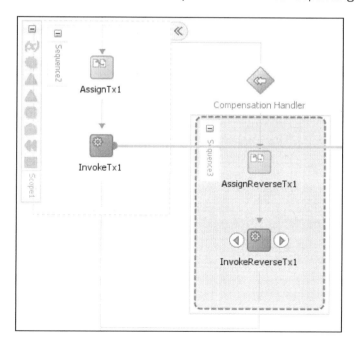

5. If a failure in an operation does not throw a fault, then create a **Throw** activity by dragging it into the scope that contains the failed operation (see step 2 of the recipe *Aborting a transaction* in this chapter).

6. Choose an appropriate fault type (see step 4 of the recipe *Aborting a transaction*).

7. Drag appropriate activities (usually an `assign` and an `invoke`) into the compensation handler to reverse the operations in the corresponding scope.

8. Add a catch block to the outermost scope (see step 3 of the recipe *Catching rollback faults*).

9. Drag a **Compensate** activity from the **Component Palette** onto the catch that was just created:

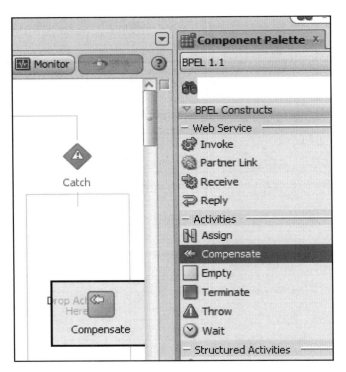

How it works...

When a `fault` is caught by `catch`, `compensate` it will cause all the operations that require reversing to be reversed.

`Compensate` can only be called from within a `catch` block. When it is called, it starts with the most recently completed `scope` and calls the `compensation handler` for that `scope` if it has one. It then looks for the previously completed `scope` and calls the `compensation handler` for that `scope`. In this way, the reversing operations are applied in the reverse order to the original operations. If a scope was not completed, its compensation handler will not be invoked.

If an operation throws a `fault`, we can `catch` it and call the **Compensate** activity. Operations may indicate failure by returning a failure status rather than throwing a `fault`. In this case, by placing a **Throw** activity inside the `scope` for which the operation failed, we can avoid the reversing operation being invoked for that `scope`.

Compensation occurs outside of transaction boundaries. So a BPEL process may be spread across several transactions, but compensation ignores this and continues to invoke compensation handlers for completed scopes regardless of the transaction context in which they were completed.

4
Mapping Data

In this chapter, we will cover the following recipes to transform data from one format to another:

- ▶ Ignoring missing elements with XSLT
- ▶ Ignoring missing elements with Assign
- ▶ Creating target elements in Assign
- ▶ Array processing with XSLT
- ▶ Array processing with BPEL Assign
- ▶ Overriding mapping of EJB data to XML
- ▶ Ignoring a Java property
- ▶ Creating a wrapper element for a Java collection or array
- ▶ Handling an abstract class

Introduction

At the heart of any solution built with SOA Suite is the transformation of data from one format to another. Within SOA Suite we have two explicit mechanisms to deal with this, namely **XML Stylesheet Transforms** (**XSLT**) or XPath Assigns. Transformation may also occur implicitly as a result of using a component or adapter, for example converting to/from Java formats when using Java components and adapters.

Comparison of XSLT and Assign

Within both the Mediator and BPEL components, we have the choice between using XSLT transformation and XPath Assigns. When we use an XPath Assign, we are manipulating the target XML document directly. This may be more efficient when we are adding or altering a small part of the target document and the target document already contains data. When we use an XSLT transform, we are replacing the target XML document with a new one generated from the transform.

Choosing between Assign and Transform

Generally when we are populating a new variable for the first time, it is best to use a transform. A transform is also easier to use when manipulating repeating elements in the target. When we wish to modify only a few elements in the target, Assign is the easiest way to do this.

A common pattern is to perform an initial mapping to a variable by using XSLT and then making subsequent additions or modifications using Assign. The reverse pattern cannot be used because an XSLT transform will completely replace a variable with new content, losing any previous assignments to that variable.

Typing in XML Schema

Although XML Schema allows for element contents to be typed, generally the data transformation process is quite lax about enforcing type constraints, and as long as the data being transformed is compatible in its string form with the target type, no errors will be thrown; for example, the string 75 may be assigned to a numeric type without error, and similarly a numeric type such as 12.5 may be safely assigned to a string.

Ignoring missing elements with XSLT

Sometimes, when we are performing an XSLT transformation, we get an empty target element because the source element was not present. If a source element is missing we may want to omit the target element from our output. We often wish to distinguish between a missing element and an empty element. In this recipe, we will show how to distinguish between a missing XML element and an empty XML element in XSLT.

It is possible that the source element might actually be an optional element in the input document, and this will be indicated by the XML element marker within square brackets, as shown in the following example:

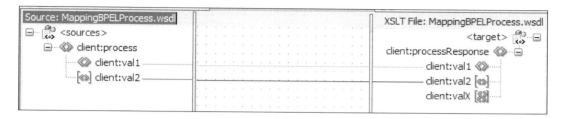

Given the following input document:

```
<inputVariable>
  <part  name="payload">
    <ns1:process>
      <ns1:val1>Only Value</ns1:val1>
    </ns1:process>
  </part>
</inputVariable>
```

The previous transform will generate the following output document:

```
<outputVariable>
  <part  name="payload">
    <processResponse>
      <client:val1>Only Value</client:val1>
      <client:val2/>
    </processResponse>
  </part>
</outputVariable>
```

Note, that this is indistinguishable from the output generated by the following input document:

```
<inputVariable>
  <part  name="payload">
    <ns1:process>
      <ns1:val1>Only Value</ns1:val1>
      <ns1:val2></ns2:val2>
    </ns1:process>
  </part>
</inputVariable>
```

This may be significant for our future processing, and so we need to be able to distinguish the two input documents, which we do by using an XSLT `if` construct.

Getting ready

Open an existing XSLT file that generates an empty element, when an element is not present in the input, to the transform.

How to do it...

1. Add an **if** function to the target element:

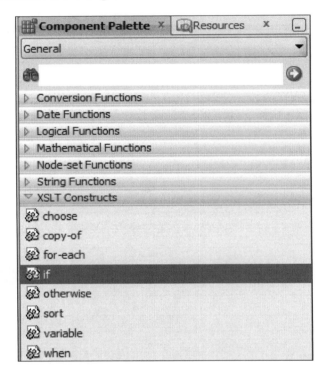

2. In the **General** section of **Component Palette** open **XSLT Constructs** and drag the **if** construct onto the target element. This will make the mapping of the target element conditional on some XPath expressions.

3. To map the source element to the target element, drag the missing source element onto the `if` construct. This makes the target element mapping conditional based on the presence of the missing source element:

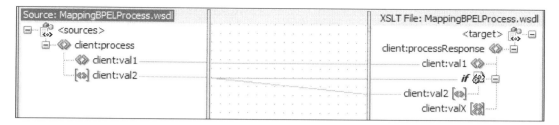

How it works...

The `if` construct acts as a conditional on any nested mappings underneath it. If the conditional evaluates to true, then the mappings underneath it are executed; otherwise they are ignored, and the elements underneath it will not appear in the output document.

There's more...

We used the `if` construct to test for the existence of an element in the source document, but we could have used it to test any Boolean expression, allowing us to put arbitrary conditional logic in our transform. In this case, rather than mapping an element to the `if` construct, we would map an XPath expression using the expression editor.

The `MiscMappings` project in the code samples has a sample XSL transformation called `CorrectedIntialTransformation.xsl` demonstrating this.

See also

▶ The *Ignoring missing elements with Assign* recipe in this chapter

▶ The *Ignoring a Java property* recipe in this chapter

Ignoring missing elements with Assign

An assignment may fail with a `selectionFailure` fault that can be caused by attempting to select a nonexistent element. In this recipe, we will show how to deal with missing elements in an assign so that we avoid the `selectionFailure` fault.

Getting ready

Open an assignment that causes `selectionFailure` faults when an element is not present in the input. It is possible that the source element might actually be an optional element in the input document, and the XML element marker being in square brackets will indicate this.

How to do it...

1. Right-click to the left-hand side of the assignment that causes the `selectionFailure` fault and select the **ignoreMissingFromData** menu item. This will cause the assignment to be ignored if the source element does not exist:

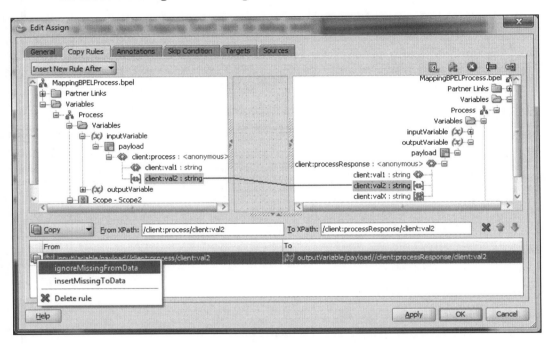

How it works...

When the `ignoreMissingFromData` attribute is set on a `copy` statement in Assign, it causes that `copy` statement to be skipped if the `from` query were to cause a `selectionFailure` fault.

There's more...

The `ignoreMissingFromData` attribute also works with all other Assign subelements, such as `insertAfter`, `insertBefore`, `copyList`, and `append`.

The `MiscMappings` project in the code samples has a sample BPEL process called `MappingBPELProcess.bpel` demonstrating this.

See also

- ▸ The *Ignoring missing elements with XSLT* recipe in this chapter
- ▸ The *Ignoring a Java property* recipe in this chapter

Creating target elements in Assign

The target of a copy must exist in Assign. In this recipe, we will show how to create that target if it does not already exist. If the target does not exist, a `selectionFault` is thrown.

Getting ready

Open an assignment that causes `selectionFailure` faults when an element is not present in the output. It is possible that the target element is not present because an earlier XSLT transform did not create it.

How to do it...

1. Right-click to the left-hand side of the assignment that causes the `selectionFailure` fault and click on the **insertMissingToData** menu item. This will cause the target element to be created if it does not already exist:

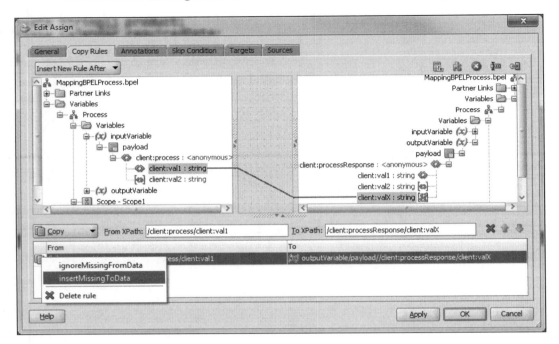

How it works...

When the `insertMissingToData` attribute is set on a `copy` statement in Assign, it causes the intended target element to be created if it does not already exist.

There's more...

The `insertMissingToData` attribute only works with the `copy assign` subelements; it cannot be used when appending or inserting elements.

The `MiscMappings` project in the code samples has a sample BPEL process called `MappingBPELProcess.bpel` demonstrating this.

See also

▸   The *Ignoring missing elements with Assign* recipe in this chapter

Array processing with XSLT

We often deal with repeating elements in XML. These repeating elements act as an array and need special processing constructs when used in XSLT. In this recipe, we show how to process an array using XSLT.

Getting ready

Create an XSLT stylesheet for an input schema and an output schema, both of which have repeating elements in them. An example schema fragment is shown as follows:

```
<element name="vendorQuote"
        maxOccurs="unbounded"
        type="tns:vendorQuoteType"/>
```

This element may repeat an unlimited number of times.

How to do it...

1.   Expand the target document until the target repeating element is visible.

2.   Drag a **for-each** construct from **Component Palette | General | XSLT Constructs** onto the repeating element in the target document (productLowestQuote in this case):

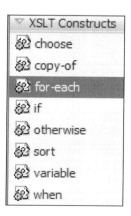

3. Drag the source repeating element (**productQuote** in the following example) onto the **for-each** construct. This will cause the output document to contain an empty target repeating element for each source document repeating element:

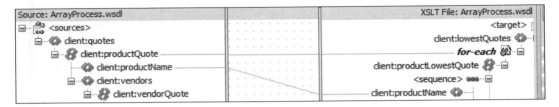

4. Now, map any nested elements and values under the source repeating element (**productName** for example) to the target elements under the **for-each** construct.

How it works...

The `for-each` construct loops over the top-level elements in the input node-set and creates an empty target element for each one. Any mappings under the `for-each` construct are done in the context of the current node from the input node-set. For example, if the input document is as shown in the following code snippet, the node-set will contain three `productQuote` nodes and a mapping from `productName` will reference each of these nodes `Revell B17G Flying Fortress 1:48 Scale`, `Monogram B29 Superfortress 1:48`, and `Airfix Avro Lancaster 1:72` in turn.

```
<productQuote>
  <productName>Revell B17G Flying Fortress 1:48</productName>
  ...
</productQuote>
<productQuote>
  <productName>Monogram B29 Superfortress 1:48</productName>
</productQuote>
<productQuote>
  <productName>Airfix Avro Lancaster 1:72</productName>
  ...
</productQuote>
```

The `ArrayProcessing` project in the code samples has a sample XSLT called `ArrayTransformation.xsl` demonstrating this.

There's more...

The `for-each` construct can reference any arbitrary node-set and does not have to be tied to the input document directly; any XPath function that returns a node-set can be used as input.

See also

- ▶ The *Array processing with BPEL Assign* recipe in this chapter
- ▶ The *Creating a wrapper element for a Java collection or array* recipe in this chapter
- ▶ The *Handling an abstract class* recipe in this chapter

Array processing with BPEL Assign

Sometimes we need to iterate over array elements in a BPEL process while performing an action such as a BPEL `invoke`. This requires us to process repeating elements outside of an XSLT transform. In this recipe, we examine how to access repeating elements in an assign statement. We will iterate over the elements in a node-set; elements in the set are indexed starting with one.

Getting ready

We will need a source XML document to iterate over, and a target XML document to update with the results of our iteration.

How to do it...

1. Create an index variable to keep track of the current index of the array. The variable should be of the integer type:

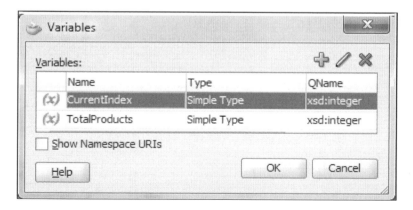

2. Create a variable to hold the number of items in the array; again this should be of the type integer.

3. Use an assign statement to initialize the current index to 0.

4. Use an assign statement to initialize the number of items to the number of elements to iterate over. The number of elements that need to be iterated over can be calculated by using the XPath `count` function and passing it to the node-set corresponding to the elements to be iterated over, as shown in the following code:

```
count(bpws:getVariableData('outputVariable',
            'payload',
            '/client:lowestQuotes/client:productLowestQuote'))
```

This can be created by dragging the expression editor onto the number of items variable, and in the **Expression Builder** by selecting **Functions | Mathematical Functions | count** and hitting **Insert Into Expression**. Then, select the elements to be iterated over and insert that XPath into the expression between the parentheses after the count function:

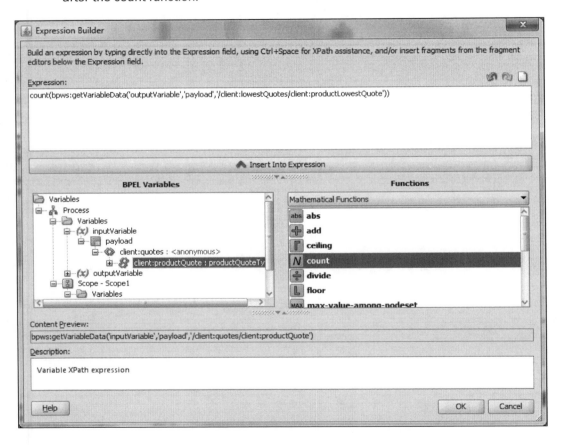

5. Create a `while` loop in the BPEL process by dragging the **Component Palette |
    BPEL Constructs | While** onto the BPEL process at the location where we want a
    loop. Open the `while` activity and use the expression editor to create a suitable loop
    condition using the loop counter variable and the number of items variable; see the
    following example:

    ```
    bpws:getVariableData('CurrentIndex') < bpws:getVariableData('Total
    Products')
    ```

6. Before using the current index variable, we need to increment it because XPath node-
    sets are indexed starting with one.

7. When we need to access the current element in the `while` loop, we do it by indexing
    the repeating element with the current index variable, as shown in the following
    sample XPath, to select a `productLowestQuote` record's product name:

    ```
    bpws:getVariableData('outputVariable','payload')
      /client:productLowestQuote
        [bpws:getVariableData('CurrentIndex')]
          /client:productName
    ```

    Note, that we can use this method to index either a source or a target variable.

How it works...

When we select an element with an XPath expression, it actually returns a node-set of zero
or more elements. If the result returns more than one node (the cardinality of the node-set is
greater than one), then we can use the index variable and the `while` loop to iterate across
the elements in the node-set. It is important to remember when selecting from a node-set that
the first element in the node-set is indexed by one.

There's more...

If we need to add elements to a sequence in an `assign` statement rather than just modify
them, we need to use **InsertAfter** to place an **XML Fragment** at the correct point in the
output document.

The `ArrayProcessing` project in the code samples has a sample BPEL process called
`ArrayProcess.bpel` demonstrating this.

See also

▶ The *Array processing with XSLT* recipe in this chapter

▶ The *Creating a wrapper element for a Java collection or array* recipe in this chapter

▶ The *Handling an abstract class* recipe in this chapter

Overriding mapping of EJB data to XML

When we use an EJB reference or the Spring component in SOA Suite, we usually want to wire it to a non-Java resource. When we do this, JDeveloper uses JAXB to create an XML representation of the parameters and return values of the methods in the Java interface we are using. Often the SOA developer is unable to modify or create mappings in EJB or Java bean itself. If we are unable to change the JAXB mapping in the EJB or Java bean, or there are no mappings provided, and we are using default mappings, then we can use this recipe to override the mappings. Overriding the default generation of the mappings allows us to specify target namespaces, rationalize the structure of the data, and remove unneeded properties from the Java classes. Some things that we may want to customize include:

▶ Specifying concrete implementations for abstract classes and interfaces in the interface

This allows us to map to the Java objects in the interface that cannot be instantiated directly. For example, often we have lists of abstract classes or interfaces; by specifying the possible concrete implementations of these classes, we can generate an XML Schema that includes additional properties available only through the concrete classes.

▶ Hiding unwanted properties

This allows us to remove properties that are not needed for our implementation, or not needed because they are convenience properties, such as the length of an array or collection, which can easily be derived from the underlying array or collection.

▶ Providing wrappers for arrays and collections

The default mapping for an array or collection is to provide a list of repeating elements. We can modify the mapping to provide a wrapper element that represents the whole array or collection, with the repeating elements appearing a level down within it.

▶ Changing WSDL namespaces

It is often necessary to change the namespaces in a generated WSDL to match a corporate standard, or to avoid conflicts with other components that are being used.

SOA Suite allows us to describe in an XML document how we want a Java interface to be mapped from Java objects into XML. The file that does this is called an **Extended Mapping (EXM)** file. When generating a WSDL and its associated XML Schema from a Java interface, SOA Suite looks for an EXM file corresponding to the Java interface that is being generated. Without this file, the mapping will be the *default* generation, which simply attempts to take each field and method in the Java code and map it to an XML type in the resulting WSDL. The EXM file is used to describe, or clarify, the mappings to XML, and uses EclipseLink MOXy to provide an XML version of the Java annotations. This means that we can apply the equivalent of the Java annotations to the Java classes referenced from the interface, giving us complete control over how the XML is generated. This is illustrated in the following diagram, which shows how the WSDL interface mapping depends on the Java interface of the EJB reference or Spring component that is being wired (obviously), but is modified by the EXM file that, in turn, may embed or reference an XML version of the JAXB annotations (using EclipseLink MOXy):

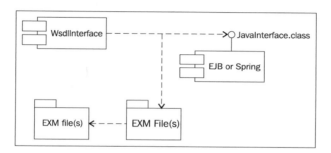

The mapping will automatically take advantage of any class annotations in the Java classes that are being mapped, but the XML descriptions can override or add to these annotations, allowing us fine-grained control over our XML interface. This allows for changes to be made without touching the underlying Java code.

Getting ready

We must identify the Java interface that we wish to override the mapping for, and understand how we wish that interface to be represented in XML. We will use the following Java interface:

```
package soa.cookbook;

public interface QuoteInterface {
    public QuoteResponse getQuotes(QuoteRequest request);
}
```

The structure of the request and response parameters is shown in the following diagram:

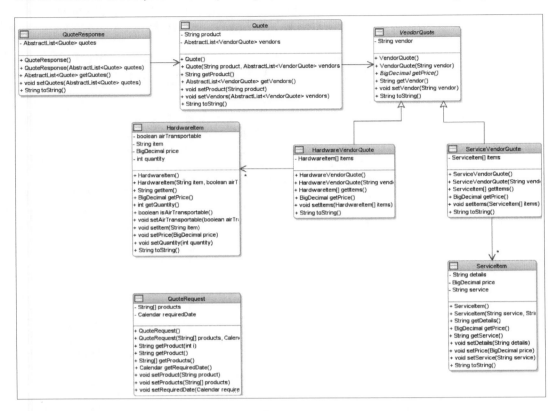

We want to create a mapping file to modify the way the interface is mapped.

How to do it...

1. Prepare JDeveloper to use the SOA JAXB mappings.

   To take full advantage of the XML element completion in JDeveloper, we must make sure that all the schema we are using are registered with JDeveloper. Under JDeveloper in **Tools | Preferences | XML Schemas**, we click on **Add** to register the schema as an XML extension:

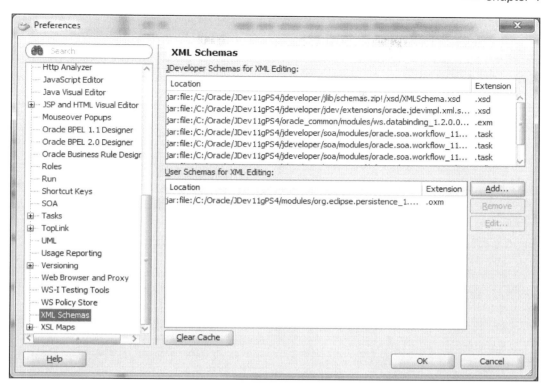

The schema is found in a JAR file located at `<JDEV_HOME>/modules/org.eclipse.persistence_1.1.0.0_2-1.jar`, and the schema is inside this jar at `/xsd/eclipselink_oxm_2_1.xsd`, so the location we register is

`jar:file:/<JDEV_HOME>/modules/org.eclipse.persistence_1.1.0.0_2-1.jar!/xsd/eclipselink_oxm_2_1.xsd` where `<JDEV_HOME>` is the location where you installed JDeveloper. Note, that the version number of the JAR file and the XML Schema vary between JDeveloper releases:

2. Change the order of the source paths in your SOA project to have `SCA-INF/src` first. This is done using the **Project Source Paths** dialog in **Project Properties**. All files related to the mapping will go here. For example, `<Project>/SCA-INF/src/com/customer/EXM_Mapping_EJB.exm`, where `com.customer` is the associated Java package:

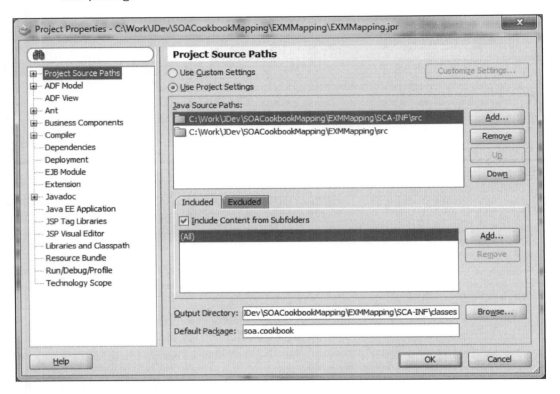

3. Create an EXM mapping file by launching the wizard to generate a base mapping (EXM) file.

   Launch the **New XML Document from XML Schema** wizard (**File | New | All Technologies | General | XML Document from XML Schema**).

4. Specify a file with the name of the Java interface and a `.exm` extension in a directory corresponding to the Java package of the interface under `SCA-INF/src`. For example, if your EJB adapter defined `soa.cookbook.QuoteInterface` as the remote interface, then the directory should be `<Project>/SCA-INF/src/soa/cookbook` and so the full file path would be `<Project>/SCA-INF/src/soa/cookbook/QuoteInterface.exm`. By using the .exm extension, we are able to use registered schema that will automatically map to the correct schema so that the future steps in the wizard will understand what we are doing:

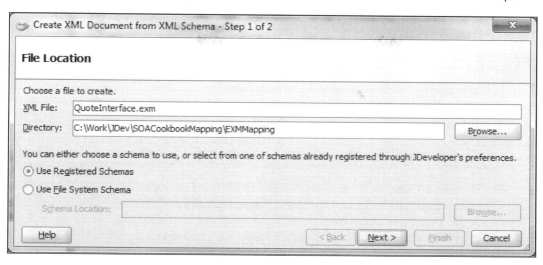

The **weblogic-wsee-databinding** schema should already be selected; select a root element of **java-wsdl-mapping** and leave **Depth** at the default value. This will give us a basic file to start working with:

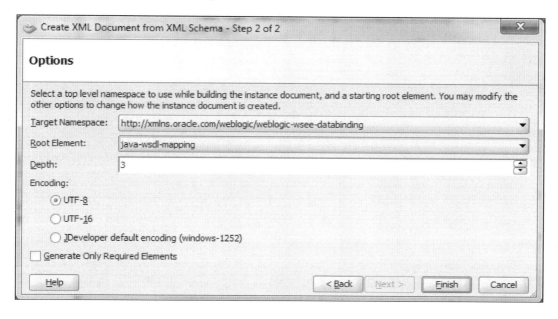

5. Import a JAXB (OXM) mapping file.

    As recommended by Oracle, separate out the mappings per package by using the `<toplink-oxm-file>` element. This will allow you, per package, to define reusable mapping files outside of the EXM file. Since the EXM file and the embedded mappings have different XML root elements, defining them separately allows JDeveloper to provide validation and completion; a sample include is shown as follows:

    ```
    <?xml version="1.0" encoding="UTF-8" ?>
    <java-wsdl-mapping xmlns="http://xmlns.oracle.com/weblogic/
    weblogic-wsee-databinding">
       <xml-schema-mapping>
         <toplink-oxm-file file-path="./mappings.xml"
                           java-package="soa.cookbook"/>
       </xml-schema-mapping>
    </java-wsdl-mapping>
    ```

6. Create an OXM file.

    Create an OXM mapping file to store custom mappings. As mentioned, these files are per package, separate from the EXM files, and reusable. We can use the **New XML Document from Schema** to create these as well. In this case, they will have an XML or OXM extension, use the persistence registered schema (`http://www.eclipse.org/eclipselink/xsds/persistence/oxm`), and be stored relative to the EXM file. That is, they can go in the same directory, or in other directories, as long as you refer to them by the relative path from the EXM file. In the following example, we have set the target namespace of the mapping.

    ```
    <?xml version="1.0" encoding="UTF-8" ?>
    <xml-bindings xmlns="http://www.eclipse.org/eclipselink/xsds/
    persistence/oxm">
       <!-- Set target Namespace via namespace attribute -->
       <xml-schema namespace=http://cookbook.soa.mapping/javatypes
                   element-form-default="QUALIFIED"/>
    </xml-bindings>
    ```

7. Rewire the existing components.

   Once complete, delete any existing wires to the Java components and rewire. You should notice the dialog box change to indicate that an extended mapping file was used:

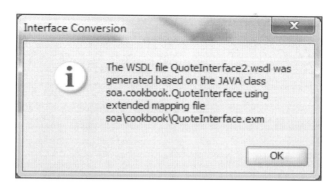

   Note that an *extended mapping file* was used.

How it works...

When a component that expects a WSDL interface is wired to a component/reference exposing a Java interface, JDeveloper will invoke the Java to the WSDL compiler. This will check the classpath to see if an EXM file exists in the path corresponding to the interface package and with a name corresponding to the interface class. If such a file exists, then it is used to override the default mappings. This file will also override any explicit JAXB annotations in the classes that are to be mapped.

This same process is done at design time in JDeveloper and again at runtime in SOA Suite. At runtime, the mapping is done the first time that the Java component is invoked.

There's more...

XML Schema can also be registered to work as an OXM extension instead of an XML extension. But if you use a .oxm extension, then in each project where you use it you must add a rule to copy .oxm files from the source to the output directory when compiling.

By using a common mapping file or files, it is possible to have consistent mapping across multiple interfaces that use the same classes. By using a different mapping file, it is possible to map classes differently depending on the interface they are used with, allowing the interface to be simplified; for example, by ignoring the properties of a class that are not needed in a given interface.

The EXMMapping project in the code samples has sample EXM (EXM_Mapping_EJB.exm) and OXM files (mappings.xml) demonstrating this.

See also

► The *Ignoring a Java property* recipe in this chapter

► The *Creating a wrapper element for a Java collection or array* recipe in this chapter

► The *Handling an abstract class* recipe in this chapter

Ignoring a Java property

Often the Java interface we are using will have *convenience* methods that appear to be additional properties but are actually just a simpler way of accessing another property. An example is shown as follows:

```java
public class QuoteRequest implements Serializable {
    ...
    private String[] products;
    ...
    public void setProducts(String[] products) {
        this.products = products;
    }
    public String[] getProducts() {
        return products;
    }
    public String getProduct(int i) {
        ...
    }
    public String getProduct() {
        return getProduct(0);
    }
    public void setProduct(String product) {
        products = new String[1];
        products[0] = product;
        return;
    }
    ...
}
```

In this example, the `getProduct` and `setProduct` methods are just simplified interfaces to the `getProducts` and `setProducts` methods in the case where there is only one product required. We would not want to generate an XML element for both the `product` and the `products` properties of this bean, so in this recipe we will show how to hide an unwanted property (`product`).

Getting ready

We need to know the class name of the bean and the name of the property that we wish to remove from the XML mapping.

How to do it...

1. Add an `<xml-transient>` element to the mapping file.

    In the OXM mapping file, we declare that a property is to be transient and not show up in the WSDL mapping by marking it as `<xml-transient>`, as shown in the following code snippet:

    ```xml
    <?xml version="1.0" encoding="UTF-8" ?>
    <xml-bindings ... >
      <java-types>
        <java-type name="soa.cookbook.QuoteRequest">
          <java-attributes>
            <!-- Can remove mappings by making them
                 transient via xml-transient element -->
            <xml-transient java-attribute="product"/>
          </java-attributes>
        </java-type>
      </java-types>
    </xml-bindings>
    ```

    The `<java-type>` name property is the Java class that has the property we want to remove. The `<xml-transient>` name property is the name of the property in the class.

2. Save the mapping file.

3. Remap the interface if necessary.

    If the interface has already been mapped, then it is necessary to regenerate the WSDL interface for the changes we have made to take effect. Do this by deleting the existing wire and then rewiring.

How it works...

`<xml-transient>` causes the named property to be ignored by the Java to XML converter. This means that no XML element will be generated for the given property.

There's more...

We may decide to ignore a property because it is not used by our particular use case. This can simplify our composite. Any mappings from XML to Java will cause the property to be initialized with a default value, usually `null`.

Ignoring a property may improve runtime performance because there is less work to do, and the resulting XML document will also be smaller.

The `EXMMapping` project in the code samples has a sample OXM file (`mappings.xml`) demonstrating this.

See also

► The *Ignoring missing elements with XSLT* recipe in this chapter
► The *Ignoring missing elements with Assign* recipe in this chapter
► The *Overriding mapping of EJB data to XML* recipe in this chapter

Creating a wrapper element for a Java collection or array

Within Java we have collections and arrays that deal with multiple objects. The collection or array has a name, but the individual objects within it do not. Because of this, the default mapping of a collection or array is just a repeating element.

Within XML, we usually like to provide a complex type element that has a sequence within it to hold the repeating elements. In other words, we want a schema that looks like the following screenshot. In this recipe, we will look at how to provide a wrapper element for our collections.

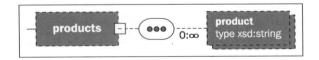

Getting ready

We need to know the class name of the bean and the name of the property that is a collection or array requiring a wrapper element.

How to do it...

1. Add an `<xml-element-wrapper>` element to the mapping file.

   In the OXM mapping file, we declare that a property requires a wrapper element in the WSDL mapping by marking it with an `<xml-element-wrapper>` as follows:

```xml
<?xml version="1.0" encoding="UTF-8" ?>
<xml-bindings ...>
  <java-types>
    <java-type name="soa.cookbook.QuoteRequest">
      <java-attributes>
        <xml-element java-attribute="products" name="product">
          <!-- Can provide wrapper element for arrays and
               collections via xml-element-wrapper element -->
          <xml-element-wrapper name="products"/>
        </xml-element>
      </java-attributes>
    </java-type>
  </java-types>
</xml-bindings>
```

   The `<java-type>` name property is the Java class that has the property we need to provide a wrapper for. The `<xml-element>` java-attribute property is the name of the Java property that needs to be wrapped, and the elements name attribute is the name we want that XML element to have in the generated schema. The `<xml-element-wrapper>` name attribute is the name we want that XML element wrapper to have in the generated schema.

2. Save the mapping file.

3. Remap the interface if necessary.

   If the interface has already been mapped, then it is necessary to regenerate the WSDL interface for the changes we have made to take effect. Do this by deleting the existing wire and then rewiring.

How it works...

`<xml-element>` is used to identify an XML element that should be generated and how it maps onto a Java bean property or class. The `<xml-element-wrapper>` property causes a wrapper XML element to be a part of the generated XML Schema. Using the `name` attribute allows us to control the name of the actual data element and the wrapper. We need this because often the Java property name will be a plural (such as products), and we want the actual data element to have a singular name (product) and would prefer the wrapper element to be plural (products).

The `EXMMapping` project in the code samples has a sample OXM file (`mappings.xml`) demonstrating this.

There's more...

If we only have a single property in a bean, then there is no need for a wrapper class because the containing class provides that function.

See also

▶   The *Array processing with XSLT* recipe in this chapter

▶   The *Array processing with BPEL Assign* recipe in this chapter

▶   The *Overriding mapping of EJB data to XML* recipe in this chapter

▶   The *Handling an abstract class* recipe in this chapter

Handling an abstract class

Within Java, we often have abstract classes and commonly use them in collections and arrays. When a class is abstract, we cannot generate XML for any derived elements because they are not known until runtime. An example of this is the following code structure:

```
public abstract class VendorQuote implements Serializable
   . . .
public class HardwareVendorQuote extends VendorQuote
   . . .
public class ServiceVendorQuote extends VendorQuote
   . . .
public class Quote implements Serializable {
   private AbstractList<VendorQuote> vendors;
   . . .
```

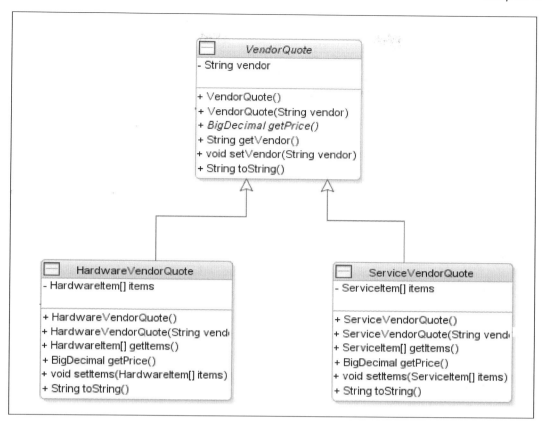

Note, that the `vendors` attribute in the `Quote` class is the collection of an abstract class. If we need our XML to differentiate between these concrete classes or create a `Quote` class (which will need concrete classes in the collection), then we need to generate XML Schema elements for the concrete derived classes `HardwareVendorQuote` and `SoftwareVendorQuote`. In this recipe we show how to achieve this.

Getting ready

We need to know the class name of the bean and the name of the property that is the abstract class.

How to do it...

1. Add the `<xml-see-also>` and `<xml-elements>` elements to the mapping file.

    In the OXM mapping file, we declare that a property has multiple possible concrete classes, and hence multiple possible elements in the WSDL mapping, by marking it with an `<xml-elements>`, as shown in the following code snippet:

    ```xml
    <?xml version="1.0" encoding="UTF-8" ?>
    <xml-bindings ...>
      <java-types>
        <java-type name="soa.cookbook.Quote">
          <!-- Indicate that we are referencing these classes
               and so generate mappings for them -->
          <xml-see-also>
            soa.cookbook.HardwareVendorQuote
            soa.cookbook.ServiceVendorQuote
          </xml-see-also>
          <java-attributes>
            <xml-elements java-attribute="vendors">
              <!-- Can provide concrete classes for
                   abstract classes via explicit type
                   attribute in xml-element -->
              <xml-element type="soa.cookbook.HardwareVendorQuote"
                      name="hwVendorQuote"/>
              <xml-element type="soa.cookbook.ServiceVendorQuote"
                      name="svcVendorQuote"/>
              <xml-element-wrapper name="vendors"/>
            </xml-elements>
          </java-attributes>
        </java-type>
      </java-types>
    </xml-bindings>
    ```

    The `<xml-elements>` `java-attribute` property is the name of the Java property that we want to associate with potential concrete classes; the `<xml-element>` elements under the `<xml_elements>` element identify the potential concrete classes for this abstract class. The `<xml-see-also>` is a list of concrete classes that we need to provide XML types for in the generated schema. The `<xml-element>` name property is the name of our concrete element and the `type` property in the concrete Java class.

2. Save the mapping file.

3. Remap the interface if necessary.

    If the interface has already been mapped, then it is necessary to regenerate the WSDL interface for the changes we have made to take effect. Do this by deleting the existing wire and then rewiring.

How it works...

`<xml-elements>` provides a list of all the possible concrete elements that may be found in the given abstract Java class. Each `<xml-element>` element is used to identify an XML element that should be generated and how it maps onto a concrete class extending the abstract Java class. The `<xml-see-also>` element is really a hint to the schema generator that it will need to create the XML elements corresponding to the listed Java classes.

The `EXMMapping` project in the code samples has a sample OXM file (`mappings.xml`) demonstrating this.

There's more...

When creating the mapping file, we need to be aware of all the possible concrete implementations that we may encounter. If we add new concrete classes to our Java implementation, we need to revisit the mapping file to add the new concrete classes.

See also

- The *Array processing with XSLT* recipe in this chapter
- The *Array processing with BPEL Assign* recipe in this chapter
- The *Overriding mapping of EJB data to XML* recipe in this chapter
- The *Creating a wrapper element for a Java collection or array* recipe in this chapter
- The *Handling an abstract class* recipe in this chapter

5
Composite Messaging Patterns

In this chapter, we will cover:

- ▶ Message aggregation within a composite
- ▶ Using dynamic partner links with BPEL 2.0
- ▶ Singleton composite
- ▶ Scheduling services
- ▶ Scheduling a service within a composite
- ▶ Deleting a scheduled service within a composite

Introduction

This chapter explores some of the more complex but relatively common message interaction patterns used in a typical SOA deployment.

While these patterns have been around for a while, some have proved cumbersome to implement in earlier versions of the SOA Suite (both 10gR3 and the initial release of 11gR1). However, later releases of the SOA Suite have introduced new features, such as aggregation, which provides better support for these patterns.

In this chapter, we take advantage of these to provide recipes for implementing patterns around message aggregation, singletons, and the dynamic scheduling of BPEL processes and services.

Message aggregation within a composite

A typical messaging requirement is to aggregate multiple related messages for processing within a single BPEL process instance. There are two parts to this recipe; the first is to route related messages through to the same instance of a BPEL process. This can be achieved using a correlation set defined against a common value present in each message.

The second is to determine when we have all the messages that belong to the aggregation. Typically, most use cases fall into two broad patterns:

- **Fixed duration**: In this scenario, we don't know how many messages we expect to receive, so we will process all those received within a specified period of time.

- **Wait for all**: In this scenario, we know how many messages we expect to receive. Once they have been received, we can process them as an aggregated message. It's usual to combine this with a timeout, so the process doesn't wait forever, if some messages aren't received.

An example of the first pattern is an order aggregation process, whereby we aggregate the orders we receive for a particular book over a period of time (for example, 24 hours) and then place a single order with the publisher for the total amount of orders received.

Getting ready

This recipe makes use of the new aggregation feature in Oracle SOA Suite 11gR1 Patch Set 5 (11.1.1.6.0), so you need to ensure that you have installed either this or a later release of the Oracle SOA Suite.

Create an SOA application with a project containing an empty composite (named WarehouseService in the following example).

How to do it...

1. Drag a BPEL process from the **SOA Component Palette** onto our composite. This will launch the **Create BPEL Process** wizard. Specify an appropriate name (**WarehouseService**, in the following screenshot), and for the template, select **Base on a WSDL**.

2. Click on the **Find Existing WSDLs** icon. This will launch the SOA Resource Browser. Browse the filesystem to select the WSDL that you wish to import and click on **OK**.

 Ideally, the WSDL should define a one-way asynchronous operation that we will use to implement our aggregation service. While synchronous operations are supported, they are not recommended and should be avoided.

For the purpose of following this example, select the
`WarehouseService_1.0.wsdl` node included with the samples for this chapter.

Ensure **Warehouse Service** is selected as the **Port Type**, and click on **OK**. This will
add BPEL Process Warehouse Service to our composite.

3. In the SOA Composite Editor, select the BPEL process service component, as
    shown next:

4. In the **Property Inspector** pane in the lower-right corner of Oracle JDeveloper, click on
    the **Add** icon (circled in the following screenshot).

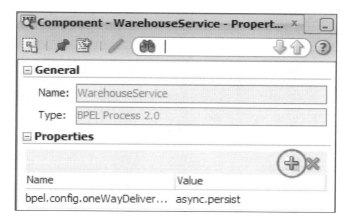

5. This will open the **Create Property** dialog. In the **Name** field, enter `bpel.config.`
    `reenableAggregationOnComplete`, and in the **Value** field, enter `true`; then,
    click on **OK**.

 If the **Property Inspector** pane is not displayed, select
Property Inspector from the **View** menu bar in JDeveloper.

6. Next, we need to create and initialize a `While` loop to process our messages. Create
    an **xsd:boolean** variable named `orderComplete` and use an **Assign** activity to set it
    to `false()`.

Create a variable named `waitUntil`, of type **xsd:dateTime**, and use an **Assign** activity to set it to the following value:

```
xp20:add-dayTimeDuration-to-dateTime(xp20:current-
    dateTime(), 'PT1H')
```

7. Next, drag a **While** activity onto the BPEL process (after the **Assign** activity) and set its `loop` condition to the following value:

```
$orderComplete = false()
```

8. Then, drag a **Pick** activity onto the **While** activity, double-click on the **OnMessage** icon to open the **Edit OnMessage** window.

   For **Partner Link**, select the same partner link used by the initial receive activity (`warehouseservice_client`, in this example), and select the same operation (`submitBookOrder`).

   Click on the **auto-create** variable (the plus icon) to launch the **Create Variable** window and give the variable a meaningful name (for example, `nextBookOrder`). Next, click on **OK**.

9. Now we need to add a step to aggregate the book orders. Drag an **Assign** activity onto the **OnMessage** activity.

   Add an expression to increment the quantity of the original order received, by the quantity of the new order; in other words:

```
origOrder/quantity = origOrder/quantity +
    nextOrder/quantity
```

   The XPath expression, should look something like the following:

```
$inputVariable.payload.ns2:bookOrder/ns2:quantity +
    $nextBookOrder.payload.ns2:bookOrder/ns2:quantity
```

10. Select the **Pick** activity and click on the **Add onAlarm** icon. Double-click on the **onAlarm** icon to open the **Edit onAlarm** window.

    Set the first radio button to **Until**, and set the second radio button to **Expression**; then, set the expression value to be `$waitUntil`.

11. Next, drag an **Assign** activity onto the **OnAlarm** activity, and assign the value `true()` to `$orderComplete`.

12. Within the **Structure** view for the BPEL process, right-click on the **Properties** folder and select **Create Property...**, as shown in the following screenshot:

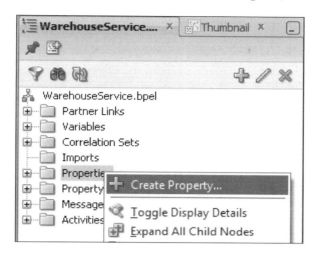

This will launch the **Create CorrelationSet Property** window. Give the property a meaningful name (for example, `isbn`), and then click on the search icon to launch the **Type Chooser** window and select the appropriate schema type (for example, `xsd:string`).

13. Click on the **Create Property Alias...** icon, circled in the following screenshot:

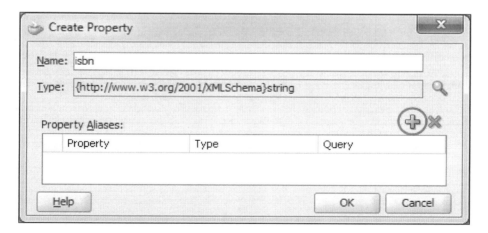

This will open the **Property Alias** window. In the **Type Explorer** window, expand the `WarehouseService_1.0.wsdl` node (under the **Project WSDL Files** folder). Next, expand the **Message Types** folder and select **Part - payload** (under `submitBookOrder`) as highlighted in the following screenshot:

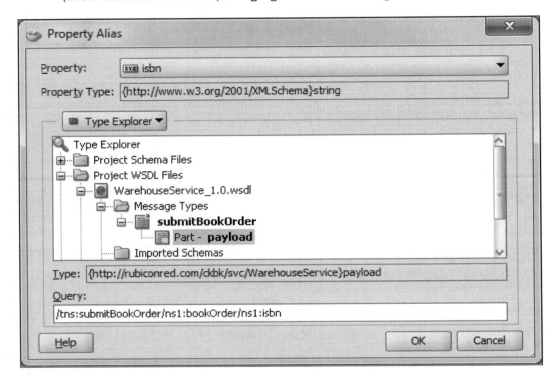

14. In the **Query** field, enter the XPath location of the ISBN in the `submitBookOrder` message, which is:

```
/tns: ns1:bookOrder/ns1:isbn
```

Then click on **OK**.

15. Within the **Structure** view for the BPEL process, expand the **Correlation Sets** folder, and then expand the **Process** folder. Then, right-click on the **Correlation Sets** folder and select **Create Correlation Set...**, as shown in the following screenshot:

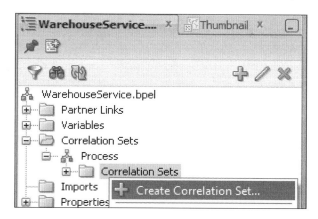

This will launch the **Create Correlation Set** window; give the correlation set a meaningful name, for example, `isbnCS`.

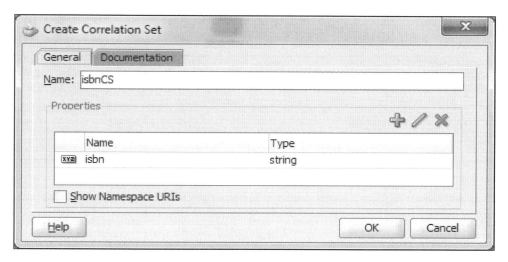

16. Next, click on the plus icon to launch the **Property Chooser** window, and select the `isbn` property created in step 12.

17. Now we need to initialize the correlation set. Within the BPEL Editor, double-click on the **receiveInput** activity to open the **Edit Receive** window, and select the **Correlations** tab.

18. Click on **Create Correlation...** (the plus icon circled in the following screenshot). This will add an empty correlation to the **Receive** activity.

19. For the **Correlation Set** field, select **isbnCS** from the drop-down list. Next, select **Yes** from the **Initiate** field dropdown, as shown in the following screenshot:

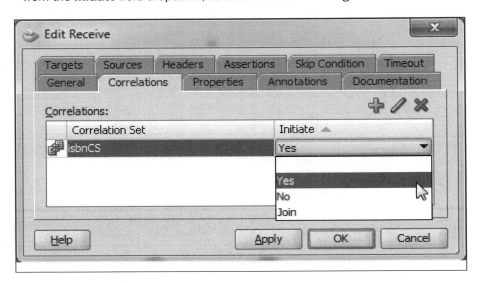

20. Within the BPEL Editor, double-click on the **onMessage** activity to open the **Edit onMessage** window, and select the **Correlations** tab.

21. Click on **Create Correlation...**, the plus icon. This will add an empty correlation to the **onMessage** activity. For the **Correlation Set** field, select **isbnCS** from the drop-down list. Next, select **No** from the **Initiate** dropdown.

22. Deploy the `WarehouseService` composite to the Oracle SOA Suite and use Enterprise Manager to submit multiple `submitBookOrder` messages.

    For book orders that contain the same ISBN number, you should see that they are routed through to the same instance of the BPEL process.

How it works...

Since the 11.1.1.6 release of the Oracle SOA Suite, Oracle BPEL Process Manager has supported a message aggregation feature. When multiple messages are routed to the same process, the first message is routed to create a new instance and subsequent messages can be routed to continue the created instance using a mid-process receive activity.

By default, this feature is disabled. To enable it, we need to set the property `bpel.config. reenableAggregationOnComplete` to true.

Prior to 11.1.1.6, the same result could be achieved by using a different name for the operation that created the process instance from the operation used to receive the second and subsequent messages.

Once we have enabled aggregation, we still have to define the key that the BPEL engine should use in order to aggregate messages. For this, we use a correlation set (isbnCS, in the previous example) that consists of one or more properties (isbn in our case). These properties are then mapped, using a property alias, to the corresponding field in the messages that are being aggregated.

The combined value of these properties at runtime should result in a unique value (at least, unique across all instances of the same process) that allows the BPEL engine to route the message to the appropriate instance of a process.

On receipt of the first message in the aggregation, we need to tell the BPEL process to initialize the correlation set, which we did by setting the initiate property to true (in step 19). This then tells the BPEL engine to route all other messages that contain the same value to this instance of the BPEL process.

There's more...

With this pattern, messages are processed in the order they are received in, by the BPEL process; this may be different from the sequence in which the messages are sent. If messages need to be aggregated in a particular order, the messages should be re-sequenced prior to processing.

Using dynamic partner links with BPEL 2.0

With most BPEL processes, partner links are **static** in that they reference a single instance of web service specified by the developer at design time (though typically configured at deployment).

In the majority of cases, this approach is fine. However, in this recipe we will consider a scenario in which a standard service contract might be implemented by multiple providers, the selection of which we want to dynamically configure at runtime.

An example of this, is the order aggregation process of our online bookstore, where at the point of placing an order with the publisher, we will need to invoke the appropriate service in order to route our book order to the correct publisher.

For this scenario, the BPEL language supports the concept of dynamic partner links, which enables the BPEL process to specify at runtime the endpoint of the web service being invoked and bind to it dynamically.

In this recipe, we will build on the order aggregation process of our online bookstore in order to route our book orders to the appropriate publisher.

Getting ready

In order to use this design pattern, you will need to define a standard WSDL to be implemented by each of your routing destinations (publishers, in our example).

For our purposes, we have defined the WSDL `Publisher_Service_1.0.wsdl`, which defines the operation `submitBookOrder`.

We have provided three basic implementations of this service, as defined in the following table:

Publisher	Endpoint
ACME	`http://<host>:7001/soa-infra/services/default /PublisherACME/publisheracme_client_ep`
Packt	`http://<host>:7001/soa-infra/services/default /PublisherPackt/publisherpackt_client_ep`
Skynet	`http://<host>:7001/soa-infra/services/default /PublisherSkynet/publisherskynet_client_ep`

These implementations are defined in the **PublisherApp** application, which is included in the sample for the book. You will need to open this sample in JDeveloper and deploy to your instance of the SOA Suite.

For the purpose of this recipe, we will extend the *Message aggregation within a composite* recipe to place the aggregated order, so you will either need to follow this sample recipe or open the sample solution with JDeveloper.

In addition, we are going to create a variable of type `Endpoint Reference`, defined in the schema `ws-addressing.xsd`. This is already defined and deployed to MDS. So, to reference this from within our BPEL process, we will need to create a file-based MDS connection in JDeveloper.

Instructions on how to do this are defined in the *Creating a file-based MDS repository for JDeveloper* recipe in *Chapter 2, Using the Metadata Service to Share XML Artifacts*.

How to do it...

1. Open the `Message Aggregation` composite and drag a web service onto the **External Reference** swimlane. This will open the **Create Web Service** window. Give it the name `PublisherService`, and then browse to the `PublisherService_1.0.wsdl` WSDL included with the samples and select it.

   When prompted to localize files, ensure that the option **Maintain original directory structure for imported files** is selected, but deselect the option **Rename duplicate files**.

   Next, wire the `WarehouseService` service to the `PublisherService` service.

2. The next step is to invoke the publisher service. Open the **WarehouseService BPEL** process, and drag an **Invoke** activity onto the end of the BPEL process (after the `while` loop).

   Open the **Edit Invoke** window, give it the name `submitPublisherOrder`, specify `PublisherService` as the **Partner Link**, and ensure **submitBookOrder** is selected as the operation.

   Create an input variable with the name `publisherBookOrder` and an output variable with the name `publisherBookOrderResponse`.

3. We now need to initialize the `publisherBookOrder` variable. Drag an **Assign** activity on to the BPEL process just before the **Invoke** activity `submitPublisherOrder`.

   Map the content of `inputVariable/payload/ns1:submitBookOrder` to `publisherBookOrder/payload/ns4:submitBookOrder`.

4. Open the **Variables** window for the BPEL process, and click on **Create**. This will open the **Create Variable** window. Specify a name for **publisherEndpoint**, specify a type of Element, and then click on **Browse Elements...** (the magnifying glass icon).

   This will open the **Type Chooser** window. Click on **Import Schema File....** This will launch the **Import Schema File** window. Click on the **Browse Resources...** icon to open the **SOA Resource Browser** window.

5. Ensure **Resource Palette** is selected from the dropdown, and then expand the following:

   ```
   IDE Connections > SOA-MDS > File Based MDS > soa > shared
     > common
   ```

Select the schema **ws-addressing.xsd** as shown in the following screenshot:

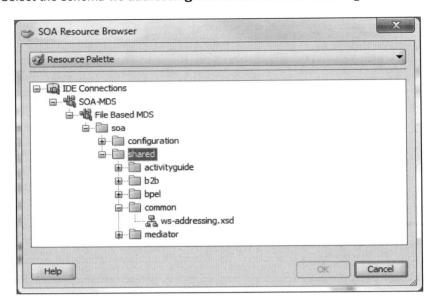

6. In the **Import Schema** file, uncheck **Copy to Project**, and click on **OK**.

    In the **Type Chooser** window, select **Endpoint Reference**, as shown in the following screenshot:

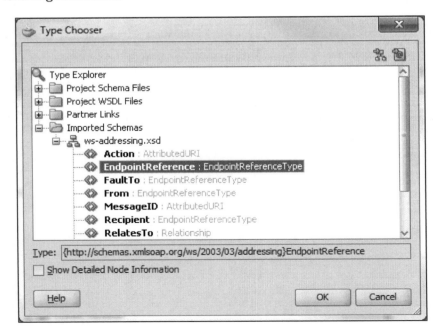

7. Next, we need to set the variable `publisherEndpoint` to contain the endpoint of the appropriate publisher service that we wish to invoke.

   To populate the `Address` element, use a transformation activity rather than an **Assign** activity. We have used a `concat` function, as shown in the following screenshot, to create the endpoint based on the publisher name and map that to the `Address` element within the `EndpointReference` variable:

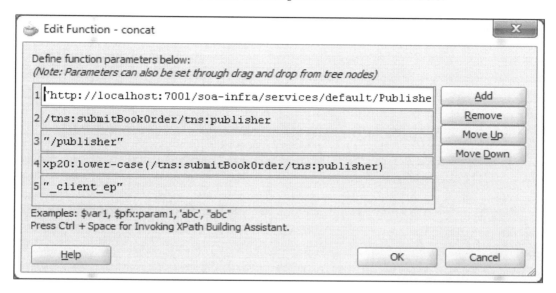

```
Edit Function - concat                                                    X

Define function parameters below:
(Note: Parameters can also be set through drag and drop from tree nodes)

1 "http://localhost:7001/soa-infra/services/default/Publishe    Add

2 /tns:submitBookOrder/tns:publisher                            Remove

3 "/publisher"                                                  Move Up

4 xp20:lower-case(/tns:submitBookOrder/tns:publisher)           Move Down

5 "_client_ep"

Examples: $var1, $pfx:param1, 'abc', "abc"
Press Ctrl + Space for Invoking XPath Building Assistant.

   Help                                         OK            Cancel
```

 In reality, we would want to use the publisher name to look up the actual endpoint; but have just taken this approach to keep it simple.

8. Open the **Variables** window for the BPEL process and click on **Create**. This will open the **Create Variable** window. Specify a name for **publisherServiceRef**, specify a type of element, and then click on **Browse Elements...**.

   In the **Type Chooser** window, select **Import Schema File...**. Browse the filesystem and select the file `ws-bpel_serviceref.xsd`, included with the samples for the *Getting ready* section for this recipe. In the **Import Schema File**, uncheck **Copy to Project**, and click on **OK**.

   In the **Type Chooser** window, select **service-ref**.

9. Drag an **Assign** activity onto the BPEL process, just before the **Invoke** activity, and give it the name `setPublisherServiceRef`.

   Map `publisherEndpoint` to `publisherServiceRef/ns6:service-ref/xsd:any`.

JDeveloper will prompt you with the following warning:

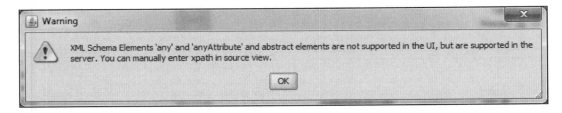

10. Double click on **To** part of the copy rule to open the **Expression Builder** window, and manually update the XPath to `$publisherServiceRef/ns5:EndpointReference`.

 Note that the namespace prefix may not be ns5; rather, you should ensure that you specify the prefix mapped to the namespace `http://schemas.xmlsoap.org/ws/2003/03/addressing`.

11. Then, right-click on the **To** part of the copy rule and select **insertMissingToData**.

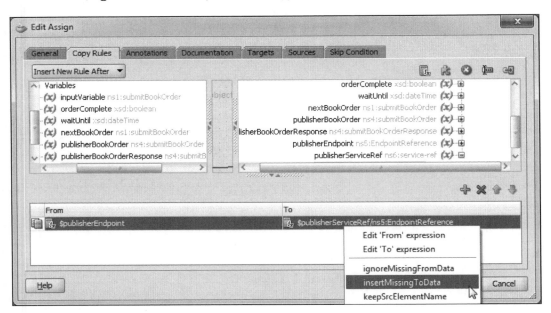

12. Next, create a copy rule to map `$publisherServiceRef` to the `PublisherService` partner link, as shown in the following screenshot:

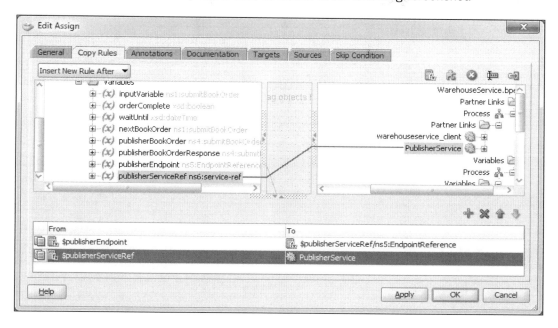

13. Deploy the updated `WarehouseService` composite to the Oracle SOA Suite and use Enterprise Manager to submit multiple `submitBookOrder` messages.

Ensure that you specify either ACME, Packt, or Skynet as the publisher , you should see that orders are dynamically routed by the Warehouse Service to the appropriate publisher service.

How it works...

BPEL 2.0 provides support for dynamic partner links. This allows a BPEL 2.0 process to override the endpoint specified at design time for a partner link, with a value determined at runtime.

While we can override the endpoint for a partner link, all other attributes of our service definition remain fixed. So, to use this approach, we must define a common WSDL interface that all of our services will implement.

To dynamically invoke the appropriate endpoint at runtime, we need to update the endpoint reference of the partner link before invoking the service. To do this, we need to create a variable of type `Service-Ref` (as defined by `ws-bpel_serviceref`) and populate it with a variable of type `EndPointReference` (as defined by `WS-Addressing`) containing just an `<Address>` element populated with the endpoint of the publisher service that we wish to invoke.

This is important, since if we create an `EndpointReference` containing any of the other optional elements, the BPEL engine will throw a fault when we try and invoke the partner link.

To do this, we used a transformation activity rather than an **Assign** activity, since **Assign** will create all optional elements as well (we could still use an **Assign**, but we would need to add a `remove` rule for each of these elements). Once done, we inserted this into the `Service-Ref` variable.

Once we have created the `Service-Ref` variable, we just map it to the partner link before invoking the service, and BPEL will dynamically route the request to the updated endpoint.

There's more...

Oracle Service Bus also enables the dynamic routing of web service invocations at runtime.

If you are implementing a solution where OSB provides a virtualization layer on top of all your external services, we would recommend that as the appropriate place to implement dynamic routing.

However, if you are only using the core Oracle SOA Suite (minus the OSB), this isn't an option. In addition, there are occasions where you may want to dynamically assemble SCA composites to build a dynamic end-to-end business process. In this scenario, dynamic partner links can prove extremely useful.

Singleton composite

A typical use case with a composite would be submitting a request to an external resource/system that only supports a single connection at a time. In such a case, we need to protect against parallel composite instances submitting concurrent requests to that resource.

This implies that we need some way to serialize requests for that resource (probably on a first-in, first-out basis). A common design pattern for achieving this is the singleton, first documented in the book *Design Patterns: Elements of Reusable Object-Oriented Software, Gang of Four* (where they use a print spooler as an example).

Now, BPEL doesn't explicitly support the notion of a singleton, however it does allow you to simulate one using a variation of the *Message aggregation within a composite* recipe, which is good enough for the purpose of what we are trying to achieve.

Getting ready

For the purpose of this recipe, we will extend the `PublisherSkynet` service used in the *Using dynamic partner link* recipe, so that we can only publish a single order to Skynet at a time.

We have extended the implementation of this composite for the BPEL process `PublisherSkynet` to invoke the BPEL process `PublisherAsyncService`. You can find the code for this extended example in the *Getting ready* section of this recipe.

For this recipe, we are going to show how to modify the `PublisherAsyncService` process to act as a singleton. So, you will need to open this composite with JDev to follow this sample recipe.

 As many components of this recipe are similar to the Message Aggregation process, for the sake of brevity, we have summarized many of the steps covered in the initial recipe.

How to do it...

1. In the SOA Composite Editor, ensure you have selected the BPEL process `PublisherAsyncService`. In the **Property Inspector** pane, in the lower-right corner of Oracle JDeveloper, click on the **Add** icon.

   This will open the **Create Property** dialog. In the **Name** field, enter `bpel.config.reenableAggregationOnComplete`, and in the **Value** field, enter `true`; then, click on **OK**.

2. Open the BPEL process `PublisherSkynet`. Open the **Assign** activity `setSubmitBookOrder`, and add a third copy rule to set the value of `token` to the following expression:

   ```
   substring( xp20:current-dateTime(), 1, 16)
   ```

   Save and close this process.

3. Open the BPEL process `PublisherAsyncService`. First, we need to create and initialize a `While` loop to process the messages in sequence. Create an **xsd:boolean** variable named **processingComplete**, and use an **Assign** activity to set it to `false()`.

   Create a variable named **waitUntil** of type **xsd:dateTime**, and use an **Assign** activity to set it to the following expression:

   ```
   xp20:add-dayTimeDuration-to-dateTime( concat
     ($inputVariable.payload/ns1:token, ':00'), 'PT1M')
   ```

Next, drag a **While** activity onto the BPEL process (after the **Assign** activity) and set its `loop` condition to the following expression:

```
$processingComplete = false()
```

4. Then, drag a **Pick** activity onto the **While** activity. Double-click on the **OnMessage** icon to open the **Edit OnMessage** window.

   For **Partner Link**, select the same partner link used by the initial receive activity (`publisherasyncservice_client`, in this example), and select the same operation (`submitBookOrder`).

   Click on the **auto-create** variable (plus icon) to launch the **Create Variable** window. Give the variable a meaningful name (for example, `nextBookOrder`).

5. Next, we need to add the logic to process the message. This is where we would typically call out to an external resource/system that only supports a single connection at a time.

   For the purpose of this recipe, we are just going to add a 10 second delay to simulate the time required by the external system to process the request. So, drag a **Wait** activity onto the **onMessage** branch, and set it to wait for 10 seconds.

6. Select the **Pick** activity and click on the **Add onAlarm** icon. Double-click on the **onAlarm** icon to open the **Edit onAlarm** window.

   Set the first radio button to **Until**, and set the second radio button to **Expression**; then, set the expression value to `$waitUntil`.

7. Within the **Structure** view for the BPEL process, right-click on the `Properties` folder and select **Create Property...**. This will launch the **Create Property** window. Give the property a meaningful name, (for example, `token`), and then click on the search icon to launch the **Type Chooser** window; select the appropriate schema type (for example, `xsd:string`).

8. Click on the **Create Property Alias...** icon. This will open the **Property Alias** window. In the **Type Explorer** window, expand the `PublisherAsyncService_1.0.wsdl` node (under the **Project WSDL Files** folder). Next, expand the **Message Types** folder and select the **Part - payload** under the `submitBookOrder` message type.

   In the **Query** field, enter the XPath location of the token in the `submitBookOrder` message, which is as follows:

   ```
   /tns:submitBookOrder/tns:token
   ```

   Then click on **OK**.

9. Within the **Structure** view for the BPEL process, expand the **Correlation Sets** folder, and then expand the **Process** folder. Then, right-click on the **Correlation Sets** folder and select **Create Correlation Set...**.

This will launch the **Create Correlation Set** window. Give the correlation set a meaningful name, for example, `tokenCS`.

Next, click on the plus icon to launch the **Property Chooser** window, and select the `token` property.

10. Next, we need to initialize the correlation set. Within the BPEL editor, double-click on the **receiveInput** activity to open the **Edit Receive** window, and select the **Correlations** tab.

    Click on **Create Correlation...**, the plus icon. This will add an empty correlation to the **Receive** activity.

    For the **Correlation Set** field, select **tokenCS** from the dropdown. Next, select **Yes** from the **Initiate** dropdown.

11. Within the BPEL editor, double-click on the **onMessage** activity to open the **Edit onMessage** window, and select the **Correlations** tab.

    Click on **Create Correlation...**, the plus icon. This will add an empty correlation to the **onMessage** activity. For the **Correlation Set** field, select **tokenCS** from the dropdown. Next, select **No** from the **Initiate** dropdown.

12. Deploy the `PublisherSkynet` composite to the Oracle SOA Suite and use Enterprise Manager to submit multiple `submitBookOrder` messages.

    For book orders that are submitted in the same minute, you should see that they are routed through to the same instance of the BPEL process.

How it works...

This recipe makes use of the message aggregation feature we introduced in the first recipe to route multiple messages to the same process instance so that we can process them sequentially, thus ensuring that only a single request is submitted at a time to our external resource.

As before, the first message is routed to create a new instance of our singleton; subsequent messages then need to be routed through to this in-flight instance that is achieved by the use of a shared **token**, which is used to correlate messages against the singleton instance.

With a typical implementation of a singleton, we would create a single instance of that object and it would live forever. However, with BPEL, we can't let the process loop forever as, over time, the size of the audit trail for the BPEL instance within the dehydration store would get too big and impact the overall performance of the BPEL engine.

Thus, in reality, we need an instance of the singleton process to run for a period of time, and then, terminate gracefully at the end of this period, to be replaced by a new instance of the BPEL process.

For the purpose of this recipe, we have assumed that an instance of the singleton will run for just 1 minute (obviously, in reality we would allow a longer duration, for example, 24 hours, but it would take a long time to test the recipe).

So, for this purpose, we are using the current time (based on a shared system clock) to create the token. Take a look at the following statement:

```
substring( xp20:current-dateTime(), 1, 16)
```

The preceding statement creates a token of the format `CCYY-MM-DDThh:mm`. Thus, every message received in the same minute will have the same token and get routed through to the same instance of the BPEL process.

The process itself will only wait until `CCYY-MM-DDThh:mm` + *1 minute* for new messages before terminating.

There's more...

It should be noted that this approach isn't perfect. An obvious issue is what happens if the singleton is sent more messages than it is able to process within its execution window.

In this scenario, the messages would be queued up for delivery, but because the singleton terminates at the end of its window, those messages would be left on the queue and would never get processed.

One answer here is for the singleton. Once it has completed its execution period to enter a second loop that retrieves each remaining message and forwards it to the singleton (via the wrapper process — PublisherSkynet in the previous example). This will generate a new token based on the new time and the message will get invoked by the new singleton.

Of course, with this scenario, there is still the possibility that a message could keep getting forwarded forever, but this would imply the throughput of messages requiring processing is greater than the external resource/system can process over a sustained period of time, and therefore, we are "resource constrained" by the backend system.

The other potential issue is that we could have a race condition between the end of one singleton process and the start of the next, with both processes trying to access the same resource at the same time. To reduce the likelihood of this, we could include a wait period at the start of the process, which comfortably allows sufficient time for the previous process to complete.

Scheduling services

A common requirement is to schedule a process or service to run at regular intervals, for example, we have an account billing composite that is required to be run once every night.

The Oracle SOA Suite doesn't provide a native scheduling component, so a common approach is to implement a BPEL process that continuously loops, with the sole purpose of launching another scheduled BPEL process.

However, as the process never dies, this will result in an ever-increasing audit trail, causing the objects persisted in the database, as well as the in-memory size of the process to grow over time, which eventually will have a negative impact on the performance of the engine.

A better approach is to use a Web Service Scheduler deployed to the Oracle SOA Suite.

Getting ready

You will need to download the Scheduler from the Rubicon Red website, which can be found at `http://www.rubiconred.com/scheduler`.

Once downloaded, follow the instructions to install the Scheduler on the WebLogic server running SOA Suite.

We are going to schedule the **StockService** process to run every hour, on the hour. This is a process that checks the stock levels for fast-selling titles and raises alerts if they are falling too low.

For the purpose of this demo, we have included a light-weight application, called `StockApp`, within the *Getting ready* samples for this recipe. You will need to open it in JDeveloper and deploy to the Oracle SOA Suite to follow along with this recipe.

How to do it...

1. Log in to Oracle Enterprise Manager and open the **StockService** dashboard. Click on the **Show WSDL and Endpoint URI** icon (circled in the following screenshot). Log in to Oracle **Enterprise Manager** (**EM**) and open a window that contains the URI for the Stock Service WSDL.

   Highlight the WSDL URL and copy it, as we will need this in a moment.

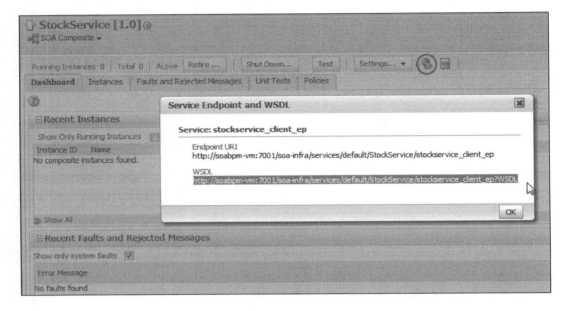

2. Log into the Scheduler at `http://<hostname>:7001/SchedulerUi/ SchedulerUIExt.html`.

   This will take you to the Scheduler dashboard. Click on the **Add Job** icon; this will open the **Edit Job** page. Enter the following information:

Field	Value
Job Name	Stock Check
Job Group	Stock
Schedule Type	Cron
Active	Ensure this is checked, otherwise the job won't be triggered.
From	Don't specify a value
Until	Don't specify a value
Cron Expression	0 * * * * ?

3. For the **Job type** field, ensure **Web service** is selected, and then within WSDL, paste the URL for the WSDL specified in step 1 and hit *Enter*. The Scheduler will parse the WSDL, and assuming it is valid, will display details of the binding and service endpoints.

4. From the **Operation** dropdown, select the **checkInventory** operation. This will populate the **Payload** field with a skeleton of the payload to be included, when the Scheduler invokes the web service. Update the content of the element **WarehouseId** to be `Main`, as shown in the following screenshot:

Create Job

Job Details:		
Job id	StockCheck	
Group	Stock	
Description	Checks stock levels of fast selling books.	
Schedule type	○ Simple ● Cron	
Active	☑ from [ ] 📅 until [ ] 📅	
Cron expression	0 * * * * ?	
Seconds	0	Minutes: *
Hours	*	Day of month: *
Month	*	Day of week: ?
Year	[ ]	

Job Definition:

Job type	● Web service ○ EDN	
WSDL	http://soabpm-vm:7001/soa-infra/services/default/StockService/stockservice_client_ep?V	
Binding	**StockServiceBinding**	Operation: checkInventory ▾
Service	**stockservice_client_ep**	Port: **StockService_pt**
Endpoint URL	http://soabpm-vm:7001/soa-infra/services/default/StockService/stockservice_client_ep	

Payload	`<stoc:checkInventory xmlns:stoc="http://rubiconred.com/ckbk/svc/StockService">`
	`  <stoc:warehouseId>Main</stoc:warehouseId>`
	`</stoc:checkInventory>`	

← Save

Once complete, click on **Save**. This will save the details of the job and return you to the dashboard.

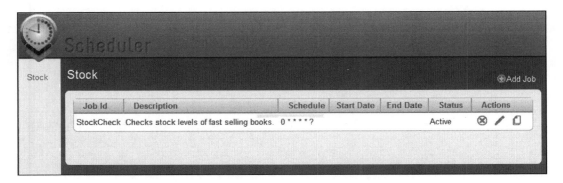

The job will now be active.

5. Log in to Enterprise Manager. Within the audit trail, we should be able to see an instance of the **StockService** process being created every 60 seconds.

How it works...

We have defined the job `Stock Check` in the `Stock` group with a cron schedule of `0 * * * * ?`.

This will create a Quartz job, under the covers, that fires every minute on the minute. When it triggers, it will cause the Scheduler to submit a web service request to the specified endpoint containing the payload that we defined.

There's more...

The Scheduler can be used to schedule synchronous and asynchronous web services deployed to the Oracle SOA Suite or Oracle Service. In addition, it can be used to schedule the publication of EDN events to the SOA Suite.

While cron expressions are powerful, they can be confusing. So, the Scheduler also supports the creation of Simple Schedules, which are simpler to understand.

The Scheduler also comes with a web service API that enables us to create schedules dynamically from within another service, which we will look at in the next couple of recipes.

This is also useful for deployment purposes, as we can use this to create scheduled jobs as part of the process of deploying composites to the SOA Suite.

Scheduling a service within a composite

A common system requirement is to dynamically schedule the future execution of a process or service relative to the occurrence of some event.

For example, we may have a customer satisfaction process, which we want to execute one month after the customer received delivery of ordered goods. Alternatively, we may want to schedule a repeating process for a specific period of time, for example, to track the status of a shipped item until it is delivered.

While this can be done using BPEL, it can cause issues when managing the dehydration store. Often, a better approach is to get the BPEL process to create a scheduled job to manage this separately.

Getting ready

You will need to download the Scheduler from the Rubicon Red website. It can be found at `http://www.rubiconred.com/scheduler`.

Once downloaded, follow the instructions to install the Scheduler on the WebLogic server running the Oracle SOA Suite.

To configure a scheduled job via the web service API, we will need the WSDL for the Scheduler. This can be found at `http://localhost:7001/RXRScheduler_2.0/util.sch.evs.Job?WSDL`.

For our purpose, we will be configuring the Scheduler to invoke our `ParcelTracker` process (as we use this in a later recipe). So, to follow the example, you will need to deploy the `ParcelTracker` composite contained within the example code for this chapter.

Once deployed, you will need the WSDL for the Parcel Tracker; this should be available at `http://localhost:7001/soa-infra/services/default/ParcelTracker/parceltrackerservice_client?WSDL`.

Create an SOA composite with a project containing a BPEL process (named **ScheduleParcelTracker** in the example detailed in this recipe).

The **ScheduleParcelTracker** process is designed to receive a request containing the `orderNo` for a parcel to be tracked and creating a scheduled job to invoke the `ParcelTracker` composite every 15 seconds to track the status of the specified order.

How to do it...

1. Drag a web service from the SOA Component Palette onto the **External References** swimlane within our composite. This will launch the **Create Web Service** wizard. Specify `Scheduler` as the name, and for the WSDL URL, enter the location of the Scheduler WSDL (see the *Getting ready* section).

    Ensure that **Port Type** is set to `util.sch.eve.Job` and click on **OK**. JDeveloper will add a reference to the Scheduler to our composite.

2. Next, drag a wire from the BPEL process to the Scheduler external reference.

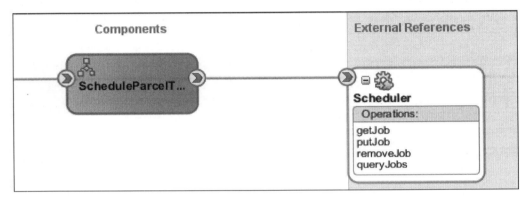

3. Open the `ScheduleParcelTracker` BPEL process and rename the default `inputVariable` variable to `orderNo`.

4. Next, drag an **Invoke** activity onto the BPEL process, double-click on it to open the **Edit Invoke** window. Give it the name `putJob`. For **Partner Link**, select `Scheduler` and select the operation `putJob`.

    For the input variable, click on the **auto-create** variable (plus icon) to launch the **Create Variable** window. Give the variable a meaningful name (for example, `putJobInput`). Do the same for the output variable.

5. Drag an **Assign** activity onto our BPEL process just before the **Invoke** activity. Double-click on it to open the **Edit Assign** window. Give it the name `setPutJob`.

6. First, we need to populate the job element with the unique identity of our job. This is a composite key defined by the elements `jobId` and `jobGroup`.

    Use the **Assign** activity to set `jobId` to contain the `orderNo` of the parcel being tracked and `jobGroup` to `ParcelTracker` (the name of our process).

    We have also set `jobDescription` to hold details of the parcel being tracked.

7. Next, we need to specify the schedule for when the job will be run. For the purpose of this recipe, we will use a basic cron schedule to run our job every 15 seconds. Use the **Assign** activity to specify the following values for the job:

Job element	Source
`ns9:startDate`	`xp20:current-date()`
`ns9:endDate`	`xp20:add-dayTimeDuration-to-dateTime(xp20:current-date(), 'P14D')`
`ns9:active`	`true()`
`ns9:jobDefinition/ns9:cronSchedule`	`'0/15 * * ?'`

We have specified that the job will only be active from the current date up to 14 days into the future (this is optional but will prevent the job from running forever, in case we forget to cancel it) and set the job to be active (otherwise it won't run).

8. Next, we need to initialize the `jobdefinition` element, which specifies the web service to be invoked and the content of the payload to be passed.

Use the **Assign** activity to initialize the attributes of the job in the element `$putJob.payload/ns8:body/ns9:job/ns9:jobDefinition`, as detailed within the following table:

Element	Source
`@jobClass`	`'WebService'`
`@responseInterface`	`'One-Way'`

We also need to use the **Assign** activity to initialize the content of the element `ns9:jobDefinition/ns9:webServiceJobDefinition`, as detailed in the following table:

Element	Value
`ns9:service/ns9:URI`	`'http://rubiconred.com/ckbk/svc/ParcelTrackerService'`
`ns9:service/ns9:localName`	`'parceltrackerservice_client'`
`ns9:port/ns9:URI`	`'http://rubiconred.com/ckbk/svc/ParcelTrackerService'`
`ns9:port/ns9:localName`	`'ParcelTrackerService_pt'`
`ns9:endpointAddress`	`'http://localhost:7001/soa-infra/services/default/ParcelTracker/parceltrackerservice_client'`

We have now configured the Scheduler to send a correctly formed SOAP message to a web service endpoint; the next step is to provide the payload to put in the message.

9. The `putJob` element contains an element called `soapRequestBody`, which is defined as `xs:anyType`. This is where we specify the request message to send to `ParcelTracker` when the Scheduler invokes it.

    To do this, we must create a variable of the same type as the message to be sent to `ParcelTracker`. This is defined in `ParcelTrackerService_1.0.wsdl`.

    Create a new global variable, named `syncParcelLocation`. Select **Message Type** as the variable type, and click on **Browse Message Types...** to open the **Type Chooser** window. From here, select **Import WSDL file** and locate the Parcel Tracker Service WSDL file. Ensure **copy to project** is selected and click on **OK**.

    Within the **Type Chooser** window, expand `ParcelTrackerService_1.0.wsdl` and select the message type `syncParcelLocation`.

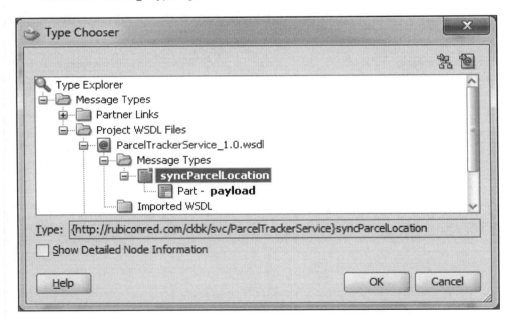

10. `syncParcelLocation` contains the element `orderNo`. Set this to be the `orderNo` contained within the variable used to invoke our BPEL process.

    Next, within the **Assign** activity, use an **Append** rule to copy the entire `syncParcelLocation` message into the `soapRequestBody` element.

11. When creating the mapping, you may have noticed a couple of choice elements, for example, `simpleSchedule` or `cronsSchedule`, and `ednJobDefinition` or `webServiceDefinition`.

By default, BPEL will create empty elements for these alternative choices at runtime, so we need to remove them to produce a valid message.

12. In the **Assign** activity, select the `simpleSchedule` element. Right-click and select **Remove**.

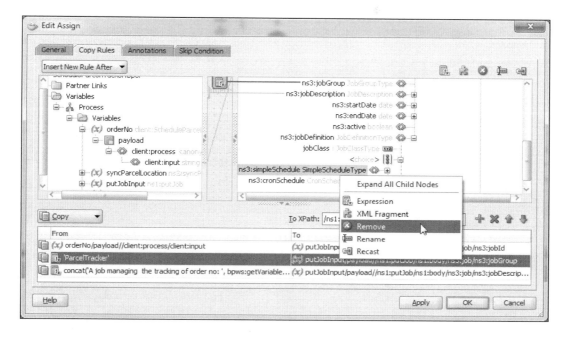

Repeat this step for the element `ednJobDefinition`.

Now that our process is complete, deploy it and run it to see the created job in action.

How it works...

When our `scheduleParcelTracker` composite is executed, it invokes the `putJob` operation against the Scheduler. The contents of the SOAP message should look somewhat like the following code snippet:

```
<job xmlns="http://rubiconred.com/ebo/util.sch.Job">
  <jobId xmlns:inp1=
    "http://rubiconred.com/ckbk/xsd/order">120699</jobId>
  <jobGroup>ParcelTracker</jobGroup>
  <jobDescription>A job managing the tracking of parcel
    120699</jobDescription>
  <startDate>2012-06-03</startDate>
  <endDate>2012-06-17</endDate>
  <active>true</active>
```

```
<jobDefinition jobClass="WebService">
  <cronSchedule>0/15 * * * ?</cronSchedule>
  <webServiceJobDefinition responseInterface="One-Way">
    <service>
      <URI>http://rubiconred.com/
        ckbk/svc/ParcelTrackerService</URI>
      <localName>parceltrackerservice_client</localName>
    </service>
    <port>
      <URI>http://rubiconred.com/
        ckbk/svc/ParcelTrackerService</URI>
      <localName>ParcelTrackerService_pt</localName>
    </port>
    <endpointAddress>http://localhost:7001/soa-infra/
      services/default/ParcelTracker/
      parceltrackerservice_client</endpointAddress>
    <soapRequestBody>
      <syncParcelLocation xmlns="http://rubiconred.com/
        ckbk/svc/ParcelTrackerService">
        <orderNo xmlns:inp1="http://rubiconred.com/
          ckbk/xsd/order">120699</orderNo>
      </syncParcelLocation>
    </soapRequestBody>
  </webServiceJobDefinition>
</jobDefinition>
</job>
```

This will cause the Scheduler to invoke `ParcelTracker` every 15 seconds. If you log in to Enterprise Manager you should be able to see a list of instances of the `ParcelTracker` composite being started every 15 seconds.

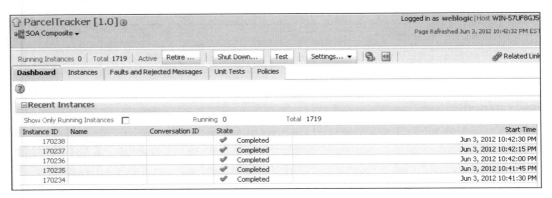

If we click on any of the ParcelTracker instances, we'll see the audit trail for a single instance of this repeatedly executed process.

There's more...

Our Scheduler exposes operations that enable the creation and management of the scheduled jobs listed as follows:

- ▶ `putJob`: Creates/updates a scheduled job
- ▶ `removeJob`: Removes a scheduled job
- ▶ `queryJobs`: Retrieves all jobs configured for a group
- ▶ `getJob`: Retrieves the configuration of a job

In this recipe we need to only use `putJob` to create a new scheduled job. If we run `putJob` for an already defined job, the Scheduler will just update that job with the new details. We will use `removeJob` to delete the job we just created, in the next recipe.

Depending on our process's requirements, we may need to use the `queryJobs` operation to fetch a list of existing jobs from the Scheduler. We can filter this by specifying the job group `groupId` (`ParcelTracker`, in this example), and we can use `getJob` to fetch the details of a specific job.

Not only is the Scheduler capable of triggering web services using an SOAP message, but we can also use it to publish an EDN event.

Deleting a scheduled service within a composite

Often, scheduled jobs that we create dynamically are temporary in nature. So, once created, we need the ability to delete them when no longer required.

Getting ready

For the purpose of this recipe, we will delete the scheduled job created in the previous recipe. So, you will need to complete that recipe before starting this.

Create an SOA application, with a project containing an empty composite (named `CancelParcelTracker` in the example detailed in this recipe).

The `CancelParcelTracker` composite is designed to receive a request containing the `orderNo` for a parcel that is being tracked and to delete the corresponding scheduled job.

How to do it...

1. Within `CancelParcelTracker`, create an external reference to the Scheduler, as described in steps 1-3 of the previous recipe.

2. Next, drag an **Invoke** activity onto our BPEL process. Double-click on it to open the **Edit Invoke** window. Give it the name `removeJob`, select `Scheduler` for the **Partner Link**, and select the operation `removeJob`.

   For the input variable, click on the **auto-create** variable (plus icon) to launch the **Create Variable** window. Give the variable a meaningful name (for example, `removeJob Input`). Do the same for the output variable.

3. Drag an **Assign** activity onto our BPEL process just before the **Invoke** activity. Double-click on it to open the **Edit Assign** window, and give it the name `setRemoveJob`.

4. We need to populate the job element with the unique identity of the job. This is a composite key defined by the elements `jobId` and `jobGroup`.

   Use the **Assign** activity to set `jobId` to contain the `orderNo` of the parcel being tracked and to set the `jobGroup` to `ParcelTracker`.

5. Now that our process is complete, deploy it and run it to delete the job we created in the previous recipe.

   You should see that no more instances of the `ParcelTracker` composite are created.

How it works...

Removing a scheduled job is as simple as invoking the Scheduler's `removeJob` operation with a request message that includes our job's key values as follows:

```xml
<?xml version="1.0" encoding="UTF-8"?>
<removeJob xsi:schemaLocation="http://rubiconred.com/
  evs/util.sch.Job util.sch.evs.Job_1.0.xsd"
  xmlns="http://rubiconred.com/evs/util.sch.Job"
  xmlns:job="http://rubiconred.com/ebo/util.sch.Job"
  xmlns:xsi="http://www.w3.org/2001/XMLSchema-instance">
  <body>
    <job:jobId>120699</job:jobId>
    <job:jobGroup>ParcelTracking</job:jobGroup>
  </body>
</removeJob>
```

6
OSB Messaging Patterns

In this chapter, we will cover:

- ▶ Dynamic binding using OSB
- ▶ Splitting out messages using OSB
- ▶ Dynamic Split-Join in OSB
- ▶ Fault handling in dynamic Split-Join in OSB

Introduction

This chapter explores some common message processing design patterns for delegation of execution to downstream services and provides recipes for implementing them using Oracle Service Bus.

Sample OSB projects are provided for each of these recipes, copies of these are provided as Oracle Service Bus Configuration Jars. For each recipe we provide two versions of the OSB project, one containing enough to get started with the recipe, the other with the completed solution.

In order to use them you will need to open an empty workspace within Eclipse, then select **File | Import**, select **Oracle Service Bus – Configuration Jar** and browse to, and import, the required project.

Dynamic binding using OSB

One of the key advantages of an Enterprise Service Bus, as well as Service Oriented Architecture in general is the quality of *Agility,* that is, the ability to easily compose new orchestrations of web service operations. In this recipe, we will consider a scenario in which a standard service contract might be implemented by multiple providers, the selection of which we want to dynamically configure at runtime.

For example, let us suppose that we are running an online bookstore and wish to automate stock order requests to multiple publishers. A stock order includes the name of the publisher, details of the book, and the quantity to order:

```
<stockOrder>
  <publisher>ACME</publisher>
  <bookOrder>
    <book>
      <isbn>1234567890123</isbn>
      <title>Barry Potter</title>
      ...
    </book>
    <quantity>Skylight vampires</quantity>
  </bookOrder>
</stockOrder>
```

This service could be fulfilled by various publishers and new publishers might be joining our network all the time. Ideally, rather than needing to re-code and publish our routing logic every time a new publisher is added, we would like to be able to keep our **Stock Order** service running with no outage and simply update the routing rules using a configuration file, such as the following:

```
<routing>
  <rule>
    <key>ACME</key>
    <serviceName>PublisherApp/PublisherACME</serviceName>
  </rule>
  <rule>
    <key>Packt</key>
    <serviceName>PublisherApp/PublisherPackt</serviceName>
  </rule>
  <rule>
    <key>Skynet</key>
    <serviceName>PublisherApp/PublisherSkynet</serviceName>
  </rule>
</routing>
```

Each of these `serviceNames` are OSB proxy services, wrapping a particular publisher's online stock ordering service. The idea is that when we want to add a new publisher, we implement a new proxy service implementing the previous service contract and add a `<rule>` element to the configuration file referencing it.

This recipe will demonstrate how this dynamic routing can be implemented in OSB.

Getting ready

In order to use this design pattern, you will need to define a standard WSDL to be implemented by each of your routing destinations (publishers in our example).

For our purposes, we have defined the WSDL Publisher_Service_1.0.wsdl, which defines the operation `submitBookOrder`.

We have provided three basic implementations of this service, as defined in the following table:

Publisher	Proxy service
ACME	PublisherApp/PublisherACME
Packt	PublisherApp/PublisherPackt
Skynet	PublisherApp/PublisherSkynet

These implementations are defined in the **PublisherApp** OSB project which is included in the sample for the book. You will need to open this sample in OEPE and deploy to your instance of OSB.

How to do it...

1. In the Eclipse IDE, open the the **PublisherApp** OSB project which is included in the samples. Define a new OSB proxy service, give it the name `PublisherService` and select **Publisher_Service_1.0.wsdl** as the WSDL.

2. The next step is to compose a simple XQuery source file containing a list of routing destinations similar to the following example:

```
xquery version "1.0" encoding "Cp1252";
(:: pragma  type="xs:anyType" ::)

declare namespace xf = "http://tempuri.org/
  PublisherApp/dynamic-routing-rules/";
```

```
declare function xf:dynamic-routing-rules()
as element(*) {
  <routing>
    <!-- dynamic-routing-rules.xq -->
    <rule>
      <key>ACME</key>
      <serviceName>PublisherApp/
        PublisherACME</serviceName>
    </rule>
    <rule>
      <key>Packt</key>
      <serviceName>PublisherApp/
        PublisherPackt</serviceName>
    </rule>
    <rule>
      <key>Skynet</key>
      <serviceName>PublisherApp/
        PublisherSkynet</serviceName>
    </rule>
  </routing>
};
```

```
xf:dynamic-routing-rules()
```

Note that in our example, `key` is the key field we will use to determine which routing rule to apply while `serviceName` indicates the exact path (within OSB) of the corresponding destination proxy service.

Save this file within your OSB project as `dynamic-routing-rules.xq`.

3. Open your proxy service and select the **Message Flow** tab. Drag in a **Pipeline Pair** followed by a **Stage**, naming the stage as `LookupDestination`. Within the new stage, add two **Assign** actions, as shown in the following screenshot:

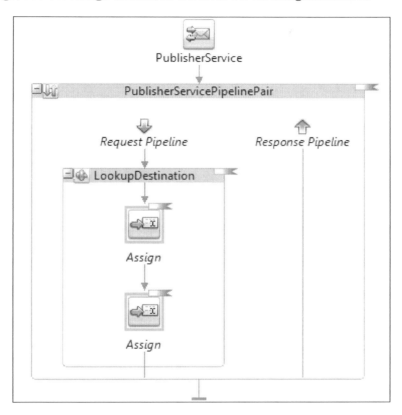

4. For the first **Assign** action, set **Variable** as `routingRules` and select `dynamic-routing-rules.xq` as the **<Expression>**.

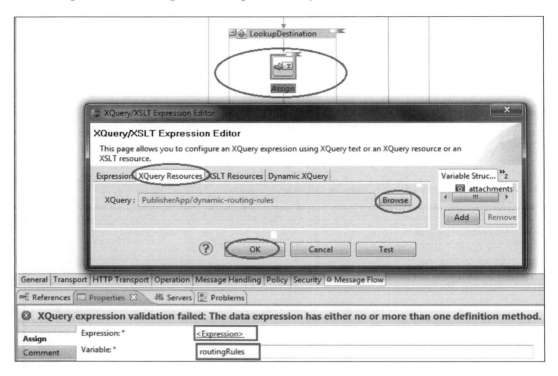

5. For the second **Assign** action, set **Variable** as `destination` and use the following XML fragment as your expression:

```
<ctx:route>
  <ctx:service isProxy="true">{
  $routingRules/rule[key/text()=$body//*:publisher
    /text()]/serviceName/text()
  }</ctx:service>
</ctx:route>
```

6. Next, drag a **Route** node to the bottom of the Message Flow and place a **Dynamic Routing** action within that. Set the **<Expression>** within the **Dynamic Routing** action as $destination.

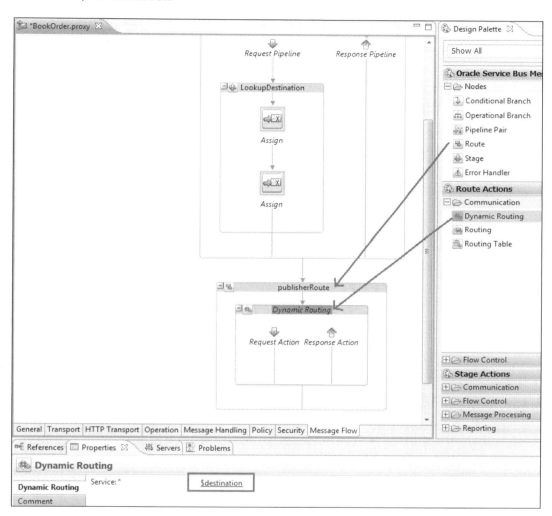

How it works...

The key feature of OSB used for this design pattern is the **Dynamic Routing** action. The expression used in this action is expected in a very specific format, as per the following XML fragment:

```
<ctx:route>
  <ctx:service isProxy="$isProxy">$serviceName</ctx:service>
  <!-- operation is optional -->
  <ctx:operation>$operationName</ctx:operation>
</ctx:route>
```

Note that `isProxy` is an `xsd:boolean`. If set to `"true"` then `serviceName` must be the complete path to an OSB proxy service, otherwise `serviceName` must be the complete path of an OSB business service. The complete path should include the OSB project and any subfolders included in the project structure.

In our example, in the `LookupDestination` stage, we've used the following XPath to determine the `serviceName`:

```
$routingRules/rule[key/text()=$body//*:publisher/
    text()]/serviceName/text()
```

This roughly reads as "return the `serviceName` corresponding to the rule in `routingRules` for which the key matches the publisher element in the request". In other words, it's a key-value lookup into our configuration file `dynamic-routing-rules.xq`.

Now, if we need to add a new publisher service, we only need to ensure that its proxy service is added to `dynamic-routing-rules.xq` and implements the same WSDL.

There's more...

The generic contract of this service comes at a price. Publisher IDs accepted by the service are not restricted and so it's possible to submit a stock order for a publisher which may not exist in the routing rules.

This is easily remedied by adding a conditional block after the `LookupDestination` stage to confirm that a valid address was retrieved before attempting to route. The expression to use for the condition is as follows:

```
fn:data($destination/*:service) = ""
```

The conditional block should include appropriate logic, such as a `Raise Error` action.

Another potential issue with this design pattern is that the destination service may not exist! This could be due to a mistake in the routing rules, or because the destination service has not been deployed for whatever reason.

If this is the case, then OSB will raise the following internal error:

```
BEA-382612: Error preparing message for dispatch
```

To detect this issue at runtime, include the following condition expression in your `Error Handler` block:

```
$fault/ctx:errorCode = "BEA-382612"
```

Splitting out messages using OSB

In this next recipe we will consider a common design pattern for processing a list of independent messages in a batch. In this scenario, a synchronous web service implemented in OSB will accept a list of messages and respond almost immediately with a response to indicate that the message was successfully received. Meanwhile, each of the individual messages will be queued for asynchronous processing by another service.

Getting ready

This recipe also assumes that the downstream, one-way service for processing individual messages from the batch has already been written using OSB.

This example builds on the result of the previous recipe, the `"BookOrder"` dynamic routing service. A sample completed version of this service is included with the code samples for the book.

How to do it...

1. Log in to the Weblogic console and select **Services | Messaging | JMS Modules**. Select **New**.

    This will open the **Create JMS System Module** window. Name the module `BookModule` and click on **Next**. Target the OSB server(s) and click on **Next**. Finally, check the box to add resources and click on **Finish**.

2. This will take us to the settings for `BookModule`. Click on **New** in the **Resources** table.

3. This will open the **Create a New JMS System Resource** dialogue. Select **Queue** and click on **Next**. Name the queue (for example, `BookOrderQueue`) and assign a JNDI name (for example, `jms.queue.bookorder`).

Click on **Next**, then click on **Create a New Subdeployment**. Accept the default name and target the existing `wlsbJMSServer`. Click on **Finish**.

4. Next, we need to modify the downstream process to use the JMS queue. Open the OSB workshop project from the previous recipe. Open the downstream proxy service (for example, `PublisherService.proxy`) and select the **Transport** tab.

    i. In the **Protocol** drop-down list, select **jms**. Change **Endpoint URI** to the queue JNDI name we created earlier, for example:

```
jms://localhost:7001/weblogic.jms.XAConnectionFactory/
    jms.queue.bookorder
```

    ii. **Save** your changes.

5. Next, we need to create a new proxy service for handling our batch requests. Give it the name `PublisherBatchService` and use `PublisherBatchService_1.0.wsdl` as the WSDL.

This WSDL defines the operation `submitBookOrderList`, which contains a list of `bookOrders` that we want to process individually.

6. Select the **Message Handling** tab and ensure **Transaction Required** is **Enabled**.

7. In the **Message Flow** tab, create **OperationalBranch** and add **Pipeline Pair** and **Stage** to the **submitBookOrderList** operation. Next, drag a **For Each** action into the **Stage**.

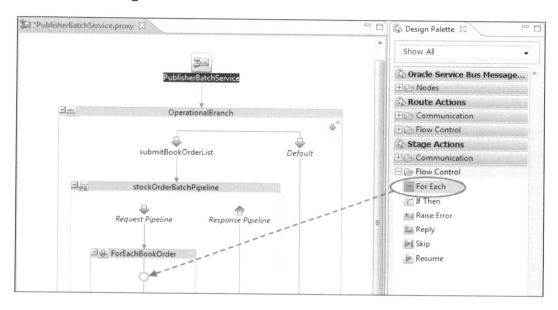

8. Set the **For Each Variable** property with a name you would like to use to reference each element of the batch, for example, `bookOrder`. Set **In Variable** to `body`. Optionally, declare index and count reference variables.

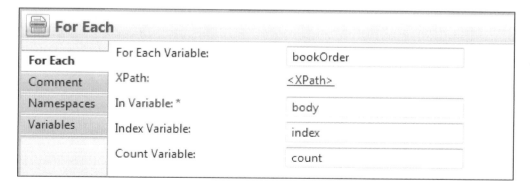

9. Next, click on the **XPath** link to open the XPath dialog.

10. Drag the repeating list member element (for example `bookOrder`) from the request body over as the XPath expression. Then click on **OK**.

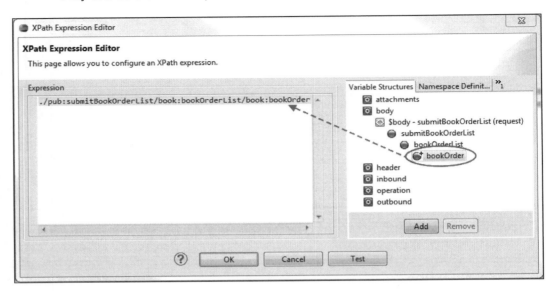

11. Drag a **Publish** action from the Design Palette into the body of the **For Each** loop. Set the **Service** and **Operation** properties of the **Publish** action to use the proxy service and operation of the downstream process (for example, `PublisherService.proxy`, and `submitBookOrder`) respectively.

12. Next, drag a **Routing Operations** action from the Design Palette into the body of **Publish** action. Within the **Routing Options**, enable **QoS** (Quality of Service) and select **Exactly Once**.

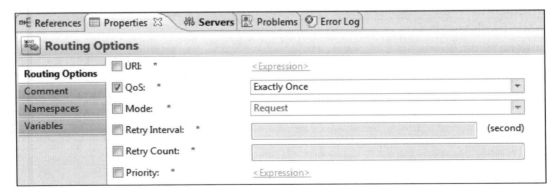

13. Finally, place a **Replace** action within the **Publish** action body and configure it to have the values listed in the following table:

Field	Value
XPath	.
In Variable	**body**
Expression	**XQuery: PublisherApp/setSubmitBookOrder**
	Select **Replace node contents**

14. Configure the expression to use the XQuery resource `PublisherApp/setSubmitBookOrder.xq` and pass in the variable `bookOrder` (set in step 10).

    This will create the payload required for the `submitBookOrder` operation invoked by the **Publish** action, based on the content of the `ForEach` variable defined earlier, for example, `bookOrder`.

15. Deploy and test your OSB projects by sending a request to your Batch processor.

How it works...

The key to the asynchronous operation of this pattern is the separation of the initial call from the bulk of the processing with a JMS queue. If not explicitly defined, OSB will dynamically generate a generic queue when the JMS transport protocol is selected, but for finer control, including auditing, repeatability, and the potential to assign a Work Manager it has been recommended in this recipe to assign a specific named queue.

The logic of the Batch process itself is relatively straightforward. The For Each loop simply divides the batch implicitly into individual list elements and passes them on to the JMS transport downstream proxy service.

A key requirement for processing our batch, is that we want to successfully split out all messages from the batch or if something fails, roll back the entire batch (so we can re-submit once the error has been resolved). For this purpose we configured the JMS Transport as follows:

- **Message handling to enable Transaction Required**: This will instruct OSB to start a new transaction if one does not exist in the request received (which it won't as this is invoked over HTTP).

- **Routing Options on the Publish action to have a Quality of Service of Exactly Once**: This will force the publication of the message to the JMS queue to be included within the transaction started by the proxy.

- **Use an XA Connection Factory for a JMS Queue**: This ensures that the transaction is propagated to JMS.

In this way, each book order is written to the JMS queue as part of the same transaction. When the proxy returns a response, then the transaction will be completed. At this point each `bookOrder` can be processed independently by the downstream proxy in a separate transaction, without interfering with the processing of other items in the list.

There's more...

Note that this pattern places very little responsibility on the Batch Processor to perform error handling. Other than syntactically validating the input request, it is not recommended to attempt any other validation on the individual list elements at this level, since one bad item might prevent the entire list from processing.

Instead, consider simply returning "success" to the caller and managing all exceptions internally, as part of the downstream process. This ensures that any valid items will still be processed and each error will be handled separately.

Fine-tuning the behavior of the JMS queue can be handled within the Weblogic console. In particular, you may wish to throttle the activity on the JMS queue to prevent the downstream process from becoming overloaded.

Dynamic Split-Join in OSB

As part of implementing a web service it is often necessary to delegate portions of the work to a number of independent subtasks. For a synchronous service, carrying out these tasks sequentially may take an unacceptable amount of time causing the client to time out waiting on the service. Therefore, the preferred approach is to process all independent tasks in parallel and consolidate the results.

This pattern is referred to as a "Split-Join" and comes in two flavors:

- **Static**: In this the subtasks are always the same. For example, in planning a holiday one needs to book both a flight and accommodation, each of which represents an independent subtask which may be completed in parallel.

- **Dynamic**: In this there are a variable number of subtasks, to be determined at runtime. For example, to complete an internet shopping order a bookstore must query each book before confirming the total price, but has no way of knowing how many different items will be required prior to reviewing the order.

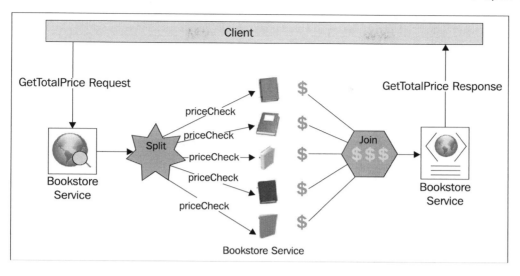

GetTotalPrice Request

priceCheck

priceCheck

Split

priceCheck

priceCheck

priceCheck

Bookstore
Service

Join
$ $ $

GetTotalPrice Response

Bookstore
Service

Bookstore Service

This recipe will guide you through a sample implementation of the second example using Oracle Service Bus.

An alternative way of implementing the previous scenario is to use a `FlowN` (BPEL 1.1) or a parallel `ForEach` (BPEL 2.0) activity within a BPEL process. As OSB is stateless, it has less overhead and, therefore, will be more performant. However, another key consideration is what happens if something goes wrong?

In the case of our example, as we are not modifying any data, our error handling is relatively straightforward. But, if we were using the Split-Join to modify data in the target system, for example splitting out an order into individual line items which are then ordered separately; then if an error occurred we may want to undo all the successfully generated line item orders.

It may be tempting to try and do all this within an XA transaction. However, this has the potential to create large distributed transactions, with significant impact on performance and scalability.

In this scenario (that is where we are modifying state) a better approach would be to implement this pattern in BPEL and use compensation for error handling.

In summary, where the Split-Join is not a modifying state, it is safe and more performant to use OSB. But, in cases where the state of the backend system is being modified you should implement this pattern in BPEL.

Getting ready

Prior to beginning this recipe, you will need to prepare the target WSDL operation which will be invoked to process individual items. In the example, this will be the `priceCheck` operation of the **Book** service, which determines how much each book should cost.

If you wish to follow along exactly with these instructions open the `BookStoreApp` (included with the code samples for the book) in Eclipse. This contains the required schema and WSDL files, as well as a mock implementation of the **Book** service.

How to do it...

1. Right-click on the **BookStoreApp** project and select **New | Split-Join** from the context menu.

2. Enter a descriptive filename (for example, `getTotalPriceSplitJoin`) and then click on **Next**.

3. Expand the project structure to select the **parent** operation used to invoke the Split-Join (for example, **BookStoreService_1.0.wsdl | BookStoreServiceBinding | operation: getTotalPrice**) and then click on **Finish**.

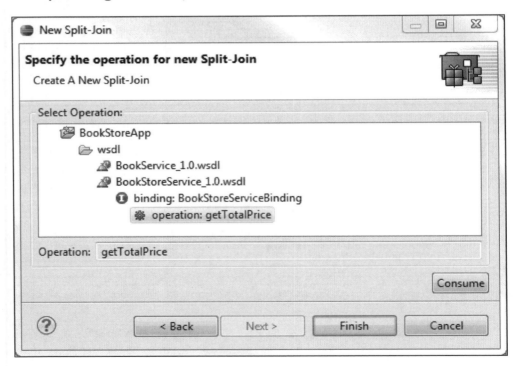

A new Split-Join flow will appear in the main editing window.

4. Select the root node and expand its properties by clicking on the small triangle on its left. Select the **request** variable and click on **Edit...**.

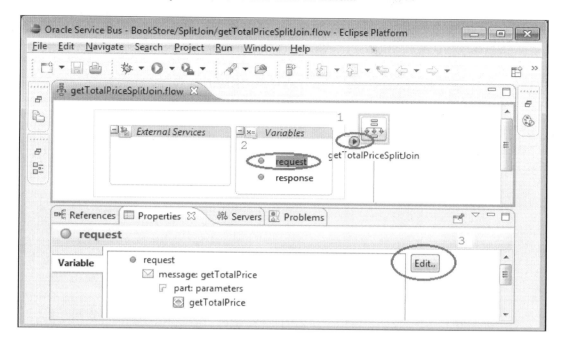

5. Rename the variable to match the parent operation (for example, `getTotalPrice`). This will help prevent ambiguity later on.

6. Repeat steps 4 and 5 to rename the **response** variable (for example, `getTotalPriceResponse`).

7. Drag an **Assign** action from the Design Palette, to between the **Receive** and **Reply** nodes.

8. Label the new scope as `Initialisation` and the **Assign** action as `Assign output variable`.

9. Click on the new **Assign** action. In the **Properties** tab (shown in the following screenshot), select the variable as the payload of the parent operation's response (for example, `getTotalPriceResponse.payload`).

10. Next, click on the **<Expression>** link. Provide an XML similar to the following and then click on **OK**.

```
<stor:priceCheckResponse
  xmlns:stor="http://rubiconred.com/ckbk/svc/BookStore">
  <stor:totalPrice>0</stor:totalPrice>
</stor:priceCheckResponse>
```

Note, that in the previous example the aggregate total has been initialized to 0.

11. Drag a **For Each** construct from the Design Palette to just below the Initialisation scope.

12. Click on the new **For Each** construct. In the **Properties** tab, set the **Counter Variable Name** field to `counter` and the starting value to 1. Click on the ellipses next to **Final Counter Value** to launch the expression editor.

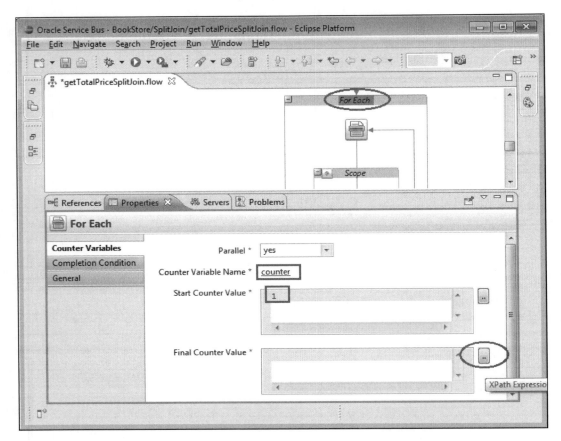

13. Select the **XPath Functions** tab, and drag the **count** function out into the **Expression** text area.

14. Click on the **Variable Structures** tab and expand the request structure to find the recurring element (for example, bookOrder) on which the split should be based. Drag it out to replace the place-holder $arg-nodeset and then click on **OK** to complete the expression.

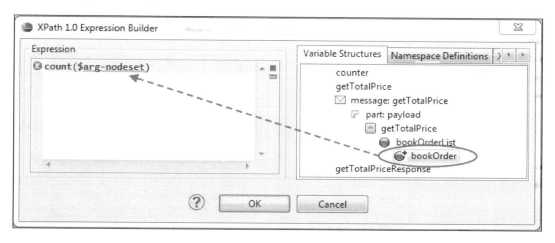

15. Drag an **Invoke Service** action into the **Scope** within the **ForEach** loop. Label it as per the child service and operation you intend to loop over (for example, Book.priceCheck).

16. In the **Properties** tab (shown in the following screenshot), select the **Operation** category. Click on **Browse**, select the child operation (for example, **BookService. proxy | priceCheck**), and click on **OK**.

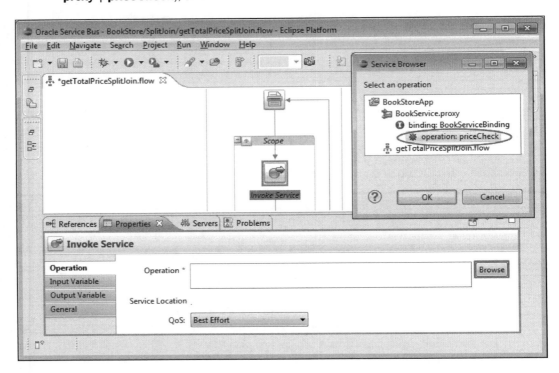

17. Select the **Input Variable** category in the **Properties** tab. From the **Message Variable** drop-down list select **Create Message Variable...**. Provide the name of the child operation (in our example, `priceCheck`) as the name and then click on **OK**.

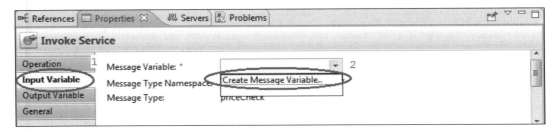

18. Use the same method to create and set the output variable (for example, as `priceCheckResponse`).

19. Drag an **Assign** action to the start of the **Loop Scope** and label it as `Extract Individual Request`.

20. Select the **Assign** action. In the **Properties** tab, set the variable as the request payload of the child operation (for example, `priceCheck.payload`) and then click on the **<Expression>** link.

21. We will use the XQuery **priceCheck.xq** to generate the input request to our call-out to the `Book.priceCheck` service. We will need to pass in the ISBN of the book using the `$counter` index defined earlier. For example:

```
$getTotalPrice.payload/book:bookOrderList/book:bookOrder[
    xs:integer($counter)]/book:book/book:isbn
```

22. Following the **Invoke Service** action, apply any aggregate logic. For our Book Store example, we would add a **Replace** action with the following properties:

Field	Value
XPath:	`./totalPrice`
Variable	**getTotalPriceResponse.payload**
Expression	`xs:float($getTotalPriceResponse.payload/bind:totalPrice) +`
	`(xs:float($priceCheckResponse.payload/ns1:price) *`
	`$getTotalPrice.payload/book:bookOrderList/book:bookOrder`
	`[xs:integer($counter)]/book:quantity)`
	Select **Replace node contents**

23. Save your progress by selecting **File** | **Save** from the menu.

24. Before the Split-Join can be used in a proxy service, it must first be encapsulated in a standard OSB Business Service.

    In the Project Explorer on the left, right-click on the Split-Join file and then select **Oracle Service Bus** | **Generate Business Service**. Accept the default name and location, and click on **OK**.

The business service is now ready for use in any OSB Proxy Service. Deploy it and test it out.

How it works...

Refer to the following, more completely labelled version of the Split-Join message flow for an end-to-end, annotated view of the final solution:

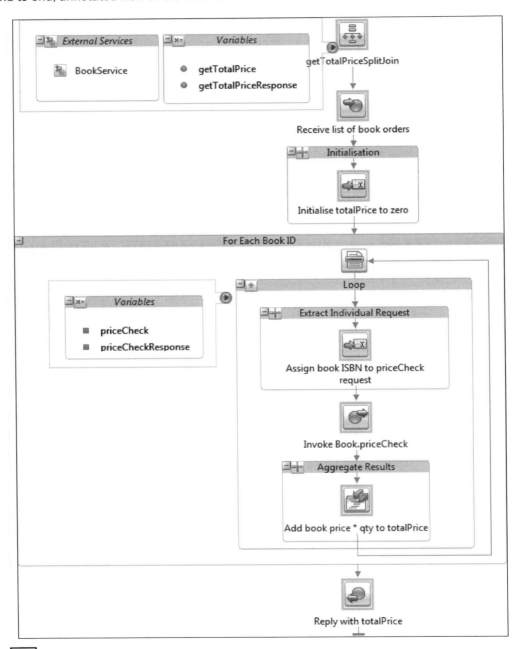

Procedurally, the pseudocode for the `BookStore` example might look to be (just going by the annotations) as follows:

```
Operation getTotalPrice( book_list ):
  totalPrice := 0
  for each order in book_list
  loop
    total_price := total_price +
      Book.priceCheck(order.isbn ) * order.qty
  end loop
  return total_price
```

The key difference is that the `For Each` section has a property called `Parallel` set by default to `yes` (note that if desired, this can be set to `no` to force sequential execution). This instructs Oracle Service Bus to execute all (or as many as it has threads) iterations of the `Loop` scope within the `For Each` statement concurrently.

Readers paying close attention will also have noticed that the `For Each` block does not actually iterate over the book IDs directly; rather the OSB determines the number of `Loop` scopes simply by counting the number of `bookOrder` nodes and then assigning each scope a different `$counter` variable integer between 1 and that total count. So, a more accurate representation of the pseudocode would be as follows:

```
Operation getTotalPrice( book_list ):
  totalPrice := 0
  for counter in 1 .. size(book_list)
  thread concurrently
    total_price := total_price +
      (Book.priceCheck(order[counter].isbn ) *
      order[counter].qty )
  end thread
  return total_price
```

Performing this addition in parallel allows the `BookStore` service to compute the total much faster, dividing the total time of `priceChecks` by the number of concurrent threads.

There's more...

This recipe represents a reasonably standard, cookie-cutter implementation of how one would use the Split-Join feature of Oracle Service Bus to iterate over a dynamic sequence of identical elements in a list. It should be enough to get you started on any similar problem. However, it only scratches the surface of the possibilities for what can be accomplished with a Split-Join message flow.

Other aggregation logic

Rather than simply summing up numerical values, you can aggregate the results of service calls any way you like. A common example is appending the results to a dynamic sequence using an **Insert** action.

More service calls

Note that you are not limited to a single **Invoke Service** action. Multiple "child" operations may be invoked sequentially or in parallel.

In fact the premise of a "Static" Split-Join is that instead of using a `For Each` loop, you would use an explicit `Parallel` construct (see Flow Control in the Design Palette) and drop a different **Invoke Service** action into each lane.

Any combination of flow constructs desired can be layered to create complex concurrent processing systems within a single Split-Join message flow.

Conflicts

With any software system involving multi-threading, there is always a possibility of deadlocks or conflicts. Although variables within a Split-Join message flow are protected from these scenarios, Oracle Service Bus does not provide any built-in mitigation tools for external systems.

It is outside the scope of this discussion to prescribe how one might resolve concurrent update issues in external systems. However, designers and developers should always be aware when there is such a possibility and take appropriate action.

Fault handling in dynamic Split-Join in OSB

Without appropriate Error-Handling logic, the first fault thrown by a service invocation within any one of the Split-Join's threads will re-raise in the Split-Join and halt the entire message flow.

In order to prevent this, **Catch** clauses need to be added to the scope of each thread as shown next.

How to do it...

1. Right-click on the loop's scope and select **Add Catch**.

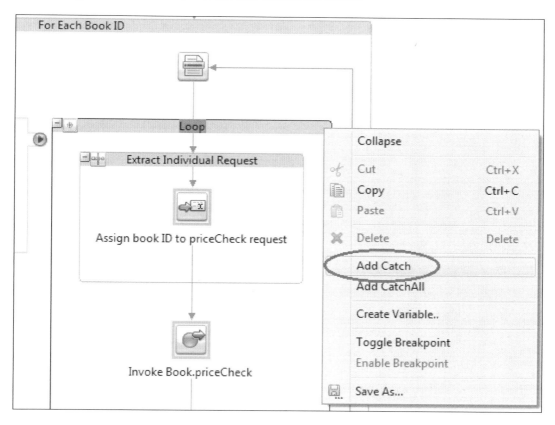

2. Select the new **Catch** block, `label` it with the name of the fault you wish to catch and then review the **Properties** tab.

3. Click on **<Soap Fault Variable Name>** and assign any name you like (the default is simply `soapFault` which should be fine).

4. Repeat this step for each expected Soap Fault.

5. Select **Define Fault** and enter the fault name and namespace of the fault you expect to catch.

6. Drag in a new **Scope** below the **Catch** and add any mitigation actions as necessary to resolve the fault. It may be appropriate to do nothing. Simply log the error, or perhaps aggregate a default value into the total. All variables available within the normal scope are also available to you within the **Catch** block.

7. Optionally, add a `Catch All` clause to the loop to capture any unexpected faults.

How it works...

Fault handling within a Split-Join in OSB is very similar to fault handling in proxy services. One simply has to define a `Catch` block for the appropriate scope and mitigate each fault appropriately.

By handling faults within the `For` loop, we ensure that each of the individual threads is managed separately, without impacting the rest of the batch.

7
Integrating OSB
with JSON

In this chapter, we will cover the following recipes for working with JSON:

- ▶ Converting between XML and JSON
- ▶ Invoking a JSON service from OSB
- ▶ Dynamically binding to a JSON service in OSB
- ▶ Exposing a proxy service as a JSON service

Introduction

Most often, when working with the SOA Suite or Oracle Service Bus, we'll be transforming data between different XML formats. It's becoming increasingly common for services to expect and provide their data in **JavaScript Object Notation (JSON)**.

JSON is a lightweight format, in that it will typically represent data in fewer bytes than the corresponding XML representation, and that it is relatively simple to generate and parse. It is also much simpler than XML, in that it has a smaller set of pre-defined data types (object, array, string, number, and the values true, false, and null) from which an object representation can be constructed.

As a result, we have the blessing and the curse of considerable freedom when deciding how to represent even quite simple values; for example, where XML provides the `dateTime` type with its standard format, we could choose to use an ISO-8601 conformant string, or the number of milliseconds since an epoch, or an object with named values for each subcomponent. All of those representations would be equally valid in JSON, requiring an agreement between the service provider and clients as to the representation to use, and the interpretation to apply.

Converting between XML and JSON

Since JSON formatted data is likely to be needed only when communicating with a partner system, we'll assume that it's most common to convert between XML and JSON in Oracle Service Bus. For working with XML, we'll use XMLBeans, as that's what OSB uses. For parsing and generating JSON, we'll use Jackson (Version 1.9.x).

Getting ready

This recipe assumes the use of an existing OSB configuration project within the OSB workshop for development. So, ensure that you have installed and familiarized yourself with it prior to beginning.

Schema

If you wish to follow along exactly with these instructions you will require a copy of the schema and WSDL files used in this recipe. Copies of these are included with the code samples for the book.

 For the purpose of this example, the JSON format will map very closely to the XML schema, but this need not necessarily be the case, and the approach demonstrated next is flexible enough to allow for arbitrarily complex mapping.

Java libraries

Oracle Service Bus uses XMLBeans to provide its XML/object mapping. We'll use the same library to make our task simpler.

In order to map between JSON and objects, we'll use the Jackson library. Download Version 1.9.x of the Jackson Core ASL and Mapper ASL libraries from `http://wiki.fasterxml.com/JacksonDownload`.

How to do it...

1. From the context menu in the **Package Explorer** view, select **New | Java Project**. For this example, the project is named `CreditCardServiceMessages`. Keep the remaining defaults and click on **Next**.

2. For the **Java Settings**, set the **Default output folder** to `CreditCardServiceMessages/build/classes`. Click on **Finish**.

3. For setting up the project structure, select **CreditCardServiceMessages** within the **Package Explorer** view, right-click and select **New | Folder**. Name the folder `dist` and click on **OK**.

4. Repeat this process to create the folders `genbuild`, `gensrc`, `lib`, `resources`, and `test` in the Java project.

   Next, we need to import the schema and WSDL files we are using for this example.

5. Within the **Package Explorer** view, select **resources**, right-click and select **Import**. This will open the Import Wizard. Select **General | File System** as the source and click on **Next**.

6. Browse to the file directory containing the code samples for this chapter, and within the directory `getting ready`, select the folder `resources`.

7. Within the **Import** window, ensure **resources** is checked and the option **Create selected folder structure** is selected (as circled in the following screenshot) and click on **Finish**.

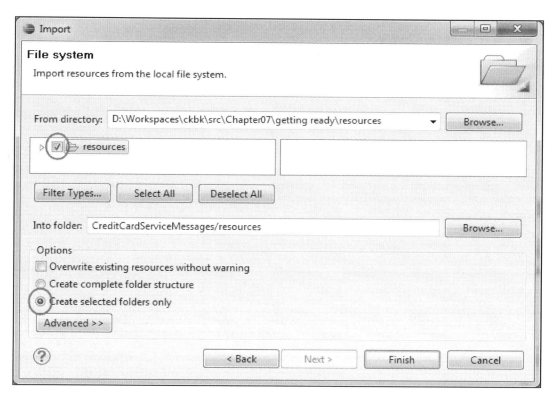

8. To import the JAR files, select **lib** within the **Package Explorer** view, right-click and select **Import**. In the **Import** wizard, select **General | File** system, and click on **Next**.

9. Browse to the directory `<MIDDLEWARE_HOME>/osb/modules`

10. Click on **OK** and select the file `com.bea.core.xml.xmlbeans_2.1.0.0_2-5-1.jar` and click on **Finish**. This will create a copy of the JAR file in the `lib` folder within the Java project.

11. Repeat this step to import the `jackson-core-asl-1.9.x.jar` and `jackson-mapper-asl-1.9.x.jar` libraries. Add the libraries to the projects build path by selecting the three files, right-clicking, and selecting **Build Path | Add to Build Path**.

The structure of our Java Project should resemble the following screenshot:

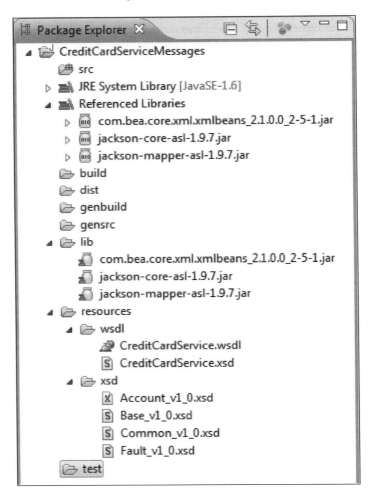

12. We'll use Ant to build our project. Within the **Package Explorer** view, select **CreditCardServiceMessages**, right-click and select **Import**. This will open the Import Wizard. Select **General | File System** as the source and click on **Next**.

13. Browse to the file directory containing the code samples for this chapter and select the folder `getting ready`. Within the **Import** window, ensure **build.xml** is checked and click on **Finish**.

    The most important target to note at this point within the `build.xml` file is `scomp`.

```
<taskdef name="xmlbean"
  classname="org.apache.xmlbeans.impl.tool.XMLBean"
  classpath="${lib}/com.bea.core.xml.xmlbeans_2.1.0.0_2-
    5-1.jar" />


<!-- Compile the config schema definition with XmlBeans
  -->
<target name="scomp" depends="init" description="compile
    xsd">
  <xmlbean srcgendir="${gensrc}"
    classgendir="${genbuild}"
    destfile="${dist}/$
      {ant.project.name}XmlBeans_1.0.jar"
    failonerror="true"
      classpathref="project.class.path">

    <fileset dir="${schemadir}"
    includes="wsdl/CreditCardService.xsd" />
  </xmlbean>
</target>
```

This compiles the schemas we have imported using **XmlBeans**, and will be required for subsequent steps.

14. To compile the schemas, select **Window | Show View | Ant** and open the Ant View in our Eclipse perspective; next drag the `build.xml` file into the Ant View, and double-click on the `scomp` target.

    This will run the `scomp` target, which will use **xmlbeans** to generate Java classes which represent the schema types in our imported schemas and package them into the JAR file, named `CreditCardServiceMessagesXmlBeans_1.0.jar`.

You should see output similar to the following, in the Console view:

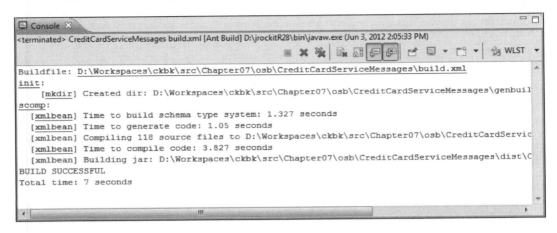

The generated JAR file will be placed in the `dist` directory (refresh the project structure view if you can't see it).

15. Right-click on this file, and select **Build Path | Add to Build Path** from the context menu, as we'll be writing classes that depend on this library later.

16. Next, we need to create **Plain Old Java Objects** (**POJOs**) that represent the JSON objects that we will later be exchanging. These classes have no knowledge of the Jackson libraries that we will be using to convert between the object and JSON representations.

For our example we will create the following classes:

- ❑ CreditCard
- ❑ DebitCreditCard
- ❑ DebitCreditCardResponse

An excerpt from the CreditCard class is shown as follows:

```
package com.rubiconred.ckbk.creditcardsvc.pojo;

public class CreditCard {

    private String cardType;
    private String cardHolderName;
    private String cardNumber;
    private Integer expiryMonth;
    private Integer expiryYear;
    private String securityNo;
```

```
public String getCardType() {
  return cardType;
}

public void setCardType(String cardType) {
  this.cardType = cardType;
}
public String getCardHolderName() {
  return cardHolderName;
}

  // ...
}
```

> Primitive types are not used for the previous numeric values.
> It is common for values in JSON objects to be optional, and
> either be omitted entirely from the serialised representation,
> or be serialised with a value of `null`. Java's primitive types
> cannot represent the absence of a value, so the object types
> should in general be used for numeric.

17. Next we need to create the Java class `CreditCardServiceMapperFactory` that will be used to convert between the previous POJOs and their JSON representations.

    A snapshot of the code to do this is shown as follows. The full source code is provided in the sample for the chapter.

```
package com.rubiconred.ckbk.creditcardsvc.json;

import ...

public class CreditCardServiceMapperFactory {

  private static ObjectMapper mapper;
  private static ObjectReader debitCreditCardReader;
  private static ObjectWriter debitCreditCardWriter;

  static {
    mapper = new ObjectMapper();

    // Include null values in generated JSON
    mapper.setSerializationConfig(
      mapper.getSerializationConfig()
      .withSerializationInclusion(Inclusion.ALWAYS));
```

```
      debitCreditCardReader =
        mapper.reader(DebitCreditCard.class);
      debitCreditCardWriter =
        mapper.writerWithType(DebitCreditCard.class);

      // ...
    }

    public static ObjectReader getDebitCreditCardReader() {
      return debitCreditCardReader;
    }

    public static ObjectWriter getDebitCreditCardWriter() {
      return debitCreditCardWriter;
    }

    // ...
  }
```

Jackson makes this very straightforward. The `ObjectReader` and `ObjectWriter` instances that we create are immutable, so they're thread-safe and can be shared as required.

The `ObjectMapper` is the object on which the details of the JSON (de-) serialization are configured. For this example, we'll configure the mapper to include `null` values, rather than omitting them.

Now that we have the necessary scaffolding in place, we can write the code that will convert between the XML format (exposed as an XMLBeans `XmlObject` instance) and the JSON format (represented by the POJOs we created earlier). This is the code that will later be invoked using **Java Callout** actions in OSB proxy services.

18. In order to convert from JSON to XML, we create a method that accepts the JSON in a String, and uses the appropriate `ObjectReader` to parse it into the POJO we created earlier.

The fields of the POJO are used to populate a new instance of the appropriate `XmlObject`. This is illustrated in the following method:

```
public static XmlObject debitCreditCardJsonToXml
    (String json) {
  ObjectReader reader = CreditCardServiceMapperFactory
    .getDebitCreditCardReader();

  DebitCreditCardDocument debitDoc =
    DebitCreditCardDocument
    .Factory.newInstance();
```

```
    DebitCreditCard jsonDebitCreditCard;
    TDebitCreditCard xmlDebitCreditCard;
    TCreditCard xmlCreditCard;

    try {
      jsonDebitCreditCard = reader.readValue(json);
      CreditCard jsonCreditCard = jsonDebitCreditCard
        .getCreditCard();
      xmlDebitCreditCard = TDebitCreditCard.Factory
        .newInstance();
      xmlCreditCard = TCreditCard.Factory.newInstance();
      xmlCreditCard.setCardHolderName(jsonCreditCard
        .getCardHolderName());
      xmlCreditCard.setCardNumber(jsonCreditCard
        .getCardNumber());
      xmlCreditCard.setCardType(jsonCreditCard
        .getCardType());

      // Set Remainder of Credit Card Details…

      xmlDebitCreditCard.setCreditCard(xmlCreditCard);

      Double trnAmount =jsonDebitCreditCard.getTrnAmount();
      if (trnAmount != null) {
        xmlDebitCreditCard.setTrnAmount(
          BigDecimal.valueOf(trnAmount));
      }
      xmlDebitCreditCard.setTrnDesc(jsonDebitCreditCard
        .getTrnDesc());

      debitDoc.setDebitCreditCard(xmlDebitCreditCard);

    } catch (JsonProcessingException e) {
      e.printStackTrace();
    } catch (IOException e) {
      e.printStackTrace();
    }
    return debitDoc;
  }
```

19. To convert from JSON to XML we simply use the following code fragment:

```
    DebitCreditCardDocument doc;
    doc = (DebitCreditCardDocument) DebitCreditCardConverter
      .debitCreditCardJsonToXml
        (DEBIT_CREDIT_CARD_JSON_STRING);

    TDebitCreditCard debitCreditCard =
      doc.getDebitCreditCard();
```

Where `DEBIT_CREDIT_CARD_JSON_STRING` contains the JSON to convert. The result of this `debitCreditCard` is an XMLBeans generated class that gives us a Java wrapper around the ML conversion of `debitCreditCard` with JavaBeans-style accessors.

20. Converting from XML to JSON uses the same approach, starting from an `XmlObject` and producing a `String` containing JSON, as illustrated in the following method:

```
public static String debitCreditCardXmlToJson
  (XmlObject xml)
{
  ObjectWriter writer = CreditCardServiceMapperFactory
    .getDebitCreditCardWriter();

  DebitCreditCard debitCreditCard = new
    DebitCreditCard();
  String json = null;
  DebitCreditCardDocument debitCreditCardDoc;
  TDebitCreditCard source = null;
  XmlObject doc = null;

  try {
    doc = XmlObject.Factory.parse
      (xml.newXMLStreamReader());

    if (doc instanceof DebitCreditCardDocument) {
      debitCreditCardDoc = (DebitCreditCardDocument) doc;
      source = debitCreditCardDoc.getDebitCreditCard();
      TCreditCard sourceCC = source.getCreditCard();
      BigDecimal trnAmount = source.getTrnAmount();

      if (trnAmount != null) {
        debitCreditCard.setTrnAmount(trnAmount
        .doubleValue());
      }
      debitCreditCard.setTrnDesc(source.getTrnDesc());
      CreditCard creditCard = new CreditCard();

      creditCard.setCardHolderName(sourceCC
        .getCardHolderName());
      creditCard.setCardNumber(sourceCC.getCardNumber());
      creditCard.setCardType(sourceCC.getCardType());
      creditCard.setExpiryMonth
        (sourceCC.getExpiryMonth());
      creditCard.setExpiryYear(sourceCC.getExpiryYear());
      creditCard.setSecurityNo(sourceCC.getSecurityNo());
```

```
         debitCreditCard.setCreditCard(creditCard);
         json = writer.writeValueAsString(debitCreditCard);
       } else {
         System.out.println
           ("debitCreditCardXmlToJson(): PARSE FAILED!!!");
       }
     } catch (XmlException e) {
       e.printStackTrace();
     } catch (JsonGenerationException e) {
       e.printStackTrace();
     } catch (JsonMappingException e) {
       e.printStackTrace();
     } catch (IOException e) {
       e.printStackTrace();
     }

     return json;
```

21. To convert from XML to JSON we simply use the following code fragment:

```
XmlObject debitCreditCardXmlObject;
debitCreditCardXmlObject = XmlObject.Factory
  .parse(DEBIT_CREDIT_CARD_XML);
String json = DebitCreditCardConverter
  .debitCreditCardXmlToJson
    (debitCreditCardXmlObject);
```

Where `DEBIT_CREDIT_CARD_XML` contains the XML to convert, the result of this JSON is a string containing the JSON representation of our XML object.

It is important to keep in mind, when implementing these conversions, that some incoming values may be `null`. One example of such an issue is when working with numeric values parsed from XML by XMLBeans; they will typically be instances of `BigDecimal` or `BigInteger`. Should you want to assign these values to a `Double` or `Integer` in your own objects, you must ensure that the returned value is not `null` before invoking the `doubleValue()` or `intValue()` methods.

Running the `dist` Ant task will produce a JAR file `CreditCardServiceMessages_1.0.j ar` in the `dist` directory. This will be used later, along with the previously generated `CreditC ardServiceMessagesXmlBeans_1.0.jar`, to perform the conversions between XML and JSON inside the OSB proxy services.

How it works...

We use XMLBeans to parse and generate XML, and we use Jackson to parse and generate JSON. We then implement an adapter that takes care of the translation between the two representations.

There's more...

It should be noted that there are other *simpler* frameworks which provide a mechanism for converting between XML and JSON, for example:

► `http://code.google.com/p/xml2json-xslt/wiki/TransformingRules`

► `http://www.bramstein.com/projects/xsltjson/`

► `http://json-lib.sourceforge.net/snippets.html#XML to JSONObject`

Given the simplicity of the previous example, any of these approaches would be fine. However, for more complex scenarios we find that Jackson provides the most control (it's also extremely fast – but that tends to be less relevant).

For example, Jackson provides many features for configuring the serialization and deserialization of your objects. In the event that the default behavior isn't appropriate for your use case, there are many options built-in, and custom (de-) serializers can be built very easily.

The final reason for leaning towards Jackson, is that it's leveraged by Coherence for its REST interface, so is a tried and tested component within the context of the Oracle stack.

Invoking a JSON service from OSB

Invoking a JSON service over HTTP from OSB is quite straightforward. Using the Java code that we built in the previous recipe will make working with the JSON messages much simpler.

Getting ready

We'll assume that you have an OSB configuration project in OEPE, and that you have the Jackson and XmlBeans JAR files referred to in the previous recipe, as well as the JAR files produced by that recipe.

How to do it...

1. We will first create an Oracle Service Bus project. Select the Oracle Service Bus perspective in Eclipse. Right-click on the OSB configuration project, and select **New | Oracle Service Bus Project**. In the dialog box, enter a name for the project (`InvokeJSONCreditCardService`) and click on **Finish**.

   We need to import the web service definition used in the Java project in the previous recipe, as we will implement the `DebitCreditCard` operation of the `CreditCardService`.

2. Right-click on the OSB project, and select **Import | Import** from the context menu.

3. In the **Import** dialog, select **General | File System** and click on **Next**.

4. Within the **Package Explorer** view, select **resources**, right-click and select **Import**. This will open the **Import** wizard. Select **General | File System** as the source and click on **Next**.

   i. Browse to the file directory containing the code samples for this chapter, and within the directory `getting ready`, select the folder `resources`.

5. Within the **Import** window, ensure **resources** is checked and the option **Create selected folder structure** is selected. Click on **Finish** to import the folder and its contents into the OSB project.

6. To import the JAR files into the project, right-click on the **InvokeJSONCreditCardService** OSB project in the **Project Explorer**, and select **New | Folder** from the context menu.

7. Enter the name `jars` for the folder in the **New Folder** dialog and click on **Finish**.

8. Now, import the following JAR files from the **CreditCardServiceMessages** project into the `jars` folder:

   ❏ `dist/CreditCardServiceMessages_1.0.jar`

   ❏ `dist/CreditCardServiceMessagesXmlBeans_1.0.jar`

   ❏ `lib/jackson-core-asl-1.9.7.jar`

   ❏ `lib/jackson-mapper-asl-1.9.7.jar`

   We now need to inform OSB of the dependencies between the JAR files.

9. Double-click on the **jackson-mapping-asl-1.9.7.jar** in the **Project Explorer**. In the **Modify Jar Dependencies** dialog, select the **jackson-core-asl-1.9.7.jar** file from the **Available jars** pane on the left, and click the **Add >** button to move it to the **Jar references** pane. Click on **OK**.

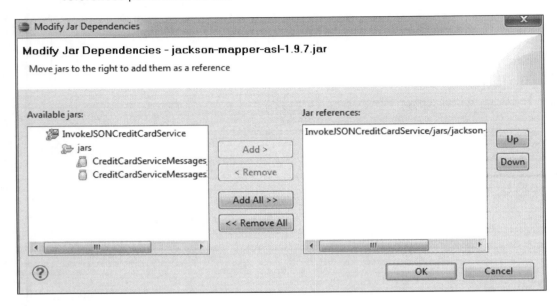

Do the same for the **CreditCardServiceMessages_1.0.jar** file, but click on the **Add All >>** button to indicate that it depends on all of the other JAR files in the projecThere will be warnings about classes from the org.joda.time package not being available. This is an optional dependency in the Jackson Mapper, and will not be a problem.

10. To create and configure a business service, right-click on the OSB project, and select **New | Business Service** from the context menu. Enter a name for the business service (CreditCardJSON_1.0) and click on **Finish**.

11. On the **General** tab, select **Messaging Service** as the **Service Type**.

12. On the **Messaging** tab, select **Text** as both the **Request Message Type** and **Response Message Type**.

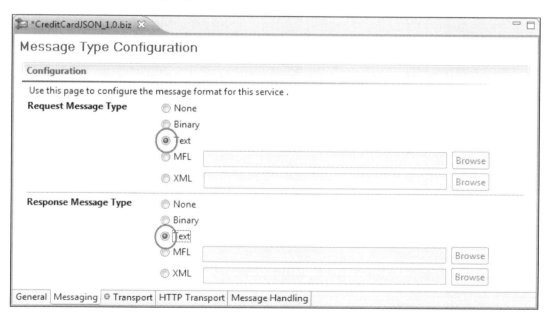

13. On the **Transport** tab, specify the **Endpoint URI** of the target service, and click on the **Add** button (for the purposes of this example, we've used the URI of a mock service that will help with testing).

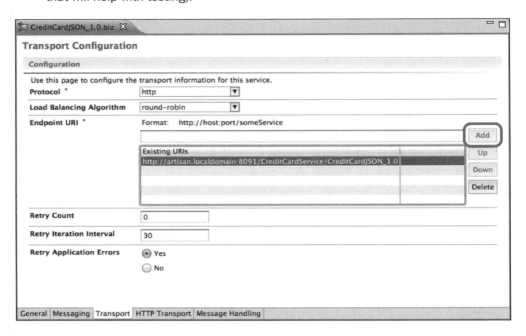

We'll accept the default values on the **HTTP Transport** and **Message Handling** tabs.

14. Click on the **Save** icon on the tool bar to save the business service.

15. To create a proxy service, right-click on the OSB project, and select **New | Proxy Service** from the context menu. In the **Create a new Proxy Service** dialog, enter a name for the proxy service (CreditCardService_1.0) and click on **Finish**.

16. Next, we will configure the proxy service.

    i.   On the **General** tab of the proxy service definition, click the **Browse** button to select the binding for the service's interface. Select the **CreditCardBinding** in the **CreditCardService.wsdl**, and click **OK**.

    ii. On the **Transport** tab, set the Endpoint URI for the service to **/ckbk/svc/CreditCard**, as specified in the WSDL.

17. On the **Message Flow** tab, drag an **Operational Branch** from the **Design Palette** and drop it under the **CreditCardService_1.0** icon.

    Give the **Operational Branch** a name (for example, CreditCardServiceOperation) and ensure that the **debitCreditCard** operation is selected.

18. Drag a **Pipeline Pair** into the **debitCreditCard** flow, and assign it a name (for example, **debitCreditCardPipelinePair**). Then, drag-and-drop a **Stage** into the **Request Pipeline**, and give that a name (for example, `debitCreditCardRequestStage`). Drag a **Java Callout** activity (under **Message Processing**) into the stage, and click on the **Browse** button in the **Properties** pane to select the Java method to be invoked.

    In the **Select an Archive Resource** dialog, select the **CreditCardServicesMessages_1.0.jar** file, and click on **OK**.

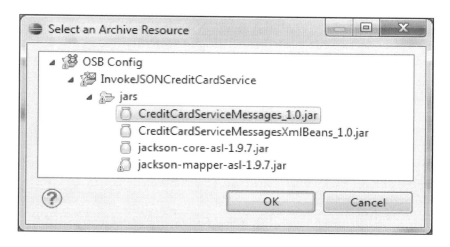

19. In the **Select a Java Method** dialog, select the **debitCreditCardXmlToJson** method in the **DebitCreditCardConverter** class, and click on **OK**.

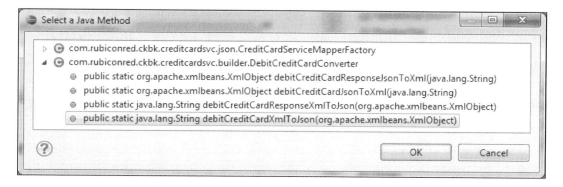

20. In the **Properties** pane for the **Java Callout** activity, set the **Expression** for the input parameter to $body. Set the **Result Value** to requestJSON; this is the variable to which the results of the Java method will be assigned.

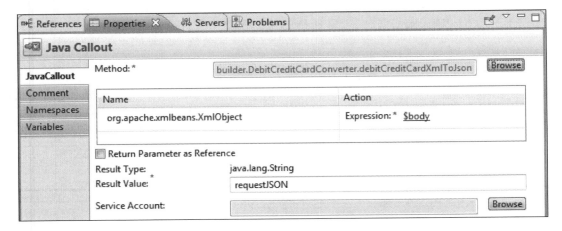

21. Insert a **Service Callout** activity after the **Java Callout**.

    i.   In the **Properties** pane for the **Service Callout** activity, click the **Browse** button, this will open the **Select a Service Resource** dialog, select CreditCardJSON_1.0.biz and click **OK**.

    ii. Enter requestJSON in the **Request Variable** field of the **Properties** pane, and responseJSON in the **ResponseVariable** field, as shown in the following screenshot:

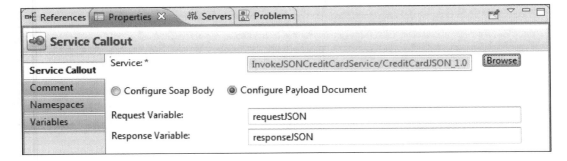

22. Drag a **Transport Header** activity into the **Request Action** flow of the **Service Callout**.

    i.   In the **Transport Headers** pane of the **Transport Header** activity, click on the **Add Header** button to add a new header to the **Outbound Request**.

    ii. Set the HTTP header **Content-Type** to have the value "application/json"; this is the standard MIME type for JSON data.

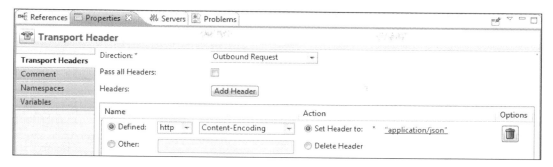

23. Create a **Stage** in the **Response Pipeline**, and give it the name
    debitCreditCardResponseStage.

    i.   Drag a **Java Callout** activity into the stage. Click on the **Browse** button
         in the **Properties** pane to select the Java method to be invoked. In the
         Select an Archive Resource dialog, select the **CreditCardServicesMess
         ages_1.0.jar** file and click on **OK**.

    ii. In the **Select a Java Method** dialog, select the
         debitCreditCardResponseJsonToXml method in the
         DebitCreditCardConverter class and click on **OK**.

    iii. In the **Properties** for the **Java Callout** activity, set the **Expression** for the
         input parameter to $responseJSON (the result of the previous **Service
         Callout**), and the **Result Value** to responseXML.

    iv. Add a **Replace** activity following the **Java Callout**, and set its properties,
         as shown in the following screenshot.

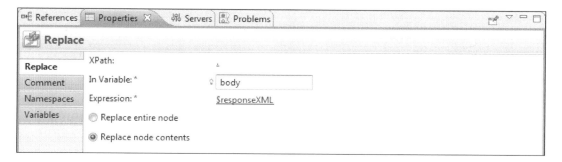

24. The proxy service and project are now complete. The project can be deployed to your Oracle Service Bus server, and tested using a mock JSON service.

> For our purposes, we created a mock service using Ruby; this is the file `mockservice.rb`, which is included with the sample code for this chapter.
>
> Before running the mock service, you will need a Ruby installation, and to also install the **JSON** gem.

How it works...

The **Java Callout** actions are used to convert between the XML and JSON message representations, using the code created in the previous recipe. The **Service Callout** makes the call through the **Business Service** to the JSON service, and uses a **Transport Header** activity to set the HTTP `Content-Type` header to `application/json`. The final **Replace** activity puts the XML response into the `body` variable, so that OSB will return it to the caller.

Dynamically binding to a JSON service in OSB

It's common for JSON services to use RESTful interface design principles; as such, the URI and HTTP method will often combine to indicate what is to be done.

This differs from the common document-literal SOAP/HTTP pattern, where the HTTP method will always be `POST`, the URI will be constant for all operations exposed by a service, and the operation will be selected by the outer-most element inside the SOAP body or the SOAPAction header.

This difference means that we'll often need to do some extra preparation before calling out to a JSON service, so that the HTTP method and the URI are correctly configured.

Getting ready

We'll be building on the previous recipes, so we'll assume that you already have an OSB project in OEPE, with an HTTP business service, and a proxy service that invokes it using a Service Callout.

How to do it...

1. The HTTP business service will have been configured to use a particular HTTP method. In the event that a different method is required, the proxy service can override the method by adding an element to the outbound variable.

2. Add an **Insert** activity to the **Request Action** path of the **Service Callout** and configure the **Properties** of the **Insert** activity described as follows:

    i. First, click on **<Expression>** to open the **XQuery/XSLT Expression Editor** and enter the following:

    ```
    <http:http-method>PUT</http:http-method>
    ```

     Here, we are specifying PUT as the HTTP method, but it could be GET, POST, or DELETE as appropriate.

    ii. Next, ensure the **Location** attribute is set to **as first child off**.

    iii. Click on **<XPath>** to open the **XPath Expression Editor**. Within the variable structure browse to **outbound | $outbound | transport | request | request – http** and drag it on to the **Expression**, as shown in the following screenshot:

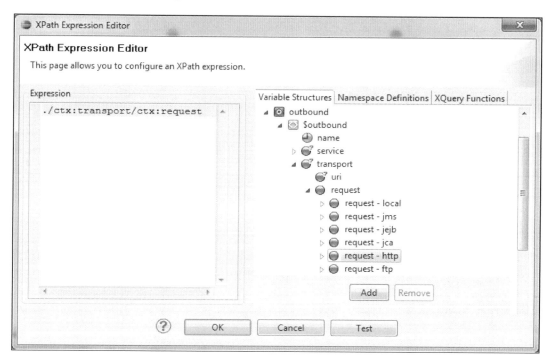

     iv. Click on **OK**.

     v. Next, set **In Variable** to outbound.

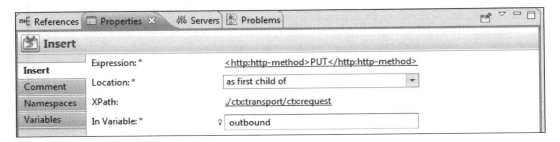

3. The business service will have been configured with a base URI to use for outgoing calls. If a suffix is required (to identify a specific resource, for example), the `relative-URI` element may be added to the outbound variable to provide this information to the business service.

   To append `/1` to the end of the URI, drag an **Insert** activity to the **Request Action** path of the **Service Callout**. Configure the **Properties** of the **Insert** activity (as in step 2) to have the values listed in the following table:

Field	Value
Expression	`<http:relative-URI>/1</http: relative-URI >`
Location	**as first child of**
XPath	`./ctx:transport/ctx:request`
In Variable	`outbound`

   If the Endpoint URI configured for the business service is `http://example.org:8091/CreditCardService/CreditCardJSON_1.0`, the outgoing call will now be made to the following URL:

   `http://example.org:8091/CreditCardService/CreditCardJSON_1.0/1.`

   It is, of course, much more likely that you will dynamically construct the relative-URI value based on the received request.

How it works...

The `./ctx:transport/ctx:request` element of the outbound variable is used to supply transport-specific metadata to the business service, to influence how it makes the outgoing service invocation.

There's more...

In some cases it will be necessary to completely override the business service's endpoint URI.

Assuming that the URI to use has been assigned to a variable `requestURI` earlier in the proxy service message flow, the endpoint URI override is performed as follows:

1. Insert a **Routing Options** activity to the **Request Action** path of the **Service Callout**. Configure the **Properties** of the **Routing Options** activity as described next.

2. First, ensure **URI** is selected, and then click on **<Expression>** to open the **XQuery/XSLT Expression Editor** and enter the text `$requestURI`.

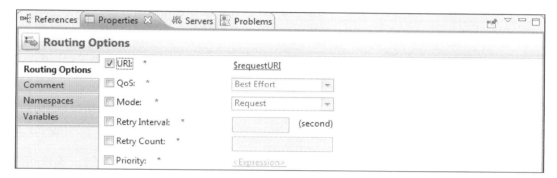

If we were using a **Route**, rather than a **Service Callout**, and we wanted to select one of a number of business services bound to different endpoint URIs, a **Dynamic Route** activity would be the one to use.

Exposing a proxy service as a JSON service

There will be times when a client is better served by providing a service with a JSON over HTTP interface, rather than the more common SOAP over HTTP. By re-using the Java code that we built in the *Converting between XML and JSON* recipe, we'll expose a JSON interface, while working with XML internally to take the best advantage of OSB's strengths.

Getting ready

We'll assume that you have an OSB configuration project in OEPE, and that you have the Jackson and XMLBeans JAR files referred to in the *Converting between XML and JSON* recipe, as well as the JAR files produced by that recipe.

How to do it...

1. Select the Oracle Service Bus perspective in Eclipse. Right-click on the OSB configuration project, and select **New | Oracle Service Bus Project**. In the dialog box, enter a name for the project (**JSONCreditCardService**) and click on **Finish**.

2. Right-click on the **InvokeJSONCreditCardService** OSB project in the **Project Explorer**, and select **New | Folder** from the context menu.

   Enter the name `jars` for the folder in the **New Folder** dialog, and click on **Finish**.

3. Now, import the following JAR files from the **CreditCardServiceMessages** project into the `jars` folder:

   - `dist/CreditCardServiceMessages_1.0.jar`
   - `dist/CreditCardServiceMessagesXmlBeans_1.0.jar`
   - `lib/jackson-core-asl-1.9.7.jar`
   - `lib/jackson-mapper-asl-1.9.7.jar`

4. We now need to inform OSB of the dependencies between the jars. Double-click on the **jackson-mapping-asl-1.9.7.jar** in the **Project Explorer**.

   In the **Modify Jar Dependencies** dialog, select the **jackson-core-asl-1.9.7.jar** file from the **Available jars** pane on the left, and click on the **Add >** button to move it to the **Jar references** pane. Click on **OK**.

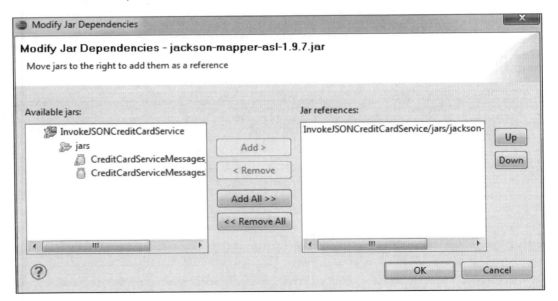

5. Do the same for the **CreditCardServiceMessages_1.0.jar** file, but click on the **Add All >>** button to indicate that it depends on all of the other JAR files in the project.

There will be warnings about classes from the `org.joda.time` package not being available. This is an optional dependency in the Jackson Mapper, and will not be a problem.

6. Right-click on the OSB project **JSONCreditCardService** and select **New | Proxy Service** from the context menu. In the **New Oracle Service Bus Proxy Service** dialog box, enter the name `JSONCreditCardService_1.0` for the proxy service and click on **Finish**.

7. On the **General** tab, configure the **Service Type** to be **Messaging Service**.

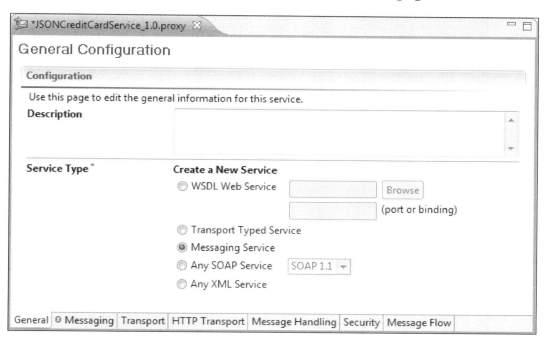

8. On the **Messaging** tab, configure the **Request Message Type** and **Response Message Type** to be **Text**.

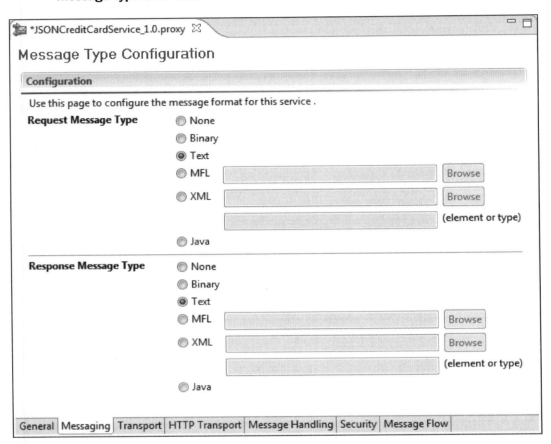

9. On the **Transport** tab, leave the **Protocol** set to **http**, replacing the **Endpoint URI** with the value **/ckbk/svc/JSONCreditCard**, and select the **Yes** radio-button for the **Get All Headers** option.

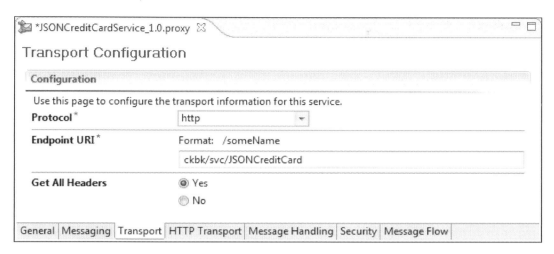

10. The **HTTP Transport**, **Message Handling**, and **Security** tabs can be left with their default values.

11. Next, we will create a conditional branch for the HTTP method. On the **Message Flow** tab, insert a **Conditional Branch** activity into the message flow, and assign it a name (HTTPMethodBranch). For this branch, we will select a path based on the incoming HTTP method – we'll only support POST for this service.

12. Click on the **Conditional Branch** subtab in the **Properties** pane and then click on the `<XPath>` value to open the XPath Expression Editor. Expand the inbound variable in the **Variable Structures** tab, as shown in the following screenshot:

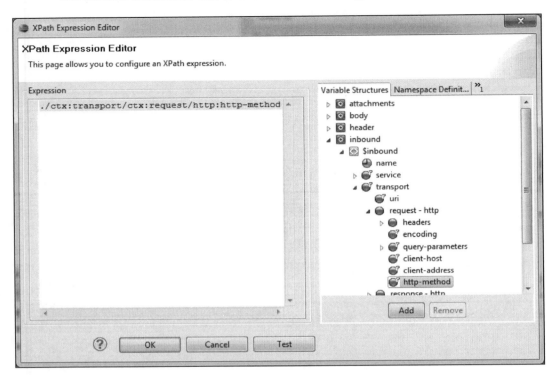

13. Drag the **http-method** into the **Expression** field to create the following expression, and then click on **OK**:

    ```
    ./ctx:transport/ctx:request/http:http-method
    ```

14. Next, enter `inbound` in the **In Variable** text field. The conditional branch should be configured as follows:

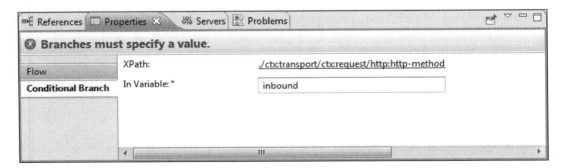

15. Next, create a **POST** branch for the JSON POST request. Click on the branch **branch1**. In the **Properties** pane, enter POST in the **Label** field, and ' POST ' in the **Value** field.

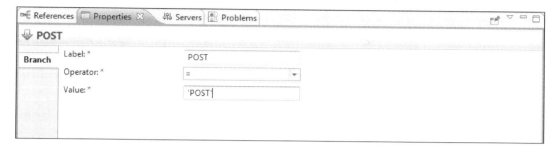

16. Add a **Pipeline Pair** to the **POST** branch, and assign it the name PostPipelinePair.

17. Add a **Stage** to the **Request Pipeline** in the PostPipelinePair, and assign it the name ProcessPutRequest.

18. Add a **Java Callout** to the ProcessPOSTRequest stage. In the **Properties** pane, click on the **Browse** button to select the method to be invoked.

    This will open the **Select an Archive Resource** dialog box. Select the CreditCard ServiceMessages_1.0.jar file in the JSONCreditCardService project and click on the **OK** button. In the **Select a Java Method** dialog box, select the method debitCreditCardJsonToXml(java.lang.String) and click on **OK**.

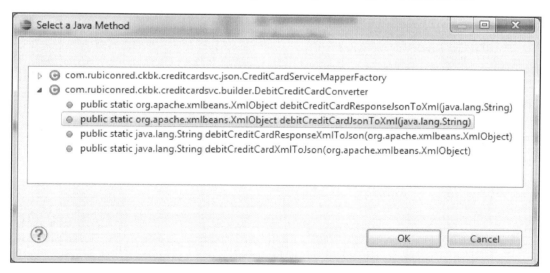

19. In the **JavaCallout** subtab of the **Properties** pane, click on the <Expression> value to specify the input parameter to the Java method. Specify the XPath expression as $body/text(). The content of the body variable is the received JSON string.

20. In the **Result Value** field of the **JavaCallout** panel, enter `requestXml`; the return value of the Java method will be assigned to this variable.

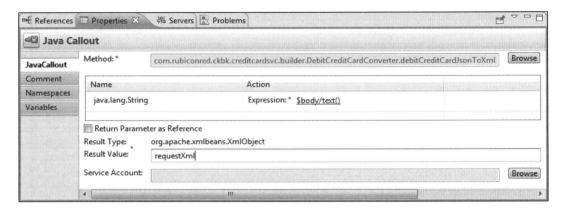

Click on the **ProcessPutRequest** stage in the **Message Flow** view, and select the **Namespaces** tab in the **Properties** pane. Add the three namespace mappings, as shown in the following table:

Prefix	URI
acc	`http://rubiconred.com/ckbk/xsd/account`
cmn	`http://rubiconred.com/ckbk/xsd/common`
ebm	`http://rubiconred.com/ckbk/ebm/CreditCard`

The result will be as follows:

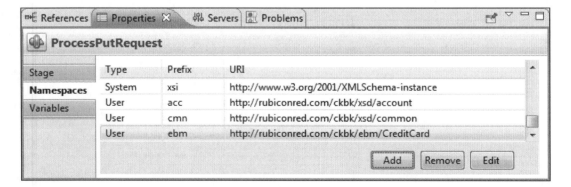

21. Add an **Assign** activity to the **ProcessPutRequest** stage, after the **Java Callout** activity. Set the **Expression** to `data($requestXml//cmn:cardNumber)`, and the **Variable** to `creditCardNumber`.

22. We have now converted the received JSON request to XML and used XPath to extract the credit card number. We will now construct an XML response, and convert it to JSON for returning to the client.

    Insert a **Stage** named **ProcessPostResponse** into the **Response Pipeline** of the `PostPipelinePair`, and add the same namespace definitions as we previously added to the **ProcessPutRequest** stage.

23. Add an **Assign** activity to the **ProcessPostResponse** stage. Set the **Expression** to the following:

```
<ebm:debitCreditCardResponse
  xmlns:ebm="http://rubiconred.com/ckbk/ebm/CreditCard"
  xmlns:cmn="http://rubiconred.com/ckbk/xsd/common">
  <cmn:cardNumber>{$creditCardNumber}</cmn:cardNumber>
  <cmn:cardAuthCode>0000</cmn:cardAuthCode>
</ebm:debitCreditCardResponse>
```

    Set the **Variable** to `responseXml`.

24. Add a **Java Callout** activity following the **Assign** activity, and select the **Java Method** in the same way as in the **ProcessPutRequest** stage, but select the method `debitC reditCardResponseXmlToJson(org.apache.xmlbeans.XmlObject)`.

    Set the **Java Callout** activity's input parameter **Expression** to `$responseXml`, and the **Result Value** to `responseJson`.

25. Add a **Replace** activity after the **Java Callout**. Set the **Properties** as follows:

    ❑ **XPath**: .
    ❑ **In Variable**: body
    ❑ **Expression**: $responseJson

Select the **Replace node contents** option.

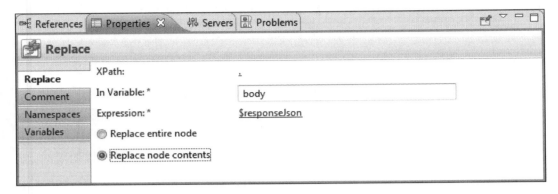

26. Next, we need to set the Content Type to JSON for the proxy response. Drag a **Transport Header** activity into the **ProcessPostResponse** stage, after the **Replace** activity.

27. In the **Transport Headers** pane of the **Transport Header** activity, set the **Direction** to `Inbound Response`. Click on the **Add Header** button to add a new header to the **Inbound Response**.

    Set the HTTP header **Content-Type** to have the value `'application/json'`; this is the standard MIME type for JSON data.

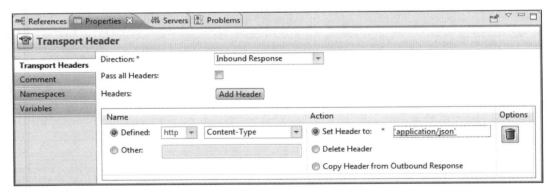

The completed **Pipeline Pair** looks like the following screenshot:

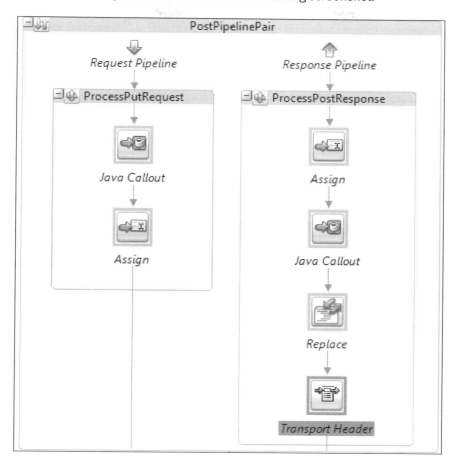

28. Your JSON service is now ready to be deployed and tested.

How it works...

Since JSON is just structured text, we can configure an OSB proxy service to accept and respond with JSON by using the Text messaging type. We then use the Jackson and XMLBeans libraries to convert between JSON and XML as required.

The **Transport Header** activity is used to set the **Content-Type** header in the response to `application/json`, in order to inform the client of the data format used for the response. It's good practice for non-SOAP HTTP interfaces to ensure that the HTTP method, status code, and headers are used correctly.

There's more...

It's possible to build services with OSB that will accept input in multiple formats, by inspecting the received Content-Type header, which can be accessed at:

```
$inbound/ctx:transport/ctx:request/tp:headers/http:Content-
   Type/text()
```

The appropriate transformation of the request payload can then be applied into a common format. Similar techniques may be used to return the response in a format chosen by the caller. The caller could indicate its preferred response format by using the **Accept** header, or by using something like a suffix on the request URI, which is accessed at:

```
$inbound/ctx:transport/ctx:request/http:relative-URI/text()
```

When adding error handling to your JSON services, you will probably want to override the HTTP status code of your response, to best communicate the error back to the caller. This can be achieved using an **Insert** activity, configured as follows:

Parameter	Value
Expression	`<http:http-response-code>404</http:http-response-code>`
Location	as last child of
XPath	`./ctx:transport/ctx:response`
In Variable	`inbound`

Where 404 in the previous table is the HTTP status code that will be returned in the response.

8

Compressed File Adapter Patterns

In this chapter, we will cover:

- ▶ Implement GZIP wrapper for OSB
- ▶ Reading compressed files with OSB
- ▶ Writing compressed files with OSB

Introduction

A reasonably common interface convention is to compress the contents of exchanged files, to reduce the impact on network traffic and archiving requirements. This is particularly common in **Business-to-Business** (**B2B**) scenarios, where network bandwidth is more of a constraint, as illustrated in the following figure:

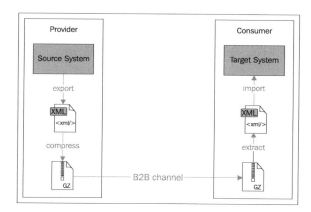

Although the Oracle Service Bus does not support such interfaces "out of the box," it is reasonably straightforward to piece together a simple adapter using existing tools.

In this chapter, we will cover recipes that enable us to read/write a GZIP file using the Oracle Service Bus.

GZIP is a data compression software application, most commonly encountered as the version implemented by the GNU Project. GZIP only natively supports the compression of one file at a time (although, of course, that file may itself be the combination of several smaller files), and has a simple format consisting of compressed binary content between a standard header and footer.

J2SE includes a standard library of compression/decompression utilities in the `java.util.zip` package, which, among other things, includes functionality for working with the GZIP data compression algorithm.

Implement GZIP wrapper for OSB

Before jumping into creating anything for OSB, we first need to create a Java library that can be used by the Oracle Service Bus to read and write GZIP files.

Getting ready

Prior to beginning this recipe, you will want to prepare some test data, consisting of XML files compressed using GZIP.

How to do it...

1. Start up Eclipse and switch to the Java perspective.

2. Right-click in the **Project Explorer** area and select **New | Java Project**. Name the project `GzipAdapter` and then select **Next**.

3. Select the **Libraries** tab and click on **Add External JARs...**. Select `com.bea.core.xml.xmlbeans_2.2.0.0.jar` from the `modules` subdirectory of your Oracle middleware installation and click on **Open**.

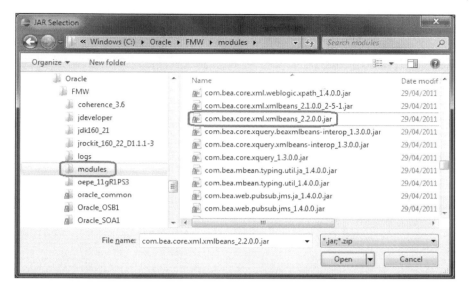

4. Click on **Finish** in the **Add External JARs** dialog box, and then on **Finish** again in the **New Java Project** dialog box.

5. Right-click on the new project and select **New | Class**. Set the package name (com.rubiconred.osb.gzip in the example) and the class name to GzipAdapter. Leave everything else as default and then click on **Finish**.

6. Replace the contents of the new file GzipAdapter.java with the following code:

```
package com.rubiconred.osb.gzip;

import org.apache.xmlbeans.*;
import java.io.*;
import java.util.zip.GZIPInputStream;
import java.util.zip.GZIPOutputStream;

public class GzipAdapter {

  public static XmlObject readGzipObject(Object param)
    throws IOException, XmlException
  {
    byte[] bytes = (byte[]) param;
    if (bytes != null) {
      InputStream input input = new
        ByteArrayInputStream(bytes);
      InputStream gzipInput = new GZIPInputStream(input);

      Writer writer = new StringWriter();
```

```
              char[] buffer = new char[1024];

          try {
            BufferedReader reader = new BufferedReader
              (new InputStreamReader(gzipInput, "UTF-8"));

            int n;
            while ((n = reader.read(buffer)) != -1)
              writer.write(buffer, 0, n);
          } finally {
            gzipInput.close();
          }

          // return the contents of the file
          return XmlObject.Factory.parse(writer.toString());
        } else {
          // input parameter is null, return null
          return null;
        }
      }

      public static byte[] writeGzipObject(XmlObject input)
        throws IOException, XmlException
      {
        ByteArrayOutputStream output = new
          ByteArrayOutputStream();
        GZIPOutputStream gzipOutput = new
          GZIPOutputStream(output);

        input.save(gzipOutput);
        gzipOutput.close();

        return output.toByteArray();
      }
    }
```

7. Right click on the GzipAdapter Java project and select **Export...**. Select **Java | JAR file** and then click on **Next**.

    Provide the **export destination** for the JAR file as GzipAdapter.jar in the directory of your choice and then click on **Finish**.

How it works...

In the previous code we have implemented two methods that allow us to convert to/from a binary format (that is GZIP) to an XML Beans Interface. As Oracle Service Bus uses the standard XMLBeans interface to manipulate XML, this provides a simple wrapper around the existing GZIP libraries that can be used by OSB to read/write GZIP data.

We will use these methods in the next two recipes to do just that.

There's more...

In addition to GZIP, the Java standard libraries also include support for the popular ZIP file format. The same design pattern can be used for this format, substituting ZIP for GZIP in the example code.

For other compression file formats (for example, RAR), there are generally open source libraries available for manipulation, with which similar approaches may be taken.

Reading compressed files with OSB

This recipe will guide you through a sample implementation of a proxy service which polls a directory for XML files compressed using the `gzip` utility, and uses the Java wrapper created in the previous recipe, to convert it to standard XML which can then be manipulated as normal within the OSB.

Getting ready

This recipe assumes you have completed the first recipe and created the `GzipAdapter.jar`. Alternatively, you can use the Jar file contained with the samples for this recipe.

Prior to beginning this recipe, you will also want to prepare some test data, consisting of XML files compressed using GZIP.

How to do it...

1. Open Eclipse and create an OSB project. Name it `GzipFileAdapter` if you want to follow the example used in this recipe.

2. First we need to import the `GzipAdapter` jar plus any of its dependencies into the project. Right-click on the **GzipFileAdapter** OSB Project in the **Project Explorer**, and select **New Folder** from the context menu.

   Enter the name `jars` for the folder and click on **Finish**.

3. Right-click on the **jars** folder and select **Import | Import...**. Select **General | File System** and click on **Next**.

   Browse to the `modules` directory under `<FMW Home>\modules` and click on **OK**. Within the import window select `com.bea.core.xml.xmlbeans_2.2.0.0.jar` (as used earlier in the first recipe), and then click on **Finish**.

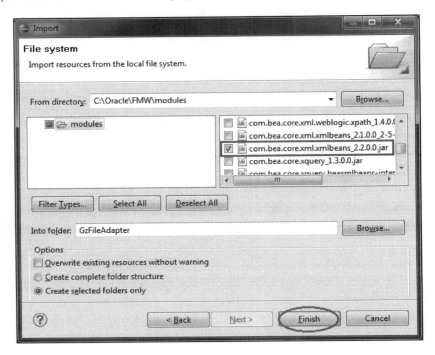

4. Right click on the **jars** folder and select **Import | Import...**. Select **General | File System** and click on **Next**.

   Browse to the directory containing the `GzipAdapter.jar`, created in the first recipe, and click on **OK**. Within the import window, select `GzipAdapter.jar` and click on **Finish**.

5. We now need to inform OSB of the dependencies between the jars. Double-click on `GzipAdapter.jar` in **Project Explorer**. In the **Modify Jar Dependencies** dialog box, select `com.bea.core.xml.xmlbeans_2.2.0.0.jar` file from the **Available jars** pane on the left, and click on the **Add >** button to move it to the **Jar references** pane. Click on **OK**.

6. The next step is to create the file adapter, as a binary file-based message proxy service, from the Oracle Service Bus IDE.

   Right-click on the `GzipFileAdapter` OSB project in **Project Explorer** and select **New | Proxy Service**. Name it `ReadGzipFile` and click on **Finish**.

7. In the **General** tab of the Proxy Service editor, select **Messaging Service** as the **Service Type**.

8. In the **Messaging** tab, select **Binary** as the **Request Message Type**. Leave **Response Message Type** as **None**.

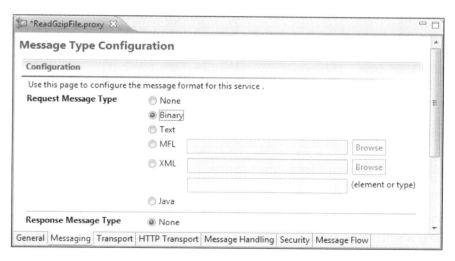

9. In the **Transport** tab, select **file** as the **Protocol** and provide a directory name where you would like to poll for files from, as the **Endpoint URI**.

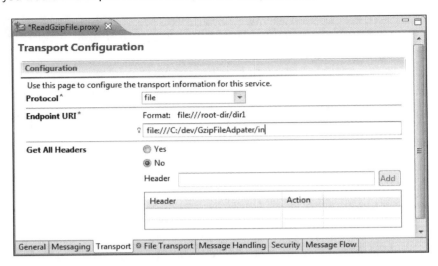

10. In the **File Transport** tab, customize the adapter to suit. In this example, we'll select a file mask of `*.gz`, as well as configuring a **Post Read Action** to be **archive** and specifying all the necessary directory file destinations.

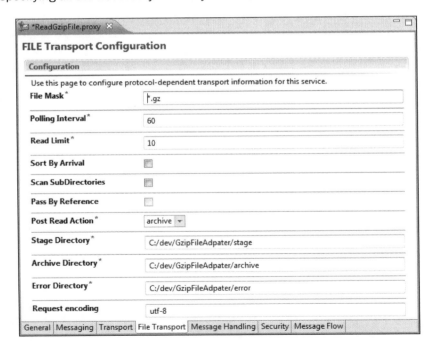

11. The next step is to incorporate a call to the `readGzipObject` Java method into the proxy service **Message Flow**.

    Start by dragging a new **Pipeline Pair** from the **Design Palette** into the **Message Flow** editor.

12. Add a new **Stage** to the **Request Pipeline** and name it `Extract GZIP`.

13. Drag an **Assign** action into the new **Stage**. In the **Properties** tab for the **Assign** action, set the **Expression** as `$body/ctx:binary-content` and the **Variable** as `gzBinaryContent`.

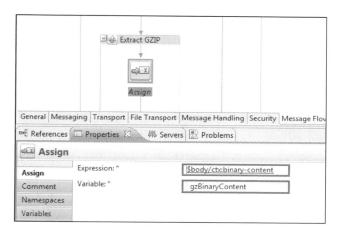

14. Drag a new **Java Callout** action from the **Design Palette** to just under the **Assign** action. In the **Properties** tab for the new **Java Callout**, select **Browse** next to the **Method** field. Select the `GzipAdapter.jar` and click on **OK**.

    In the **Select a Java Method** window, select the `readGzipObject` method and click on **OK**.

15. With the **Properties** tab, click on **< Expression>** for the only parameter and specify `$gzBinaryContent`. Set the **Result Value** variable to `payload`.

16. To test the new file adapter, you can place a GZIP'd file in the input directory and confirm the contents are read successfully by following these additional steps:

 i. Create a new **Reporting** stage below the GZIP Extract stage and drag a new **Log** action in.

 ii. Set the log **Expression** as $payload and the **Annotation** as GzipFileAdapter message payload.

 iii. Change the **Severity** to Error so that it is guaranteed to appear on your weblogic's console output.

 iv. Deploy the service to your server, copy a GZIP'd text file to the input directory you specified earlier, and observe that the contents are written to the console.

How it works...

OSB's binary message format capability allows us to accept files of any type, and extract the binary content using the built-in constructs which are generated by the engine.

From there, the **Java Callout** allows us to manipulate and parse the content using standard libraries. Note, that the return type from the **Java Callout** is org.apache.xmlbeans. XmlObject, the standard XMLBeans interface which OSB uses to manipulate XML. By using this return type (as opposed to a String) we are able to immediately start manipulating the returned content as XML using all the standard OSB message processing actions.

There's more...

In some cases, multiple files may be included in the same compressed archive. There are a couple of viable strategies for manipulating these files using OSB:

 ▶ Use a 2-stage process with two file adapters, one to decompress and write the files out, and the other to read the uncompressed files in separately

 ▶ Use a single file adapter which reads all the contained files in a single pass, then concatenates the contents inside a batch XML element for a downstream process to separate

Writing compressed files with OSB

In this next section we will consider the inverse scenario, in which files are written using the same GZIP compression algorithm to the filesystem.

This recipe will demonstrate how a simple proxy service which accepts XML content and writes GZIP'd XML files can be built using OSB.

Getting ready

This recipe assumes you have created an OSB project **GzipFileAdapter** and carried out steps 1 to 5 in the previous recipe, as well as completed the first recipe and created the GzipAdapter.jar.

How to do it...

1. Right-click on the **GzipFileAdapter** OSB project in the **Project Explorer** and select **New | Business Service**. Name it GzipFileWriter and click on **Finish**.

2. On the **General Configuration** tab, select **Messaging Service** as the **Service Type**.

3. On the **Messaging** tab, select **Binary** as the **Request Message Type**. Leave the **Response Message Type** as None.

4. On the **Transport** tab, select **file** as the **Protocol**. Enter a directory you would like to write to as the **Endpoint URI**, then click on **Add**.

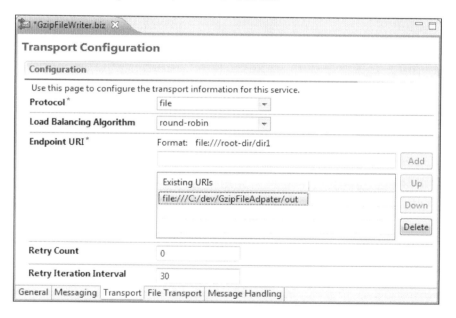

5. On the **File Transport** tab, set the **Suffix** as `.xml.gz`.

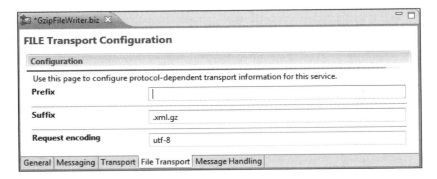

Save your changes.

6. Right-click on the **GzipFileAdapter** OSB project in the **Project Explorer** and select **New | Proxy Service**. Name the service `WriteGZipFile` and select on **Finish**.

7. On the **Message Flow** tab, drag a **Route** node from the **Design Palette** into the main editor.

8. Next, drag a **Routing** action into the route. Set the **Service** property to **GzipFileWriter.biz**.

9. Drag a new **Java Callout** action from the **Design Palette** into the *Request Action* section of the **Routing** action. In the **Properties** tab for the new **Java Callout**, select **Browse** next to the **Method** field. Select the **GzipAdapter.jar** and click on **OK**.

    In the **Select a Java Method** window, select the `writeGzipObject` method and click on **OK**.

10. With the **Properties** tab, click on **< Expression>** for the only parameter and set it to `$body` and set **Result Value** to `gzContent`.

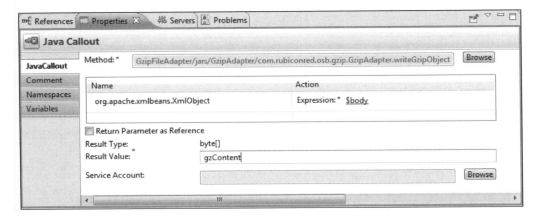

11. Next, add a **Replace** action after the **Java Callout**, and set its properties as follows:

Field	Value
XPath	.
In Variable	body
Expression	$gzContent
	select **Replace node Contents**

12. Drag a **Transport Headers** action into the **Request Action** section, after the **Replace** action.

13. In the **Properties** tab, click on **Add Header**. Select the file category and fileName element and then Set Header to your desired filename. This could be a string variable or a constant.

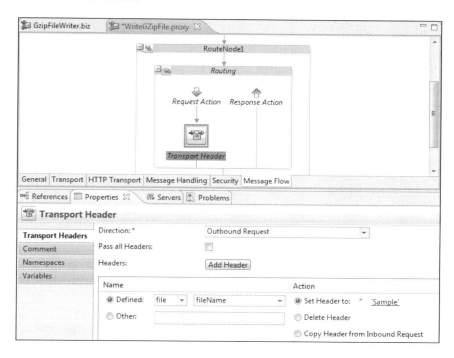

Note, that if a constant filename is used, then subsequent uses of the business service will automatically append an integer to the filename so as not to overwrite existing files.

14. Deploy your project and test out the proxy service. You should see the GZIP'd XML files being produced containing the content you place in the body of the request.

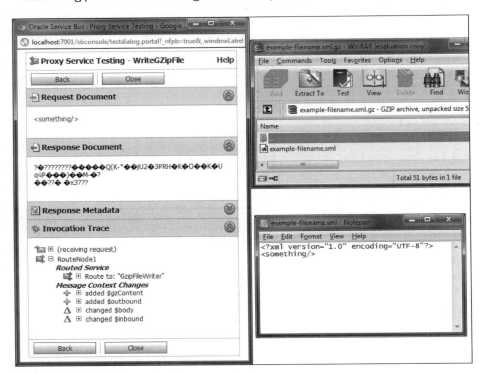

How it works...

The `writeGZipObject()` method converts the input XML into an output stream; in our case, the `GZIPOutputStream` which compresses the content into the output stream it wraps.

By using the `byte[]` return type for our **Java Callout**, we leverage OSB's binary content capability to include a reference to the raw data produced by our GZIP compression code.

Passing this to a binary messaging business service then automatically pushes the content out into the file, exactly as expected.

Note, the use of transport headers to set the filename. This is necessary meta-info, and should usually be used to name the file using variable content.

There's more...

In addition to GZIP, the Java standard libraries also include support for the popular ZIP file format. The same design pattern can be used for this format, substituting `ZipOutputStream` for `GZIPOutputStream` in the example code.

For other compression file formats (for example, RAR), there are generally open source libraries available for manipulation with which similar approaches may be taken.

9
Integrating Java with SOA Suite

In this chapter, we will examine the following recipes that allow us to integrate Java code into our SOA composites:

- ▶ Creating a custom XPath function for SOA Suite
- ▶ Calling an EJB from an SOA composite
- ▶ Using a Spring bean in an SOA composite
- ▶ Using an EJB reference in a Spring component
- ▶ Accessing the SOA runtime environment from BPEL

Introduction

Java is a widely used and popular programming language; indeed, SOA Suite is written in Java. Often we have existing Java code that we wish to use in our composites. The point about Service Oriented Architecture is that it is language neutral and encourages re-use, so it is natural to want to re-use existing Java artifacts. In addition to re-using existing artifacts, we may want to use Java to handle some tasks that are too complicated to handle easily in XML. The following list summarizes the ways in which we may interact with Java from within the SOA Suite, and the purpose for which they should be used:

- ▶ Spring container
  - ❑ Allows the use of existing Spring beans and other Java objects
  - ❑ Allows the implementation of a WSDL interface in Java
- ▶ EJB reference
  - ❑ Allows composites to call an Enterprise Java Bean

- ► Java Exec
    - ❏ Allows a BPEL process to access an executing environment

- ► Custom XPath function
    - ❏ Allows custom Java code to be embedded in assign statements and XSLT transforms

- ► EJB service
    - ❏ Allows a composite to be invoked by Java code as though it were an EJB

The following use cases outline when to use the different types of Java integration.

Use Case 1 – adding complex logic to XPath

Sometimes, the existing XPath functions are insufficient for our needs. In this case, we can write custom XPath functions in Java code. These XPath functions can be used in XQuery, XSLT, and Assign operations in the same way as built-in XPath functions. This allows complex logic to be embedded in XML processing without requiring complex XPath or Xquery logic to be added to it; it also helps to avoid having to make callouts to Java code through other mechanisms and hides the fact that Java is being used from the user of the XPath function.

Use Case 2 – calling existing Java code

Existing Java code can be classified as an EJB, a Spring bean, or some other Java object. Other Java objects can be wrapped in a Spring bean to make them consumable by SOA composites. It is possible to select methods to be exposed from existing code. Methods to be exposed should have only simple types or Java beans as input and output parameters. Java beans have no argument constructors. If the methods do not meet these criteria, then it will be necessary to wrap the methods with a Spring bean interface that does meet these criteria if the method is to be called from non-Java components.

The following flowchart helps you decide how to re-use existing Java code, identifying if there is a need to wrap the code to make it usable by non-Java components. Use the flow chart to determine how to re-use your existing Java. Depending on your answers to the questions in the flow chart, it will suggest if you need to create a Java bean wrapper for your resource to convert parameter and return types into simple Java types and Java beans. It will also identify how the resource should be consumed within the SOA Suite, such as by an EJB reference or as a Spring component.

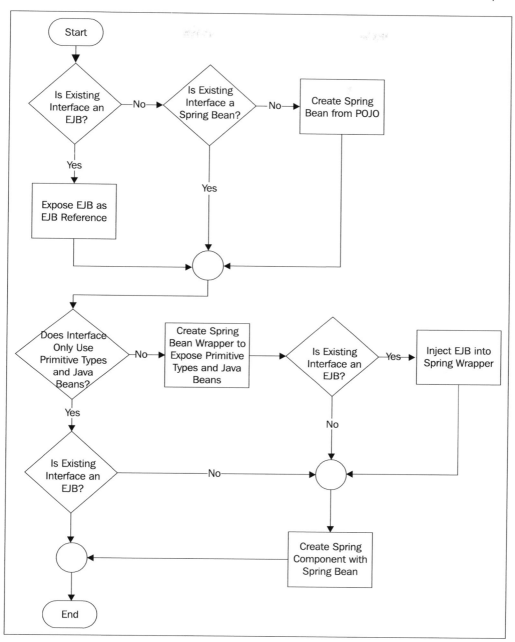

Use Case 3 – implementing a service in Java

SOA Suite is generally concerned with orchestrating services together, but it can also be used to implement the services. Sometimes, we have existing interfaces that need a concrete implementation behind them that may best be provided in a 3GL, such as Java. In this scenario, instead of writing a Java web service, deploying it, and operating it separately to our SOA infrastructure, it may be better to implement the interface in a Spring component inside an SOA composite. This keeps the service in a managed environment while taking advantage of Java.

Use Case 4 – accessing BPEL and composite information

Sometimes, we need to access information about the composite or BPEL process that is exposed through Java APIs but not available through built-in XPath functions. We could use custom XPath functions to access this information, but sometimes we want quick, one-off access that will not be re-used. In this case, we can use a Java Exec activity in a BPEL process to execute Java code as part of our BPEL process. This code has access to the BPEL and composite environment.

Creating a custom XPath function for SOA Suite

In this recipe, we will create a custom XPath function in java that can be used by any composite component in an assign or transform. This enables us to add complex logic into our XPath expressions without making an explicit call to Java. We will use the example of calculating the mean and standard deviation of a set of numbers.

Getting ready

Our XPath function will have a signature, as shown in the following code snippet:

```
double getStdDev(values as node-set)
```

It will take the value of each node in the input node set, calculate it, and return the standard deviation.

How to do it...

1. Create a project with the appropriate libraries that are required by XPath.

    In JDeveloper create a new Java project. From the new projects **Project Properties**, choose the **Libraries and Classpath** tab and choose **Add Library** to add the **SOA Runtime** library and the **Oracle XML Parser v2** library to the project. Click on **OK** until the **Project Properties** dialog closes.

2. Create a new **Java Class** in the project and add a static method to the class that takes an `oracle.xml.parser.v2.XMLNodeList` as the input parameter (this is the input to our function) and returns a `java.lang.Double` (the output of our function). The method name is the name of our XPath function.

This is the method that we will use to provide the implementation of our custom XPath function. It is also the method we will register with the XSLT engine.

A sample class is shown as follows:

```
package soa.cookbook.xpath;

import oracle.xml.parser.v2.XMLNodeList;

public class StdDev {
  public static double getStdDev(XMLNodeList nodes)
  {
    return null;
  }
}
```

3. Access the input values.

   The input parameter to our XPath function is a list of nodes that we can iterate over through each node:

   ```
   for (int i = 0; i < nodes.getLength(); i++) {
     try {
       Node node = nodes.item(i);
   ```

   We can then check that the node is of the expected type; in our case we expect an element:

   ```
   if (node.getNodeType() == Node.ELEMENT_NODE) {
   ```

4. Get the input value.

   We can then access the value of the element as a string and parse it into the double we expect:

   ```
   double value = Double.parseDouble(node.getTextContent());
   ```

   We wrap the parameter processing in a try-catch block so that we can ignore any unexpected data types.

   ```
     }
   } catch (Exception e) {
     ; // Ignore non-numeric values
   }
   ```

   We can now manipulate the data passed in to our function.

5. Add the required libraries.

Our implementation makes use of the Apache Commons Math library, and so we need to add that library to our **Project Properties** by going to the **Libraries and Classpath** tab and choosing **Add Library**. We can then click the **New** button to add a new library to JDeveloper.

On the **Create Library** dialog, we can specify a name for the library and then choose the **Class Path** and click **Add Entry** to bring up the **Select Path Entry** dialog, which will allow us to choose the JAR file or classpath that we need to add to find the classes in the library.

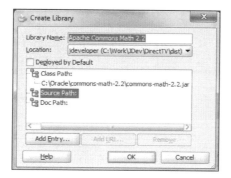

We can then specify the **Source Path** and **Doc Path** if those are also available for the library. Finally, we add the library by clicking on **OK** and then select the library from the **Add Library** dialog to include it in our project.

6. Implement the function logic.

To implement the function logic, we begin by executing the initialization code before we start iterating over the nodes in the `XMLNodeList`.

```
DescriptiveStatistics stats = new DescriptiveStatistics();

for (int i = 0; i < nodes.getLength(); i++) {
```

```
XMLNodeList nodes = (XMLNodeList)list.get(0);
```

Within the iteration of `XMLNodeList`, we then add the value of the element to the statistics we are gathering.

```
double value = Double.parseDouble(node.getTextContent());
stats.addValue(value);
```

Finally, we return the standard deviation as the result of the XPath function by passing it out as the return value of the method.

```
return stats.getStandardDeviation();
```

7. Create a BPEL and Mediator wrapper function.

BPEL and Mediator components can use custom XPath functions, but they have a slightly different interface than custom XSLT XPath functions, so we will now implement that interface—`oracle.fabric.common.xml.xpath.IXPathFunction`.

We modify our class to implement the interface by right-clicking on the class name and choosing **Source | Implement Interface**. We then use the **Hierarchy** browser in the **Implement Interface** dialog to select the `IXPathFunction` interface.

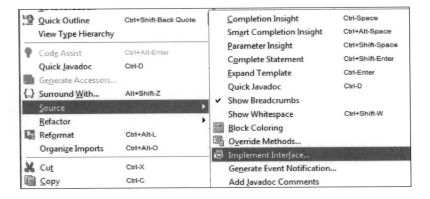

This creates a new method in our class:

```
public Object call(IXPathContext iXPathContext,
                   List list) throws XPathFunctionException {
   return null;
}
```

The call method takes an `IXPathContext` and a `List` as the input parameters and returns an `Object`. The method should declare that it throws an `XPathFunctionException`.

8. Get a single parameter.

The input parameters to the XPath function are available in the list parameter of our method.

We have only one parameter, so we can access it by getting the first item in the list and casting it to the expected type, an `XMLNodeList`:

```
NodeList nodes = (NodeList)list.get(0);
```

The `iXPathContext` provides access to the calling component (Mediator and BPEL) and to any variables declared in that component.

We need to pass the function input parameters to the static method we previously implemented, so we'll just call that method from the new method:

```
return getStdDev(nodes);
```

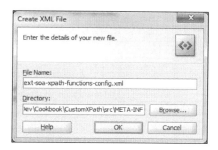

9. Create the custom XPath descriptor file.

To tell both JDeveloper and SOA Suite about our custom XPath functions, we must create their description in an XML file. The file is called `ext-soa-xpath-functions-config.xml` and must be created in the project's `src/META-INF` directory.

This file must have the following content:

```
<?xml version="1.0" encoding="UTF-8"?>
<soa-xpath-functions
  xmlns="http://xmlns.oracle.com/soa/config/xpath"
  xmlns:stat=
"http://www.oracle.com/XSL/Transform/java/soa.cookbook.xpath.
StdDev" >
```

The `soa-xpath-functions` element is in the `http://xmlns.oracle.com/soa/config/xpath` namespace and must specify a target namespace prefix (with a name of our choosing) that references a namespace made up of two parts. The first part of the namespace must be `http://www.oracle.com/XSL/Transform/java/` and the final part must be the canonical class name of the class implementing the static XSLT function, called `soa.cookbook.xpath.StdDev`.

10. Define the XPath function name.

   The `function name` element is used to register the name of the function. The function name is used by XSLT to identify the static method in the class that was previously identified.

   ```
   <function name="stat:getStdDev">
   ```

11. Identify the function implementation class.

   The `className` element identifies the class that implements the BPEL and Mediator call method.

   ```
   <className>soa.cookbook.xpath.StdDev</className>
   ```

12. Define the XPath function's return type.

   The `return` element identifies the return type of the function.

   ```
   <return type="number"/>
   ```

13. Define the XPath function's parameters.

   The `params` element lists the parameters of the function, identifying their names and types.

   ```
   <params>
     <param name="data" type="node-set"/>
   </params>
   ```

14. Provide the XPath function's description.

   The `desc` element provides the function summary that will appear in the brief description in JDeveloper.

   ```
   <desc>Returns the Standard Deviation of the values of the
         input node-set</desc>
   ```

   The `detail` element provides the detailed description that appears in JDeveloper.

   ```
   <detail>Returns the Standard Deviation of the values of
           the top level elements in the node-set passed as
           a parameter. </detail>

     </function>
   </soa-xpath-functions>
   ```

15. Packaging the XPath functions in a JAR file.

Having created the descriptor file, we now package the XPath function into a JAR file by going to **Project Properties** and selecting the **Deployment** tab. Here, we create a **New** deployment that will be used to package the XPath function we have created.

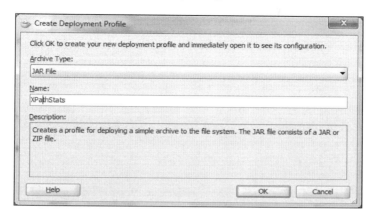

In the **Create Deployment Profile** dialog, we give the profile a name and choose it to be of the type **JAR File**, and then click on **OK**.

16. Add additional libraries to Deployment Profile.

In the **Edit JAR Deployment Profile Properties** dialog, we go to the **Contributors** section of the **Project Output** section in **File Properties** and click on the **Add** button to add a new contributor. Here, in the **Add Contributor** dialog, we enter the path for any libraries that need to be included in our custom XPath library; in our case we add the Apache Math library.

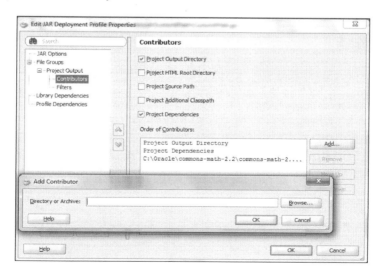

17. Generate the JAR file.

Having created the profile, we can now deploy it by right-clicking on the project and selecting **Deploy** to generate our JAR file.

18. Register the XPath functions with JDeveloper.

To use the custom function in JDeveloper, we must go to **Tools | Preferences** and choose the **SOA** section.

Clicking on **Add** allows us to locate our newly created JAR file in the deploy directory of our project and register it with JDeveloper.

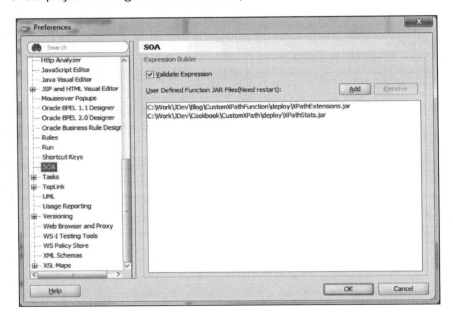

19. Register the XPath functions with SOA Suite.

To use our custom XPath functions in an SOA Suite installation, we need to copy the generated JAR file to $ORACLE_HOME/soa/modules/oracle.soa.ext_11.1.1.

20. Use the XPath functions.

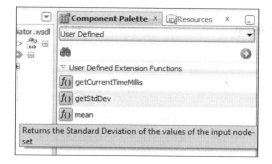

We can use our custom XPath function just like any other XPath function by choosing it from **Component Palette**. It will be listed under the **User Defined** section.

How it works...

When we register our XPath JAR file with JDeveloper and SOA Suite, they look in the `META-INF` directory for a configuration file that will tell them what functions are being registered and which classes implement those functions. The name of the configuration file varies according to which component types we want to allow to access our XPath function. The format of the file is the same for all the components; the name of the file and the component types they apply to are shown in the following table:

Filename	Registered Component			
	XSLT	**BPEL**	**Mediator**	**Human Workflow**
`ext-soa-xpath-functions-config.xml`	Yes	Yes	Yes	Yes
`ext-mapper-xpath-functions-config.xml`	Yes	No	No	No
`ext-bpel-xpath-functions-config.xml`	No	Yes	No	No
`ext-mediator-xpath-functions-config.xml`	No	No	Yes	No
`ext-wf-xpath-functions-config.xml`	No	No	No	Yes

If we do not wish to register our function with the XSLT mapper, because for instance it made use of the name of the currently active composite or component, we would need to provide three identical files to register with BPEL (`ext-bpel-xpath-functions-config.xml`), Mediator (`ext-mediator-xpath-functions-config.xml`), and Human Workflow (`ext-wf-xpath-functions-config.xml`).

When our function is called from XSLT, the parameters to the function map directly onto the parameters of our static method. The parameter mappings from the XSD type in our XPath function to the Java type in our static method are shown as follows:

XPath Function Parameter Type (XSD)	Java Method Parameter Type
`String`	`java.lang.String`
`Boolean`	`boolean` or `java.lang.Boolean`
`Number`	`int` or `java.lang.Integer` or `float` or `java.lang.Float` or `double` or `java.lang.Double`
`node-set`	`oracle.xml.parser.v2.XMLNodeList`
`tree`	`oracle.xml.parser.v2.XMLDocumentFragment`

A node set will have multiple XML elements at the same level and is useful for when we want to operate across multiple elements; in our example, we used it to pass multiple values for statistical analysis. A tree has a single, top-level XML element that will usually have a number of nested XML elements.

When our function is called from BPEL, Mediator, or Human Workflow, the list of parameters are packaged up into a `java.util.List` and passed as a single parameter to our registered class' `call` method.

There's more...

If we have more than one parameter, we can iterate over the list using a `for` statement:

```
For (Object o : list) {
    ...
}
```

The `IXPathContext` parameter for the XPath functions registered with BPEL and Mediator is used to pass information about the calling component. In particular, it can be used to determine the type and name of the calling component, and provides access to any variables in that component.

Calling an EJB from an SOA composite

In this recipe, we will call an Enterprise Java Bean Session Bean from within a composite. This is useful if we have an existing EJB that we wish to re-use.

Getting ready

Make sure that you have opened the composite to which you will add the EJB reference. There will be one item in the list for each parameter of our function.

How to do it...

1. Add an EJB reference.

    Open the composite in JDeveloper and drag the **EJB Service** from the **Component Palette** onto the **References** section of the composite.xml **Design View**.

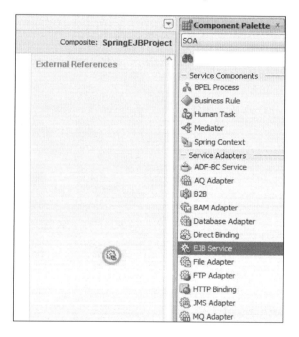

2. Start configuring EJB.

   Select a **Name** for the EJB reference. Select the **Type** as **Reference**. Select the **Version** of an EJB specification that the EJB has implemented. Set the **Interface** to be **Java**.

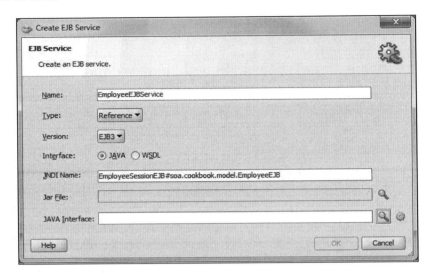

3. Select the EJB JAR file.

   Click on the magnifying glass 🔍 and use the **SOA Resource Browser** to find your EJB JAR file. After selecting your file and clicking on **OK**, you will be asked if you want to copy the file into your project. Click on **Yes** to copy the file into your project.

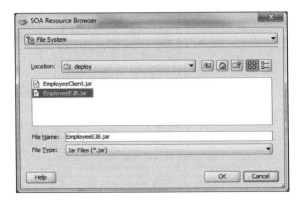

4. Select the Java interface that you want to use.

   Click on the magnifying glass 🔍 and use **Class Browser** to find your EJB's interface in the class **Hierarchy**. Select the interface you want and click on **OK**.

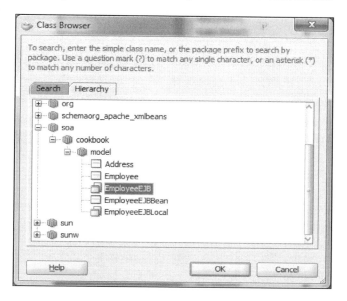

5. Complete the EJB reference creation.

   After reviewing your **EJB Service** settings, you can click on **OK** to complete the creation of the reference.

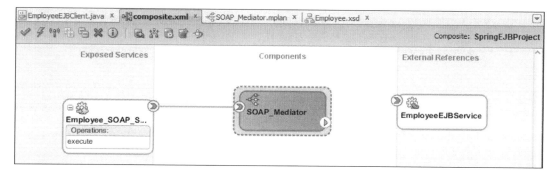

6. Wire the EJB reference to a component.

   Wire an EJB reference to a component by selecting the inbound service arrow 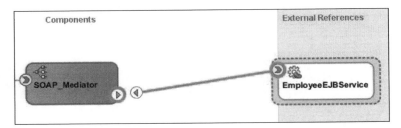 on the EJB reference in the **External References** section of the **Design** view, and drag it onto a component in the **Components** section. The outbound reference arrow will automatically appear as you move close to a component.

If the component is not a Java component, a dialog box will appear telling you that a WSDL file was generated for you based on the EJB interface chosen.

The EJB reference is now ready to be used in the selected component. It can be accessed just like any other reference.

How it works...

The EJB reference is given the **Java Naming and Directory Interface** (**JNDI**) location of an EJB that implements the given Java interface. At runtime, the container will look this JNDI location up to obtain a reference to the EJB. If this reference is of type "Java", it can be used by other Java components without requiring any additional translation. If the reference is of type Java and is consumed by a non-Java component, such as a Mediator or BPEL process, then a mapping from XML to Java is generated to allow consumption of the EJB by the non-Java component. Finally, if the type is "WSDL", the Java interface is translated to XML for all the consumers, and the Java components will access the EJB through a WSDL interface.

The Java-to-XML translation can only be generated if the EJB interface has simple types or Java beans as the input parameters and return value. For example, the schema element for a generic object type cannot be autogenerated. Similarly, all exceptions thrown must only contain simple types and/or Java beans. Java beans must have a public no parameter constructor and only consist of simple types and other Java beans. Finally, the entire object graph must be instantiated in order for the Java object to be converted to XML, so lazy loading is not supported.

There's more...

EJBs with complex interfaces can be consumed by other Java components, and so one way to provide access to an EJB with complex interfaces is to inject it into a Spring component that provides a wrapper interface to convert the interface into one for which SOA Suite can automatically generate Java/XML conversions. This approach shows the EJB dependency in composite.xml, but allows us to use complex Java interfaces.

When consuming an EJB with a non-Java component, we can control the way the Java interface parameters are mapped onto an XML schema by use of EXD files.

See also

- ▸ The *Customizing the XML mapping of an EJB* recipe in this chapter
- ▸ The *Using an EJB reference in a Spring component* recipe in this chapter

Using a Spring bean in an SOA composite

In this recipe, we will call a Spring bean from within a composite. This is useful if we have an existing Spring bean that we wish to use; it is also a useful way to wrap other Java code.

Getting ready

Make sure that you have a composite open to add the Spring component.

How to do it...

1. Copy Java libraries to a composite.

    Copy any JAR file you will be using to the `SCA-INF/lib` directory and any class that is not in a JAR file to the `SCA-INF/classes` directory of your project. Open the **Project Properties** by right-clicking on the project name in the **Application Navigator**. Select the **Libraries and Classpath** section and click on the **Add JAR Directory** button, and select the JAR file in the `SCA-INF/lib` directory or the `SCA-INF/classes` directory and add it to the project.

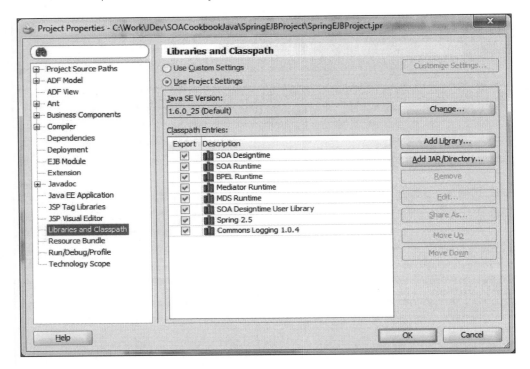

2. Add **Spring Context** to the composite.

    Open the composite in JDeveloper and drag the **Spring Context** from the **Service Components** section of the **Component Palette** onto the **Components** section of the `composite.xml` **Design View**.

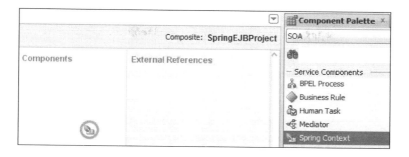

3. Start configuring **Spring Context Component**.

    Select a **Name** for the **Spring Context Component**. Select **Create New Context** and provide a name for the Spring Context XML file. Then click on **OK** to create the Spring component.

4. Add a **bean** to **Spring Context**.

    Double-click on the Spring component to start configuring Spring Context. This will open a **Source** view of the Spring Context XML file. Drag **bean** from **Component Palette** onto the Spring Context XML file immediately after the `<!--Spring Bean definitions go here-->` comment.

5. Configure the bean.

   Click on the newly created `<bean/>` tag and then use **Property Inspector** to set **id** of the bean.

   Click on the down arrow ⌄ next to the **class** property and choose **Edit...** from the pop up. This will launch the **Edit Property: class** dialog from where you can browse the class hierarchy for the bean class, as shown in the following screenshot:

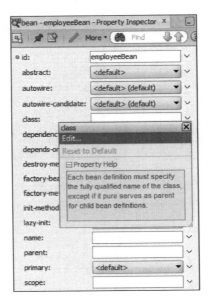

   Your bean should now look like this:

   ```
   <bean id="employeeBean" class="soa.cookbook.EmployeeEJBClient"/>
   ```

6. Configure a service on Spring Context.

   Having loaded a bean into our Spring Context, we can now make it available to other components by dragging a service from the **Component Palette** onto our Spring Context XML.

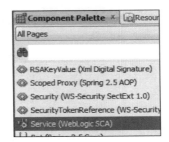

This will bring up the **Insert Service** dialog where we can enter a **name** for the service, a **target** bean that will receive service requests (the previously created bean), and the interface **type** that is being exposed (which must be implemented by the previously created bean). The **type** can be selected by using the hierarchy browser accessed via the ellipsis button to the right-hand side of the **type** input field.

7. Wire Spring Context to a component.

Wire a Spring component to another component, by selecting the inbound service arrow ⊚ on the Spring component in the **Components** section of the **Design** view and dragging it onto a component in the **Components** section. The outbound reference arrow will automatically appear as you move close to a component.

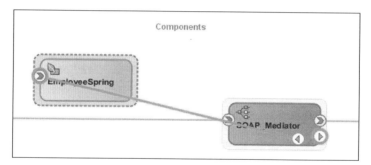

If the component is not a Java component, then a dialog box will appear telling you that a WSDL file was generated for you based on the Java interface that was chosen.

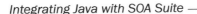

The Spring container is now ready for use in the selected component. It can be accessed just like any other component.

How it works...

The Spring Context file is a standard Spring Context, and within it we have access to the full power of Spring. When we wire another component in our application to Spring Context, we have access in our context to a new interface that can be injected as a parameter to an existing Spring bean. This has a couple of benefits; first, it makes it easy to consume other components and references in our Spring bean, and secondly, it makes our dependencies visually obvious by having them appear as wires in our composite visual editor. It is always better to have visible references because then developers and maintainers of the code can clearly see what dependencies exist. There is minimal, if any, runtime overhead to making Spring dependencies explicitly visible in the composite.

There's more...

Spring is a very powerful development framework for Java that plays well with the JEE platform that SOA Suite is built on. If we need to implement new functionalities in Java, the Spring component is a good way to implement that, because the SOA framework takes care of all the details of deployment and context, and leaves the Spring bean implementer free to concentrate on providing the business service logic in Java.

See also

▶   The *Using an EJB reference in a Spring component* recipe in this chapter

Using an EJB reference in a Spring component

In this recipe, we will configure a Spring bean to use an EJB reference from within a composite as a constructor argument. This is useful if we have a Spring bean that references an EJB, because it shows the dependency on the composite diagram.

Getting ready

Make sure that you have a composite open to configure the Spring component.

How to do it...

1. Wire Spring component to the EJB reference.

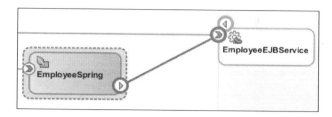

In the **design** view of composite.xml, drag the reference link from the Spring component to the service link of the EJB reference.

This will generate a new reference in Spring Context, as shown in the following code snippet:

```
<bean id="employeeBean"
      class="soa.cookbook.EmployeeEJBClient"/>
<sca:service name="employeeSpringService"
             target="employeeBean"
             type="soa.cookbook.EmployeeEJBBean"/>
<sca:reference type="soa.cookbook.model.EmployeeEJB"
             name="EmployeeEJBService"/>
```

2. Use a reference in Spring Context.

Open the composite in JDeveloper and drag the **Bean Constructor Argument** from the **Component Palette** onto the bean in the Spring Context **Structure** view. This will add a constructor to the bean.

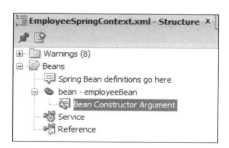

3. Configure a constructor argument.

   Use the **Bean Constructor Argument – Property Inspector** window to set a **ref**. The **ref** should be the name of the generated sca:reference element in Spring Context.

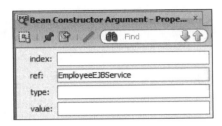

This will generate the code, shown as follows, that wires the constructor argument of the bean to the EJB:

```
<bean id="employeeBean"
      class="soa.cookbook.EmployeeEJBClient">
  <constructor-arg ref="EmployeeEJBService"/>
</bean>
<sca:service name="employeeSpringService"
             target="employeeBean"
                type="soa.cookbook.EmployeeEJBBean"/>
<sca:reference type="soa.cookbook.model.EmployeeEJB"
               name="EmployeeEJBService"/>
```

Your bean is now ready to use.

How it works...

When we wire another component service or reference to a Spring bean, then we create a new interface within Spring Context that can be injected into other Spring beans. In this case, we injected the EJB interface as a parameter to the constructor of our Spring bean, avoiding the need to use a JNDI lookup in our Spring code.

There's more...

If we were to wire up a reference from our Spring Context to a non-Java component, then JDeveloper would generate a JAXB mapping to make available the WSDL reference as a Java interface in our Spring Context. This makes it easy for our Spring Context to interact with any other portion of SOA Suite without us having to perform complex, object-XML mapping.

Accessing the SOA runtime environment from BPEL

In this recipe, we will embed a snippet of Java code into our BPEL process.

How to do it...

1. Open your BPEL process in the BPEL process editor.

2. Drag a **Java Embedding** activity from **Component Palette** under the **Oracle Extensions** section onto the BPEL process, to create an Exec activity.

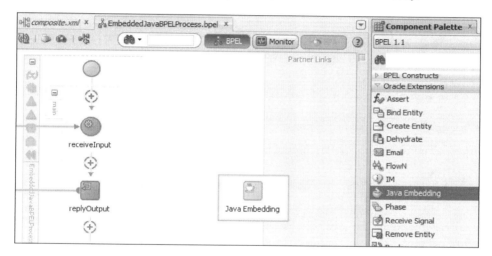

3. Access the BPEL process variables.

   Double-click the Java activity to open the **Edit Java Embedding** dialog, and enter the Java code to be executed.

BPEL variables can be read by using the `getVariableData` method that is predefined. This method takes three parameters, namely the variable name, the message part (if it is a message variable), and the XPath expression (if any). The XPath expression must use appropriate namespace prefixes declared in the BPEL process.

```
org.w3c.dom.Element elem = (org.w3c.dom.Element)getVariableData("i
nputVariable", "payload", "/client:process/client:input");
```

The `setVariableData` method is used to write to variables in the BPEL process. This takes up to four parameters, with the fourth parameter being the data that we need to store in the BPEL variable.

```
setVariableData("outputVariable", "payload", "/
client:processResponse/client:result", "Response");
```

How it works...

The Java embedding activity causes the Java code to be included in the code that is generated when the BPEL process is compiled. This is actually an instance of an extension of the `com.collaxa.cube.engine.ext.bpel.v1.nodes.BPELXExecLet` class. This class is part of the BPEL process and is used to implement the Exec activity. Any namespace prefixes in the scope of the BPEL process may be used in XPath expressions in the embedded Java code.

There's more...

Generally, it is more flexible to write a custom XPath function than use Java embedding, because a custom XPath function can be re-used across BPEL and Mediator components in different composites.

10
Securing Composites and Calling Secure Web Services

In this chapter we will cover:

- ▸ Restricting a composite to authenticated users with HTTP Basic Security
- ▸ Creating a new, group-based authorization policy
- ▸ Restricting a composite to authorized users
- ▸ Adding keys to a credential store
- ▸ Invoking an HTTP Basic secured web service

Introduction

In this chapter, we will examine recipes that allow us to secure composites or to invoke secured web services.

Web Services Manager

Oracle Web Services Manager (**WSM**) is the component that is used by SOA Suite to act as the policy manager and enforcement agent. WSM is installed as an integral part of SOA Suite.

Key security terms

When dealing with secured services, it is useful to know the terms that are used. The definitions that follow are those needed to understand how security works in SOA Suite. If this were a cookbook on identity management, then we would need to be more precise.

User

A user is a person or application program. Typically, the user and their associated attributes, such as credentials (see next section), are stored in an LDAP directory such as Oracle Internet Directory or Microsoft Active Directory. The default store is the internal WebLogic LDAP directory.

Credential

A credential is the token used for validating the identity of a user. This may be a password or the public certificate for a user.

Group

A group refers to a set of users.

Principal

A principal can be a user or a computer system. A principal is the combination of a user and a validated credential for that user, and the authenticated resource that is requesting access to a service.

Role

A role is an abstract name given to a set of permissions required to access a resource. It is normally granted to a user or a group.

Authentication

Authentication is the task of verifying the identity of a user to create a principal, and may be done in a variety of ways, including, but not limited to, a password, a client certificate, or a Kerberos token. Multiple methods of authentication (multifactor authentication) may be required for this.

Authorization

Authorization is the task of verifying if a principal has the right to access a resource.

Policy

A policy is a collection of security steps or assertions that are applied to an endpoint, which may be a service or a reference endpoint.

Basic model

The basic security model goes through the following steps:

1. A service request is constructed by a client.
2. The client adds the user identifier (username) and credentials (a password for example, usually encoded).
3. The service request is received by the service.
4. The service validates the credentials against the provided user identifier, and if they are valid, creates a principal.
5. The service validates that the principal is authorized to access the service, usually by checking that the principal has been granted the required role.
6. After authenticating and authorizing the principal, the request is acted upon by the service.

Note, that in this sequence, we have not identified if SOA Suite is the client or if it is providing the service. If SOA Suite is providing the service, then security policies are enforced when the request is received and the policy was applied to a service. If SOA Suite is invoking a service, then the security policies are enforced when the request is sent and the policy is applied to a reference.

Identity store

The identity store holds details of users and their associated credentials, groups, and roles. The identity store is provided through **Oracle Platform Security Services** (**OPSS**) and is usually an LDAP server, either the embedded LDAP in WebLogic or an external LDAP, such as Oracle Internet Directory or Microsoft Active Directory. The identity store is configured at the application server level. WebLogic may have multiple identity stores, but WSM just uses the first unless the Oracle Virtual Directory flag is set. The identity store is where the users, groups, and roles are stored.

Policy store

The policy store holds the web service manager policies that may be applied to composites. At runtime, the policy store is maintained in the **Meta-Data Repository** (**MDS**). At design time, the policy store may be held in the filesystem locally to JDeveloper, or JDeveloper may reference MDS.

Credential store

The credential store holds the credentials required to construct principals in systems that will be called by SOA Suite.

Secure Sockets Layer (SSL)

WSM is not required to provide basic message integrity and security by using SSL. SSL allows the communication between service and requestor to be protected from eavesdropping. At this level, SSL can be thought of as a secure communication channel. By default, a server-authenticated SSL only validates that the server has a certificate matching its hostname, and allows for encryption of all traffic between the client and the server. SSL with client authentication may be used to identify the requestor to the service. This requires client certificates to be kept in the identity store of the target service.

The use of client authentication in SSL can be taken advantage of by WSM, but it still does not identify whether the authenticated client has the right to access a particular service. For this, we require the WSM policies to be applied to the service.

SSL can be used to simplify security by ensuring that communication between machines is encrypted, potentially removing the need for encryption to occur at a higher level. However, there may be a performance penalty associated with this, although most modern processors have special instructions for the symmetric key portion of SSL communication, and the only significant cost these days is in the establishment of an SSL connection in the first place.

Restricting a composite to authenticated users with HTTP Basic Security

This recipe will show how to restrict access to a service, to clients that are able to authenticate themselves as a valid user in the WebLogic domain.

Getting ready

Choose the composite and service endpoint in the composite that you wish to protect.

How to do it...

1. Open the **Configure SOA WS Policies** dialog.

    In the composite, right-click on the service you wish to protect and choose the **Configure WS Policies...** option.

    This will bring up the **Configure WS Policies** dialog:

2. Add an HTTP authentication policy.

    Click on the plus (✥) icon next to **Security** to bring up the **Select Server Security Policies** dialog. Choose **oracle/wss_http_token_service_policy** and click on **OK**.

    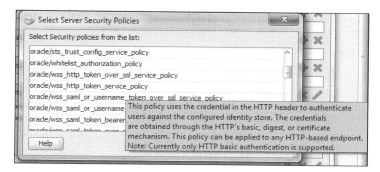

3. Confirm that the policy is attached.

    Verify that the selected policy appears in the **Security** section of the dialog box and select **OK**.

4. Deploy and test the composite.

The composite can now be deployed and the test screen can be used to verify that the service cannot be called without providing a valid username and password recognized by the WebLogic domain. Go to the **Test Web Service** screen and test the service endpoint without providing the credentials. You should get a **Webservice invocation failed** dialog box. Expand the **Show Additional Trace Information** link to see the full error. Note that there is a **Bad response: 403 Forbidden** message indicating that access to the page has been denied:

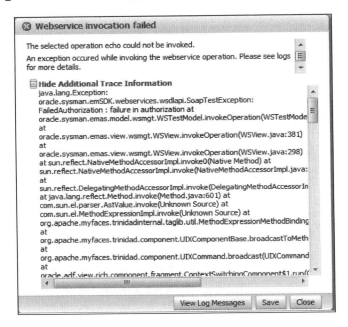

Close the dialog and expand the **Security** section of the **Test Web Service** page. Select the **HTTP basic Auth** radio button and provide the **Username** and **Password** of the user in the WebLogic domain. Then submit the request.

How it works...

We began by attaching a policy to a service in a composite. This tells the WSM agent that it must apply a particular policy to this endpoint. All requests to this endpoint will be validated against this policy.

In this case, our policy is to perform HTTP Basic authentication. This policy does two things:

- ▶ It authenticates the incoming request
- ▶ It denies access to the service unless the request can be authenticated

We can think of the policies as acting as filters. In this case, the policy filters out all the requests to the service that are not authenticated via HTTP Basic authentication.

Note, that the policy **oracle/wss_http_token_service_policy** that we used has a particular name structure:

- ▶ **oracle/** identifies it as a built-in, Oracle-provided, policy.
- ▶ **wss** identifies it as associated with web service security.
- ▶ **http** tells us that the policy is based on HTTP transport properties.
- ▶ **token** means that there is some kind of credential being passed.
- ▶ **service** tells us that the policy is restricted to service endpoints and cannot be used with references. There are usually corresponding *client* policies that request WSM to inject credentials into a request made through a reference.

Note, that this naming convention is exactly that, a convention, and we could create our own policy called `antonys_special` that does exactly the same thing. Following the convention is a good idea as it makes it easier to identify the policies that are appropriate for our particular requirements.

There's more...

All restrictions of access have some form of authentication policy. There are more ways of authenticating than just HTTP Basic authentication for example, but they all have the same filtering effect.

Alternative authentication methods

This table outlines some other out of the box authentication policies that are available in SOA Suite. I have omitted the **oracle/** prefix and **_policy** suffix for the policy names in the interest of brevity. The Service Policy Name column is used to identify the policy that protects the resources in SOA Suite. The Client Policy Name column is used to identify the corresponding policy that injects credentials into requests to references:

Service Policy Name	Client Policy Name	Notes
wss_http_token_service	wss_http_token_client	HTTP Basic authentication
wss_username_token_service	wss_username_token_client	Username/password in WS-Security headers
wss10_saml_token_service	wss10_saml_token_client	SAML tokens are passed in the SOAP message
wss10_saml20_token_service	wss10_saml20_token_client	SAML 2.0 tokens are passed in the SOAP message
wss11_kerberos_token_service	wss11_kerberos_token_service	Kerberos authentication using **Service Principal Names** (**SPN**)

The SAML authentication policies mentioned previously are only secure if used across an SSL connection. To enforce the delivery of a message across an SSL connection, WSM provides a number of *_over_ssl_* policies such as **oracle/wss_http_token_over_ssl_service_policy**. These policies only allow messages through if they have used, or will use, the SSL protocol. If a message is received from a non-SSL connection, then it will be rejected without even an attempt at authentication.

Other policies have a *_with_message_protection_* description that uses WS-Security to encrypt parts of the message, providing a mechanism for secure passage of messages through untrusted intermediaries.

Using a different authentication method

This recipe used HTTP Basic authentication to validate the credentials of a requestor. To use a different mechanism, such as **oracle/wss_saml_token_over_ssl_service_policy**, just replace the policy selected in step 2 of the recipe with the desired recipe.

- The *Creating a new, group-based authorization policy* recipe in this chapter
- The *Invoking an HTTP Basic secured web service* recipe in this chapter

Creating a new, group-based authorization policy

In this recipe, we will create a policy that will only allow access to a service if the requestor has been authenticated as the member of a particular group. Note, that all the screens say that it is a role, but actually the mapping is to a group.

Getting ready

Log in to Fusion Middleware Control.

How to do it...

1. Copy an existing policy.

   In Fusion Middleware Control, expand the Farm and **WebLogic Domain**, and then right-click on the domain name to bring up the menu. Select **Web Services | Policies**:

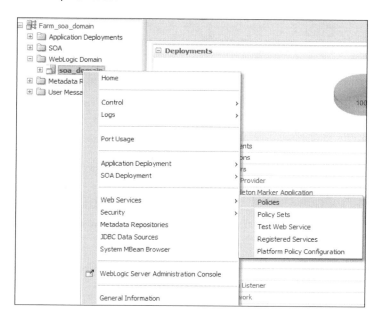

On the **Web Services Policies** screen, select the policy **oracle/binding_ authorization_permitall_policy** and click on the **Create Like** button to make a copy of the policy:

2. Modify the policy.

   Change the **Name** of the policy. Accept all the default settings. In the **Assertions** section, select the **J2EE services Authorization** line, and then on the **Settings** tab change **Roles Authorization Setting** to **Selected Roles**. Click on the plus (✚) sign to **Add** a role.

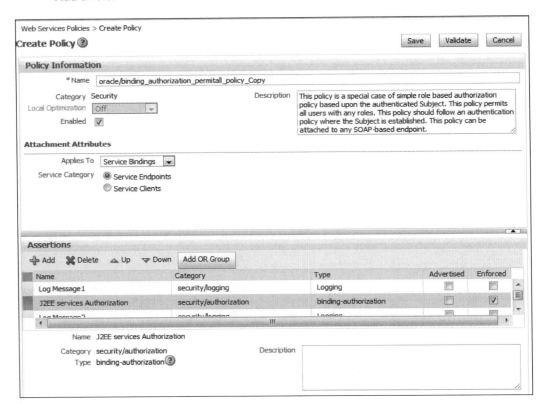

3. Authorize a role.

Choose the group, or groups, you wish to authorize from the **Roles Available** list, and click on the **Move** arrow to move them to the **Roles Selected to Add** list. Then click on **OK**.

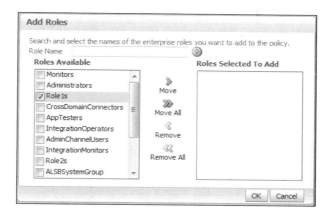

The policy may now be saved by clicking on **Save**.

4. Synchronize the policy with JDeveloper.

   In order to use our new policy in JDeveloper, we must make sure that JDeveloper is retrieving the list of policies from the policy store in the WebLogic domain. To do this in JDeveloper, go to the **Tools** menu and select **Preferences...**.

5. Choose to synchronize with App Server.

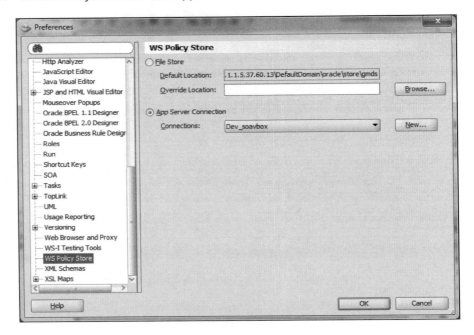

Choose the **WS-Policy Store** section and select the **App Server Connection** radio button, and choose a connection from the **Connections** drop-down list to the domain where you just created the new security policy. Then click on **OK**.

How it works...

Rather than creating a new policy from scratch, we always copy an existing policy and modify it to suit our needs. Changing a policy will automatically modify the behavior of all the endpoints that are using the policy.

The authentication policy we created restricts access based on the group that a user is a member of. We created this policy in the policy store of the SOA Suite runtime environment. To make this available to JDeveloper, we could have exported the policy from the SOA Suite runtime and then imported it into JDeveloper. Instead we chose to point JDeveloper to the SOA Suite run time policy store. This has the advantage that when we add any additional policies in the future, they will automatically be available in our JDeveloper environment.

Restricting a composite to authorized users

In the previous recipe, we allowed any authenticated user in the WebLogic domain access to our service. In this recipe, we will further restrict access to only those users that have a particular role.

Getting ready

Ensure that a suitable policy has been created for the role that we want to use to restrict access to a service.

How to do it...

1. Add an authentication policy.

    Follow the steps given in the *Restricting a composite to authenticated users with HTTP Basic Security* recipe in this chapter to add an authentication policy to the service you want to protect.

2. Add an authorization policy.

    Repeat the previous step, except this time choose the policy that you created to grant access to a particular group.

You should now have an authentication and authorization policy applied to the service.

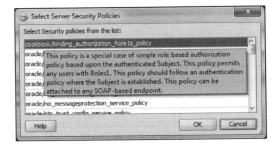

3. Confirm that both the policies are attached.

Verify that the two selected policies appear in the **Security** section of the dialog box and select **OK**.

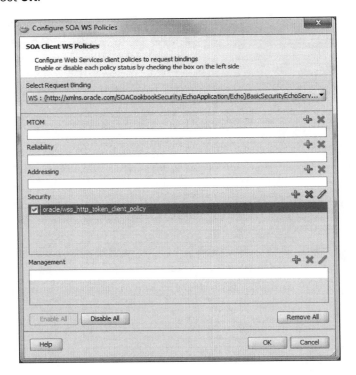

4. Deploy and test the composite.

The composite can now be deployed and the test screen used, to verify that the service cannot be called without providing a valid username and password recognized by the WebLogic domain and the user belonging to the specified group:

   i. Go to the **Test Web Service** screen and test the service endpoint without providing the credentials for it.

   ii. You should get a **Webservice invocation failed** dialog box.

   iii. Expand the **Show Additional Trace Information** link to see the full error.

   iv. Note, that there is a **Bad response: 403 Forbidden** message indicating that access to the page has been denied.

Now, provide a valid username and credentials for a user that is not a member of the allowed group:

   i. You should get a **Webservice invocation failed** dialog box.

   ii. Expand the **Show Additional Trace Information** link to see the full error.

   iii. Note, that there is a **Failed Authorization** message indicating that access to the page has been denied.

Close the dialog and provide the username and password of the user in the WebLogic domain that is a member of the requisite group. Then submit the request. This process should now succeed.

How it works...

An authorization policy is an additional filter on requests. Not only must a client be a recognized user, as determined by the authentication policy, the principal must also belong to a particular group.

Authorization policies should always be applied along with an authentication policy. The authentication policy is required to construct the principal that will be used in the authorization policy.

There's more...

In addition to the basic, role-based authorization, there is an authorization policy called **oracle/whitelist_authorization_policy** that also allows requests from the local network to be automatically approved, or to automatically approve requests that have a valid SAML Sender Vouches token.

Policies may also be changed at runtime using the Fusion Middleware Control console.

Adding keys to a credential store

In this recipe, we will examine how to add the credentials required to access an external system.

How to do it...

1. Navigate to the security credentials store.

   From Enterprise Manager, expand the Farm and WebLogic domain and right-click on the domain name. Choose the **Security** item in the menu and then click on **Credentials**.

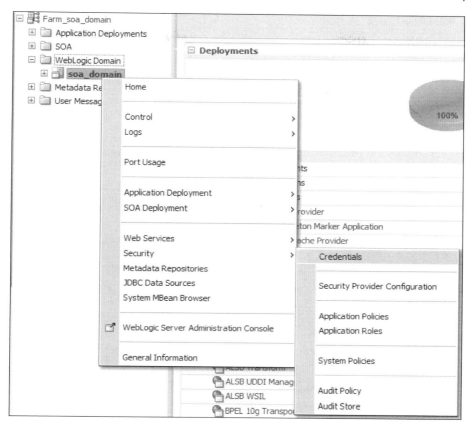

2. Add the Web Services Manager map.

   If the **oracle.wsm.security** map does not exist, then click on **Create Map**.

3. Name the map.

   Enter **Map Name** as `oracle.wsm.security`, then click on **OK**.

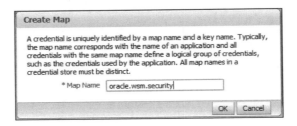

4. Create a key.

   From the **Credential Store Provider** section, click on **Create Key**. In the **Create Key** dialog:

   i.   In **Select Map** choose **oracle.wsm.security** from the drop-down list.

   ii. In the **Key** field, give the key a name.

   iii. Choose **Type** as **Password** from the drop-down list.

   iv. Provide **User Name** to be passed as part of the service invocation.

   v.   Provide **Password** to be passed to the remote system, and **Confirm Password**.

   vi. Provide a **Description** that will remind you of which credentials are associated with this key.

   vii. Click on **OK** to create the key.

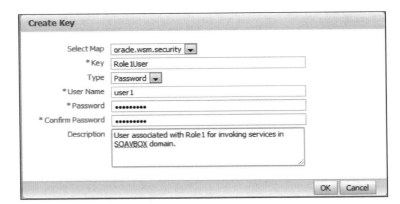

How it works...

The credential store allows us to securely store the credentials of the remote systems that we will need to invoke. By putting the credentials in a central resource, multiple references can use the same credentials. The consumer of the credentials can be separated from the user of the credentials, reducing the number of individuals that know the credentials required to access a particular system.

Invoking an HTTP Basic secured web service

In this recipe, we will consume a web service protected by HTTP Basic authentication.

How to do it...

Create a reference to the web service that is protected by HTTP Basic authentication. Ensure that you have created a credential key that can be used to identify the requestor.

1. Configure WS Policy.

    Right-click on the reference that requires HTTP Basic authentication, and select **Configure WS Policies...**.

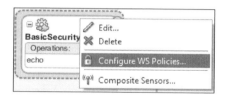

2. Attach the HTTP token client policy.

    In the **SOA Client WS Policies** dialog, click on the plus (✛) icon next to **Security**. Choose **oracle/wss_http_token_client_policy** and click on **OK**.

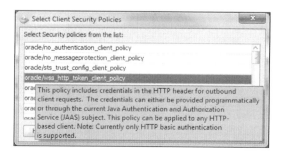

3. Configure the HTTP token client policy.

Select the policy in the **SOA Client WS Policies** dialog and then click on the pencil (✐) icon to bring up the **Config Override Properties** dialog.

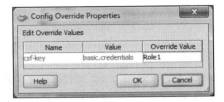

Set the **csf-key** property to be the name of the credential key, previously created, by entering the name into the **Override Value** field. Click on **OK** to set the value of the key.

4. Finally, in the **Configure SOA WS Policies** dialog, click on **OK** to apply the policy to the reference.

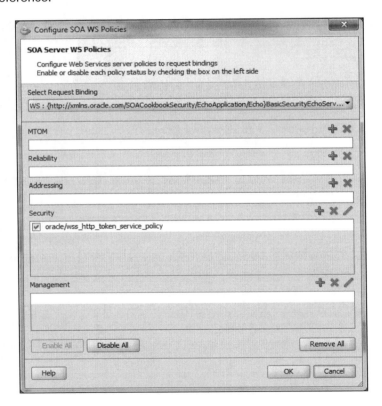

How it works...

After attaching the policy to the outbound endpoint (reference), we needed to identify the particular set of credentials that we need to use. We did this by pointing to a set of credentials we previously created in the credential store.

The entry in the credential store can be re-used across multiple references in the same or different composites.

11
Configuring the Identity Service

In this chapter, we will cover how to configure SOA Suite to use the following LDAP providers for authentication and authorization:

- ▸ Configuring the SOA Identity service to use Oracle Internet Directory
- ▸ Configuring the SOA Identity service to use Oracle Virtual Directory
- ▸ Configuring the SOA Identity service to use Active Directory
- ▸ Configuring the SOA Identity service to use the Sun iPlanet server

Introduction

Oracle Platform Security Services (**OPSS**) provides a **Java Enterprise Edition** (**Java EE**) platform-independent identity service. The Oracle SOA Suite uses the identity services provided by OPSS for all its identity related activities, for example when a user logs in to the BPM worklist application.

When the Oracle SOA Suite is deployed on WebLogic, OPSS (and therefore the Oracle SOA Suite) uses the authentication providers defined in WebLogic.

Oracle WebLogic includes an embedded LDAP server, which is the default identity provider for all security related services, such as user authentication and authorization. By default, the embedded LDAP server stores all information including users, groups, credential mappings and role mapping, and role mapping providers.

Most enterprises already have one or more identity stores that are typically based on LDAP or Active Directory. Rather than replicating the existing identity store in WebLogic, the best practice is to configure WebLogic to use the external identity store, such as Oracle Internet Directory, Microsoft Active Directory, or Sun iPlanet, along with the default authenticator.

This will then become the authentication and identity provider for the SOA Suite (via the OPSS layer). In this chapter, we will examine recipes that allow us to configure WebLogic, and, therefore, the SOA Suite to use an external identity store as an authentication provider.

Use one or more authentication providers

The WebLogic Security Framework supports multiple authentication providers in a security realm in WebLogic. Where multiple authentication providers are defined, WebLogic will attempt to authenticate a user against each provider in turn, according to its control flag, which can be set to one of the following values:

> ▸ **REQUIRED**: The authentication test is always called and must *succeed*. Regardless of whether the authentication succeeds or fails, the authentication process continues to the next authentication provider in the list of providers.

> ▸ **REQUISITE**: The authentication test must succeed. If it succeeds, the authentication process continues to the next authentication provider in the list of providers. If it fails, the authentication process fails and the control is returned to the application.

> ▸ **SUFFICIENT**: The authentication test need not succeed. If it succeeds, the authentication process is successful and returns the control to the application. If it fails the authentication process continues to the next authentication provider in the list.

> ▸ **OPTIONAL**: The authentication test need not succeed. Regardless of whether it succeeds or fails, the authentication test proceeds down the list.

> Although you can configure multiple authentication providers for Oracle WebLogic, the Oracle Platform Security Services does not support multiple LDAP authentication providers. As a result, the provider you want to use for the Oracle SOA Suite must be the first one in the list of authentication providers.

Configuring the SOA Identity service to use Oracle Internet Directory

In this recipe, we will address how to configure **Oracle Internet Directory** (**OID**) as an alternative authentication provider and create users and groups in the authentication provider using Oracle Directory Services Manager.

Getting ready

You will need to have an instance of OID installed and configured; you will also need to have installed and configured an instance of **Oracle Directory Services Manager** (**ODSM**), OVD, and Oracle SOA Suite running on Oracle WebLogic.

How to do it...

We need to use the WebLogic Admin console to add our new authentication provider. To do this:

1. Log in to Oracle WebLogic Server Admin Console at `http://host:port/console` as a user with administrator privileges, such as `weblogic`.

   Once logged in, within the **Domain Structure** select **Security Realms**; this will list the currently defined security realms.

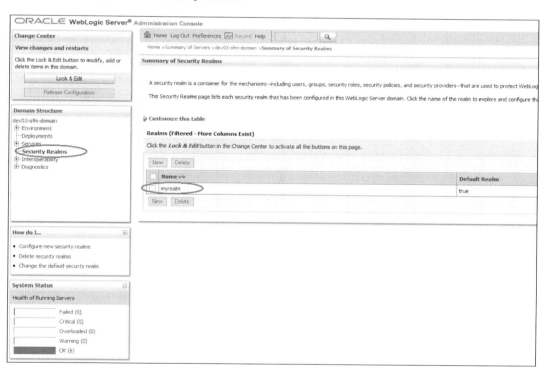

2. Select **myrealm**; this will display the settings for **myrealm**.

    Click on **Lock & Edit** to edit the session. Then select the **Providers** tab, and within that select the **Authentication** tab. This will list the authentication providers currently defined for **myrealm**.

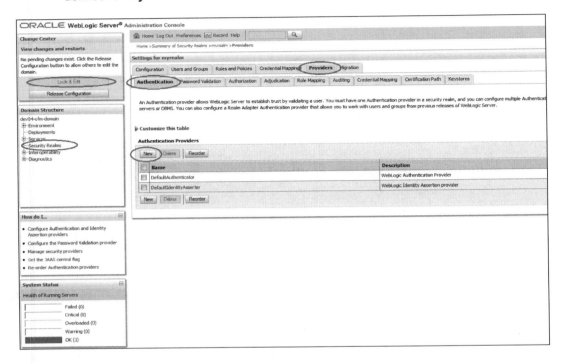

3. Click on the **New** button to create a new authentication provider. This will open the Authentication Provider configuration page.

    Enter a name, such as `OID LDAP`, and select **Type** as **OracleInternetDirectoryAuthenticator** as the authentication provider type and click on **OK**.

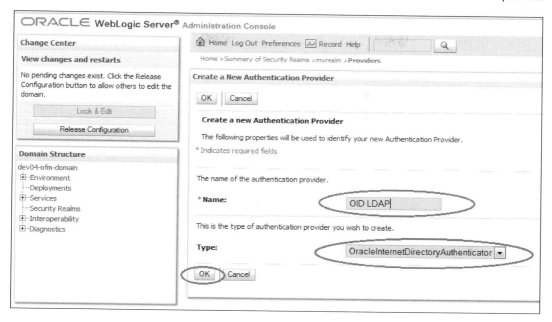

This will return us to the list of authentication providers; here we can see our newly created OID authentication provider.

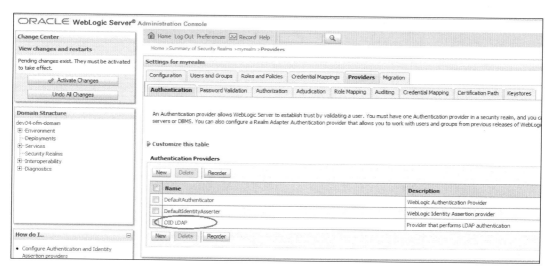

4. The authentication providers are listed in the order in which they will be called. We need to move the **OID LDAP** authentication provider to the top of the list.

   To do this, click on **Reorder**, ensure **OID LDAP** is selected, then click on the up arrow to move it to the top of the list and then click on **OK**.

5. Now, we need to configure our OID Provider to connect to our instances of OID; select **OID LDAP** from the authentication provider list and click on the **Configuration** tab. From here select the **Provider Specific** tab.

   Here we need to provide our OID-specific connection details as well as the location of our users and groups within the identity store, as shown in the following table:

Field	Description
Host	The host of the machine hosting the Oracle Internet Directory LDAP server.
Port	The port number on which the Oracle Internet Directory LDAP server is listening.
SSLEnabled	If the connection to Oracle Internet Directory uses SSL, select **SSLEnabled**.
Principal	The Distinguished Name of the LDAP user that the WebLogic server should use to connect to the LDAP server.
Credential	The credential (password) used to connect to the LDAP server.
User Base DN	The base Distinguished Name of the tree in the LDAP directory that contains users.
Group Base DN	The base Distinguished Name of the tree in the LDAP directory that contains groups.

The settings for your OID Authenticator should look similar to the following:

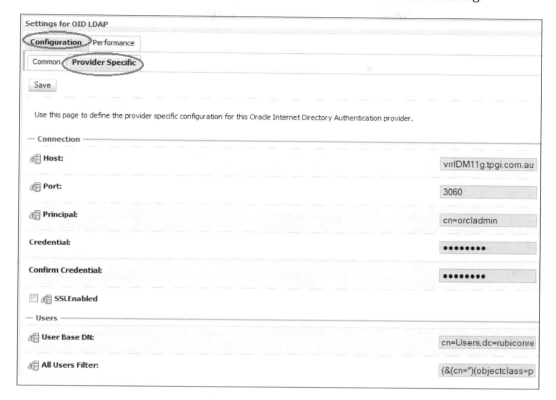

6.   Next, select the **Common** tab, and set **Control Flag** to **SUFFICIENT** and click on **Save**.

7.   Finally, we need to set **Control Flag** to **SUFFICIENT** for our default authenticator.

Select **Default Authenticator** from the authentication provider list, click on the **Configuration** tab, and then select the **Common** tab. From here set **Control Flag** to **SUFFICIENT** and click on **Save**.

8. The final step is to put our changes into effect. Within the **Change Center**, click on **Activate Changes**.

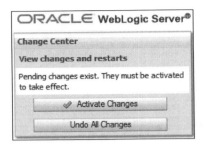

Next, shut down and restart the Oracle WebLogic Admin Server and related managed servers.

9. Next, we will create the `demo` user and group `Administrators` in OID and configure them with the appropriate privileges to log in to the WebLogic Server Admin Console and Fusion Middleware Control (EM Console).

   Log in to Oracle Directory Service (`http://oidhost:port/odsm`), select **Connection to OID** , select the **Data Browser** tab and click on **New Entry**.

   This will open the **Create New Entry** dialog. On the **Entry Properties** page, click on the green + icon to add **Object Class** and select **inetOrgPerson**.

   For **Parent of the entry** specify the User Base Distinguished Name; this should be the same value we specified in step 5 and click on **Next**.

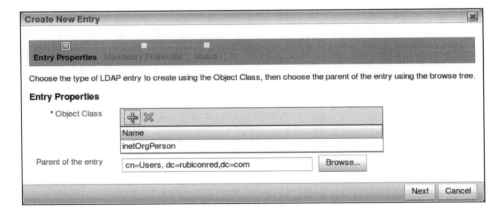

10. This will take us to the **Mandatory Properties** screen; enter `demo` for both **cn** and **sn**, and set the **Relative Distinguished Name** to **cn**. Click on **Next** and then **Finish** on the **Status** page.

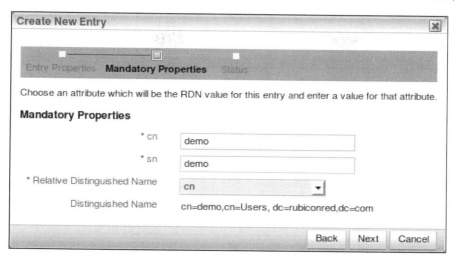

We should see our newly created user under **Data Tree**.

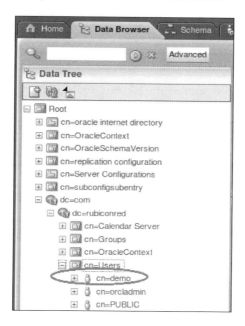

11. Open **cn=demo** in the data tree, and then click on the **Attributes** tab; from here click on the **Optional Attributes** icon.

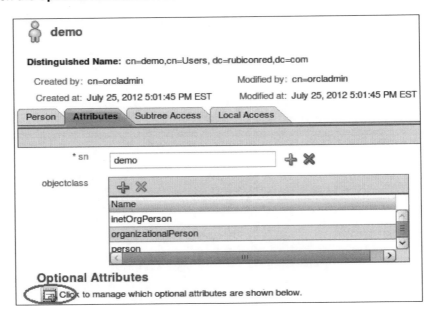

In the **All Attributes** list, select **userPassword** and move it to the **Shown Attributes** list and then click on the **Add Attributes** button.

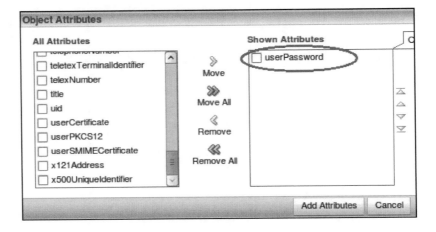

Enter the password for the demo user in the **Password** textbox and click on **Apply**.

12. Next, we will create the group `Administrators` in OID, select **Data Browser** tab, and click on **New Entry**.

    This will open the **Create New Entry** dialog on the **Entry Properties** page; click on the green + icon to add **Object Class** and select **groupofNames** as the object class and click on **OK**.

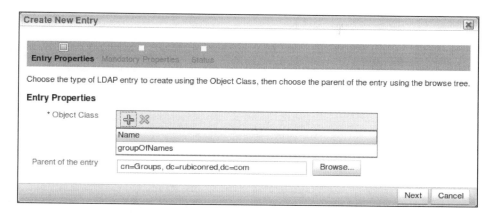

    For **Parent of the entry** specify Group Base Distinguished Name; this should be the same value we specified in step 5 and click on **Next**.

    Enter `Administrators` in the **cn** textbox and select **cn** from the **Relative Distinguished Name** list and then click on **Next**, then click **Finish**. We should see our newly created group in the data tree.

13. The final step is to add the `demo` user to the `Administrators` group. From the **Data Tree**, open **cn=Administrators**, select the **Group** tab and click on the green + icon next to **Members**. Select DN of `demo`, click on **OK**, and then click on **Apply**.

14. Now, we should be able to log in to Oracle WebLogic Admin Console by using the `demo` user we created or as the user `weblogic` (via the embedded LDAP server).

How it works...

We have defined two authentication providers, the first being the OID authentication provider with the control flag **SUFFICIENT**, and the second being the default authenticator defined against the embedded LDAP.

When we log in as the `demo` user, WebLogic will attempt to authenticate the user against OID. Assuming the password is correct, the authentication will be successful and the user will be logged into the application.

When we log in as `weblogic`, authentication will fail against OID, but because the OID authentication provider is defined as **SUFFICIENT**, WebLogic will attempt to authenticate the user against the embedded LDAP at the point at which it succeeds and the user will be logged into the application.

There's more...

If we configure OID as the sole authentication provider, we introduce a point of failure into our WebLogic configuration. Since WebLogic must authenticate the administrative user as part of the server startup process, if OID or the network connection to OID is not available, then the server will be unable to start.

To prevent this, you may want to keep the default authenticator to provide additional resilience; alternatively, you can configure OID to be highly available to protect against this scenario.

Configuring the SOA Identity service to use Oracle Virtual Directory

Many enterprises have multiple identity stores; this can include LDAP, Active Directory, as well as application specific databases. **Oracle Virtual Directory** (**OVD**) allows us to provide a virtual LDAP layer on top of these disparate identity stores and presents a single unified view across these data stores.

In this recipe, we will configure OVD to provide a virtual LDAP layer on top of **Oracle Internet Directory** (**OID**), and then configure OVD as the authentication provider for WebLogic.

Getting ready

You will need to have an instance of OID installed and configured; you will also need to create the `demo` user and add them to the `Administrators` group as described in the previous recipe.

You will also need to have installed and configured an instance of **Oracle Directory Services Manager** (**ODSM**), OVD, and Oracle SOA Suite running on Oracle WebLogic.

How to do it...

1. The first step is to launch ODSM and create a connection to OVD. Enter the URL
   `http://host:port/odsm` into your browser's address field.

   Next, click on **Create a New Connection**. This will open the **New Connection** dialog.
   Enter the details specified in the following table:

Field	Value
Directory Type	**OVD**
Name	OVDConnection
Server	hostname or IP address of OVD server
Port	8899 (default OVD admin SSL port)
SSL Enabled	checked
User Name	cn=orcladmin
Password	Your Password
Start Page	**Home**

Then click on **Connect**.

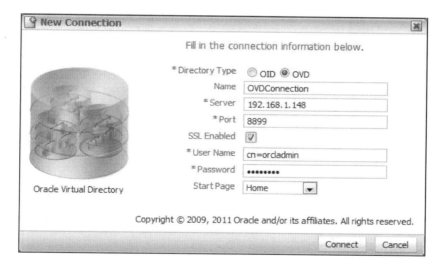

2. We can configure OVD to connect to a variety of identity stores, including LDAP, Active Directory, an OVD local store, or database. In this recipe, we will create an adapter for an LDAP server and configure it to connect to the OID server used in the previous recipe.

   Within ODSM, select the **Adapter** tab, and then click on the **Create Adapter** icon. This will launch **New Adapter Wizard**.

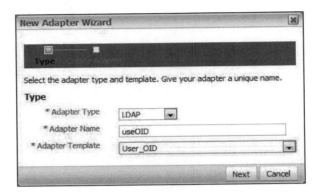

   Click on the **Create Adapter** button in the left-hand side pane.

   Select **Adapter Type** as **LDAP**, give it the name useOID, and select **User_OID** as the **Adapter Template**. Then click on **Next**.

3. This will open **New LDAP Adapter Wizard**. Leave **Use DNS for Auto Discovery** set to **No** and click on the **Add Host** icon.

   Enter the OID hostname and port for your OID server and leave **Weight Value** set to **100**.

   For **Server proxy Bind DN** and **Proxy Password** enter the admin DN (cn=orcladmin, cn=Users, dc=rubiconred,dc=com in our example) and password for your OID server.

   Leave **Use SSL/TLS** unchecked and click on **Next**.

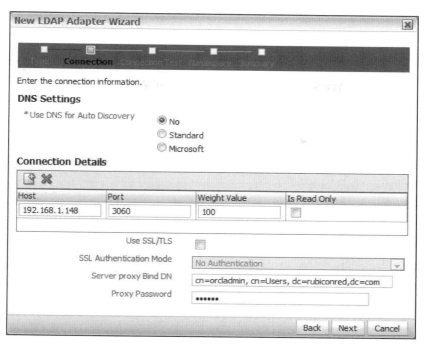

4. OVD will now test the connection to the OID server. You should see **Success!! Oracle Virtual Directory connected to all hosts**.

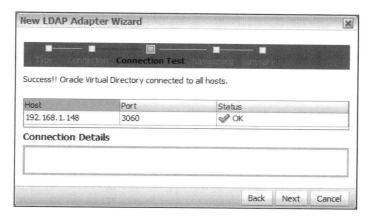

If **Status** is not **OK**, select **Status** to get details of the error.

5. If the **Status** is **OK**, click on **Next**. This will take us to the **Namespace** page. Here we need to map the namespace of where we want to connect in the tree of the base directory (OID) to the namespace we want to appear in OVD.

   In this demo, we are using the same namespace (`dc=rubiconred,dc=com`) in both the directories. Set **Pass Through Credentials** to **Always** and click on **Next**.

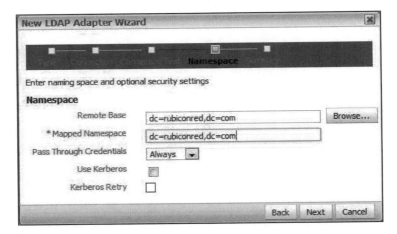

6. Review the values and if everything is fine click on **Finish**.

7. The next step is to create an authentication provider in WebLogic to connect to OVD.

8. Log in to Oracle WebLogic Server Admin Console (`http://host:port/console`) with the user that has an administrator privilege, such as `weblogic`.

   Once logged in, within **Domain Structure** select **Security Realms**. Next, select **myrealm**. This will display the settings for **myrealm**.

   Click on **Lock&Edit** to edit the session. Then select the **Providers** tab, and within that select the **Authentication** tab. This will list the authentication providers currently defined for **myrealm**.

9. Click on the **New** button to create a new authentication provider. This will open the authentication provider configuration page.

   Enter a name, such as `OVDProvider`, and select the **OracleVirtualDirectoryAuthenticator** type as the authentication provider type and click on **OK**.

This will return us to the list of authentication providers; we can see here our newly created OVD authentication provider.

10. The Authentication Providers are listed in the order in which they will be called. We need to move the **OVDProvider** authentication provider to the top of the list.

    To do this, click on **Reorder**, ensure **OVDProvider** is selected; then click on the up arrow to move it to the top of the list and then click on **OK**.

11. Now, we need to configure our OVD Provider to connect to our instances of OVD; select **OVDProvider** from the authentication provider list, and click on the **Configuration** tab. From here, select the **Provider Specific** tab.

    Here, we need to provide our OVD specific connection details, as well as the location of our users and groups within the identity store, as detailed in the following table:

Field	Description
Host	The host of the machine hosting Active Directory.
Port	The port number on which Active Directory is listening.
Principal	The admin DN (for example `cn=orcladmin`) that the WebLogic server should use to connect to OVD.
Credential	The credential (password) used to connect to OVD.
User Base DN	The base Distinguished Name of the tree in the LDAP directory that contains users.
Group Base DN	The base Distinguished Name of the tree in the LDAP directory that contains groups.

    Next select the **Common** tab, and set the **Control Flag** to **SUFFICIENT** and click on **Save**.

12. Finally, we need to set **Control Flag** to **SUFFICIENT** for our default authenticator.

    Select **Default Authenticator** from the authentication provider list, click on the **Configuration** tab, and then select the **Common** tab. From here set **Control Flag** to **SUFFICIENT** and click on **Save**.

13. The final step is to put our changes into effect. Within **Change Center**, click on **Activate Changes**. Next, shutdown and restart the Oracle WebLogic Admin Server and related managed servers.

How it works...

This is similar to our first recipe, in that WebLogic is still authenticating against OID, the difference being that it is now going via OVD, as this has been defined as the first authentication provider.

When we log in as the `demo` user, WebLogic will attempt to authenticate the user against OVD, which in turn will pass the request to OID. Assuming the password is correct the authentication will be successful and return control to the application.

When we log in as `weblogic`, authentication will fail against OVD, but because the OVD authentication provider is defined as **SUFFICIENT**, WebLogic will attempt to authenticate the user against the embedded LDAP at the point at which it succeeds and control is returned to the application.

There's more...

It may seem a bit pointless having WebLogic go via OVD to authenticate a user against OID. However, OVD offers a number of advantages. Firstly it can be used to present non-LDAP data as LDAP data to WebLogic (or any other LDAP client); this includes identity information available via a web service call or in a database (such as PeopleSoft HR or Seibel UCM).

In addition, where an enterprise has multiple identity stores we can use OVD to present a single unified view.

Although you can configure multiple authentication providers for Oracle WebLogic, the Oracle Platform Security Service does not support multiple LDAP authentication providers.

As a result, the provider you want to use for Human Workflow authentication must be the first one listed in the order of authentication providers. Using OVD allows us to work around this limitation.

Configuring the SOA Identity service to use Active Directory

In this recipe, we will demonstrate how to configure **Active Directory** (**AD**) as an alternative authentication provider for WebLogic.

Getting ready...

Ensure that you have an instance of Active Directory installed and configured and has the group administrator defined. For the purpose of following this recipe, create the demo user and add it to the Administrators group.

You will also need to have installed and configured an instance of Oracle SOA Suite running on Oracle WebLogic.

How to do it...

1. Log in to Oracle Weblogic Server Admin Console (http://host:port/console) with the user that has an administrator privilege, such as **weblogic**.

   Once logged in, within the **Domain Structure** select **Security Realms**; this will list the currently defined security realms.

2. Next, select **myrealm**. This will display the settings for **myrealm**.

   Next, click on **Lock&Edit** to edit the session. Then select the **Providers** tab, and within that, select the **Authentication** tab. This will list the authentication providers currently defined for **myrealm**.

3. Click on the **New** button to create a new authentication provider. This will open the authentication provider configuration page.

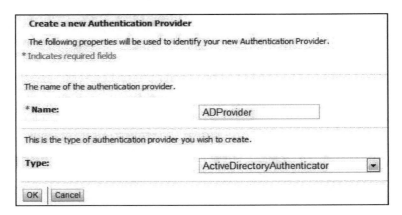

Enter a name, such as `ADProvider`, and select **Type** as **ActiveDirectoryAuthenticator** as the authentication provider type and click on **OK**.

4. The authentication providers are listed in the order in which they will be called. We need to move **ADProvider** to the top of the list.

   To do this, click on **Reorder**, ensure **ADProvider** is selected; then click on the up arrow to move it to the top of the list and then click on **OK**.

5. Now we need to configure our **ADProvider** to connect to our instances of AD; select **ADProvider** from the authentication provider list, and click on the **Configuration** tab. From here, select the **Provider Specific** tab.

   Here, we need to provide our Active Directory specific connection details, as well as the location of our users and groups within the identity store, as detailed in the following table:

Field	Description
Host	The host of the machine hosting Active Directory.
Port	The port number on which AD is listening (6501 is the default).
Principal	The Distinguished Name of the LDAP user that WebLogic server should use to connect to Active Directory.
Credential	The credential (password) used to connect Active Directory.
User Base DN	The base Distinguished Name of the tree in the AD directory that contains users.
Group Base DN	The base Distinguished Name of the tree in the AD directory that contains groups.

Next select the **Common** tab, and set **Control Flag** to **SUFFICIENT** and click on **Save**.

6. Finally, we need to set **Control Flag** to **SUFFICIENT** for our default authenticator.

    Select **Default Authenticator** from the authentication provider list, click on the **Configuration** tab, and then select the **Common** tab. From here, set **Control Flag** to **SUFFICIENT** and click on **Save**.

7. The final step is to put our changes into effect. In the **Change Center**, click on **Activate Changes**.

    Next, shutdown and restart the Oracle WebLogic Admin Server and related managed servers.

How it works...

We have defined two authentication providers, the first being Active Directory authentication provider with control flag **SUFFICIENT**, and the second being the default authenticator defined against the embedded LDAP.

When we log in as the `demo` user, WebLogic will attempt to authenticate the user against AD. Assuming the password is correct the authentication will be successful and the user will be logged in to the application.

When we log in as `weblogic`, authentication will fail against AD, but because the OID authentication provider is defined as **SUFFICIENT**, WebLogic will attempt to authenticate the user against the embedded LDAP at the point at which it succeeds and the user will be logged in to the application.

Configuring the SOA Identity service to use Sun iPlanet server

In this recipe, we will demonstrate how to configure Sun iPlanet as an alternative authentication provider for WebLogic.

Getting ready

Ensure that you have an instance of iPlanet installed and configured that has the group administrator defined. For the purpose of following this recipe create the `demo` user and add it to the `Administrators` group.

You will also need to have installed and configured an instance of Oracle SOA Suite running on Oracle WebLogic.

How to do it...

1. Log in to Oracle WebLogic Server Admin Console (`http://host:port/console`) with the user that has an administrator privilege, such as `weblogic`.

    Once logged in, within **Domain Structure** select **Security Realms**; this will list the currently-defined security realms.

2. Next select **myrealm**; this will display the settings for **myrealm**.

    Next, click **Lock&Edit** to edit the session. Then, select the **Providers** tab, and within that select the **Authentication** tab. This will list the authentication providers currently defined for **myrealm**.

3. Click the **New** button to create a new authentication provider. This will open the authentication provider configuration page.

    Enter a **Name**, such as `iPlanetProvider`, and select **Type** as **IPlanetAuthenticator** as the authentication provider type and then click on **OK**.

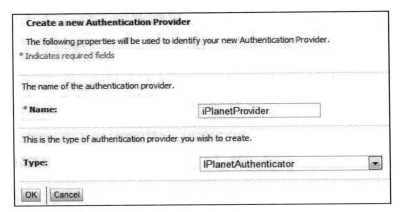

4. The authentication providers are listed in the order in which they will be called. We need to move **iPlanetProvider** to the top of the list.

    To do this, click on **Reorder**, ensure **iPlanetProvider** is selected; then click on the up arrow to move it to the top of the list and then click on **OK**.

5. Now, we need to configure our iPlanet Provider to connect to our instances of iPlanet; select **iPlanetProvider** from the authentication provider list, and click on the **Configuration** tab. From here, select the **Provider Specific** tab.

    Here, we need to provide our iPlanet-specific connection details, as well as the location of our users and groups within the identity store, as detailed in the following table:

Field	Description
Host	The host of the machine hosting the iPlanet server.
Port	The port number on which the iPlanet server is listening.
Principal	Distinguished Name of the LDAP user that WebLogic server should use to connect to iPlanet.
Credential	The credential (password) used to connect to iPlanet.
SSLEnabled	If the connection to iPlanet uses SSL, select **SSLEnabled**.
User Base DN	The base Distinguished Name of the tree in the `LDAP` directory that contains users.
Group Base DN	The base Distinguished Name of the tree in the `LDAP` directory that contains groups.

Next select the **Common** tab, and set **Control Flag** to **SUFFICIENT** and click on **Save**.

6. Finally, we need to set **Control Flag** to **SUFFICIENT** for our default authenticator.

   Select **Default Authenticator** from the authentication provider list, click on the **Configuration** tab, and then select the **Common** tab. From here set **Control Flag** to **SUFFICIENT** and click on **Save**.

7. The final step is to put our changes into effect. Within the **Change Center**, click on **Activate Changes**.

   Next, shutdown and restart the Oracle WebLogic Admin Server and related managed servers.

How it works...

We have defined two authentication providers, the first being the iPlanet authentication provider with the **Control Flag** set to **SUFFICIENT**, and the second being the default authenticator defined against the embedded LDAP.

When we log in as the `demo` user, WebLogic will attempt to authenticate the user against iPlanet. Assuming the password is correct, the authentication will be successful and the user will be logged in to the application.

When we log in as `weblogic`, authentication will fail against iPlanet, but because the iPlanet authentication provider is defined as sufficient WebLogic, it will attempt to authenticate the user against the embedded LDAP at the point at which it succeeds and the user will be logged in to the application.

Now, we are able to use Sun iPlanet for authentication. We should be able to see the users from iPlanet in WebLogic Administration Console.

12
Configuring OSB to Use Foreign JMS Queues

In this chapter we will cover:

- ▶ Creating an OSB proxy service to consume JMS messages from OC4J
- ▶ Creating an OSB business service to publish JMS messages to OC4J
- ▶ Using WebLogic JMS Store-and-Forward for inter-domain messaging
- ▶ Configuring OSB to consume JMS messages from JBoss Application Server 5.1

Introduction

Message Oriented Middleware (**MOM**) enables applications distributed over heterogeneous platforms that span multiple operating systems and network protocols, to exchange information asynchronously with each other in the form of messages.

MOM enables this through the provision of a distributed communications layer that insulates the application developer from the details of the various operating systems and network interfaces. MOM is not a new concept, with IBM MQSeries being one of the better known MOMs launched by IBM in 1992.

Java Message Service (**JMS**) is a standard-based Java API defined as part of the Java Enterprise Edition specification. It enables applications that use the JMS API to send or receive messages using any MOM that supports the JMS API (for example, Oracle WebLogic JMS, IBM MQ, and JBoss JMS).

Many legacy integrations into today's IT infrastructure are built on top of a variety of JMS providers; as a result, it is a common requirement to integrate Oracle Service Bus with a variety of JMS providers. In this chapter of the cookbook, we will look at how to integrate OSB with some of the more common JMS providers found within the application infrastructure.

Creating an OSB proxy service to consume JMS messages from OC4J

Prior to Oracle's acquisition of BEA, the underlying application server for Oracle SOA Suite and many Oracle applications such as E-Business Suite, JD Edwards was Oracle Internet Application Server (aka OC4J).

As a result, it is a common requirement for Oracle Service Bus to consume messages that have been published to OC4J. In this recipe, we will configure a proxy service on Oracle Service Bus to consume messages published to a JMS provider running on OC4J.

The core of this recipe requires us to configure Oracle Service Bus and its **Java Naming and Directory Interface (JNDI)** provider in the WebLogic server to access a remote JNDI provider (on OC4J). Once configured, we can then implement a proxy service to consume JMS messages as if it was on a local queue.

Getting ready

For this recipe, we have assumed you have a working knowledge of the OC4J JMS provider, WebLogic server, and JMS itself.

To prepare for this recipe, make sure you have access to the OSB server's console and the console of your JMS provider, as you'll need access to the required Java libraries.

To configure OSB to connect to OC4J, you will need to have the JNDI details of a connection factory and queue (or topic) on OC4J.

You need to ensure that Oracle Service Bus has access to the same Java client libraries as any normal JMS client would. For OC4J, you will need the following JAR files:

- `oc4j-internal.jar`
- `optic.jar`

These are located in the `[OC4JHOME]/j2ee/home/lib` directory.

How to do it...

1. Copy the library files listed in the *Getting ready* section of this recipe to the `lib` directory of your OSB domain; this should be located at the following location:

    `[ORACLE_HOME]/user_projects/domains/[OSB DOMAIN]/lib`

2. You must update your classpath for the OSB Admin server and your OSB server (if you've split them out during your domain's creation). To do this, you must edit your `setDomainEnv.sh` (or `.cmd` for Windows) file in the following location:

    `[ORACLE_HOME]/user_projects/domains/[OSB DOMAIN]/bin`

3. Add a line, like the following, to the end of your `setDomainEnv.sh` or `setDomainEnv.cmd` file (all in one line):

    ```
    export CLASSPATH=$CLASSPATH${CLASSPATHSEP}${DOMAIN_HOME}/lib/
    optic.jar${CLASSPATHSEP}${DOMAIN_HOME}/lib/oc4j-internal.jar
    ```

4. For Windows, edit `setDomainEnv.cmd` with a line like the following:

    ```
    set CLASSPATH=%CLASSPATH%%CLASSPATHSEP%%DOMAIN_HOME%/lib/optic.
    jar%CLASSPATHSEP%%DOMAIN_HOME%/lib/oc4j-internal.jar
    ```

5. If your OSB domain is currently up, now would be a good time to restart; otherwise start the domain up before continuing.

6. From the domain structure in the WLS console, expand the **Services** menu and select **Foreign JNDI Providers** from the **Administration** console of your OSB domain.

    Click on **New** and give it a descriptive name (**IAS** in the following example), click on **Next** where you should target this to the OSB server or cluster, and click on **Finish**.

7. Next we need to configure our foreign JNDI provider to point it at the JMS queue on OC4J. To do this, click on the provider you just created.

This will take you to the **JNDI configuration** window; here we need to specify the JNDI client details of our OC4J JMS provider, as shown in the following table:

Property	Value
Initial Context Factory	`oracle.j2ee.rmi.RMIInitialContextFactory`
Provider URL	`opmn:ormi://[HOSTNAME]:[PORT]:[Container Name]`
User	Username of an account with privileges to access these JMS resources on your OC4J server
Password/Confirm Password	The password for the user

Your foreign JNDI provider should look somewhat like the following screenshot:

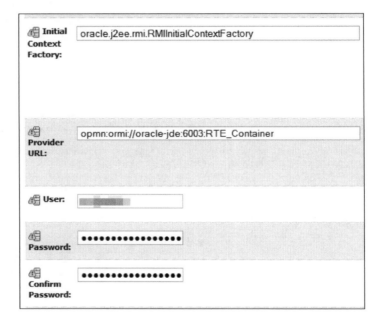

8. Next we need to configure local JNDI links for the OC4J queue or topic that we wish to consume messages from.

Click on the **Links** tab of the foreign JNDI provider you created previously, and click on **New**. Give the link a descriptive name for the queue or topic that you're going to link into your OSB's JNDI tree.

For **Local JNDI Name**, enter a JNDI name for which this resource will appear in OSB's JNDI tree.

For **Remote JNDI Name**, enter the JNDI name of the resource in your JMS provider's JNDI tree. Once this is done, click on **OK**.

Repeat this process to create a link for the connection factory of the queue or topic. Once completed, our **Foreign JNDI Links** window should look somewhat like the screenshot, shown as follows:

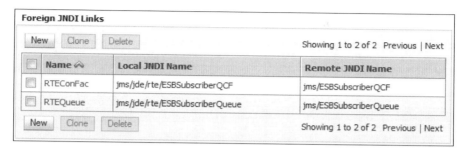

9. Create a proxy service in the OSB console or Eclipse, as you usually would, but at the **Transport Configuration** screen in the wizard, select **jms** as your **Protocol** and **EndPoint URI** should be something like **jms://[OSBHOST]:[PORT]/[LINKCF]/ [LINKQUEUE]**.

   Where LINKCF and LINKQUEUE are the local JNDI names of the connection factory and queue respectively, which you have defined in the previous step.

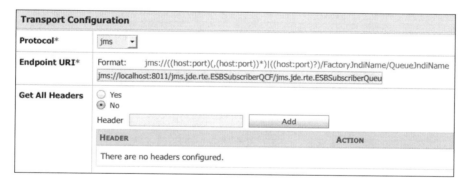

Ensure the correct **Destination Type** is selected in the next screen and continue with the wizard as usual. For testing purposes, add a simple log or report action step to the pipeline to write out the content of the JMS message.

You can now deploy and test your OSB proxy service; once you have validated that the proxy service is successfully consuming a message from the OC4J JMQ queue, you can then implement the remainder of your proxy service as required.

How it works...

The foreign JNDI provider and the links work by linking the local names in our JNDI tree to the remote ones we've configured. The important thing to note is that you need to include the classes normally required by this remote JNDI provider to Oracle Service Bus because, even though it's locating the JNDI reference locally, it is still acting as a remote client to the JMS provider. It will make JMS server connections directly to the providing server via the connection factory.

Once configured, the OSB proxy service *thinks* it's accessing the JMS destination as a local resource.

There's more...

For those readers more experienced with the WebLogic server, you might note that we had to add the classes to the classpath and not just drop them into the domain's `lib` folder; this is because of the WebLogic server's (and Java's) class loading hierarchy. When the WebLogic server loads the JARs in the `lib` directory, it loads them as a child to the system class loader for all J2EE applications. We need these classes loaded in the system class loader to be available for the server itself, and so we had to adjust the classpath.

For those readers who have used Oracle's **JD Edwards** (**JDE**) product and are not on the WebLogic server yet, this solution would give your OSB installation access to JDE **Realtime Events** (**RTE**) and provide a gateway to SOA Suite for performing business logic based on the events in JDE.

Creating an OSB business service to publish JMS messages to OC4J

This recipe provides an example of how to use OSB to publish a message to a remote JMS queue on OC4J via a JMS message bridge. The JMS message bridge will forward messages from a local JMS queue to the remote OC4J queue. An advantage of using a JMS message bridge is that it keeps your OSB configuration clean and simple, and all of the gory details for connecting to the remote JMS location are configured and managed by the WebLogic server. Also, the same bridge could be used by multiple JMS clients should this be required.

Getting ready

You will need to adjust your OSB domain's classpath, as we detailed in the *Creating an OSB proxy service to consume JMS messages from OC4J* recipe given in this chapter, to bridge between a local JMS queue and a remote OC4J queue.

You will also need the connection details and the JNDI names for a connection factory and a queue on your OC4J server. The connection factory should *not* be an XA-enabled connection factory.

How to do it...

1. First we create the local queue in our OSB domain from where messages will be forwarded by the JMS bridge. From the domain structure in the WLS console, expand the **Services** menu and the **Messaging** submenu and select **JMS Modules**. Click on the **New** button, and you will be presented with the **Create JMS System Module** wizard.

2. For **Name** enter OC4JBridge and click on **Next**.

3. Target this JMS module to your OSB-managed server (normally osb_server1), and click on **Next**.

4. Select **Would you like to add resources to this JMS system module** and click on **Finish**. You will be presented with a summary of resources.

5. Click on the **New** button to start the **Create a New JMS System Model Resource** wizard.

6. Select **Connection Factory** and click on **Next**.

7. Set **Name** to OC4JLocalCF and **JNDI Name** to /jms/OC4JLocalCF and click on **Next**, followed by clicking on **Finish** (you must not just click on **Finish**, otherwise the connection factory will not get its default target). You will be taken back to the summary of resources where you should see your connection factory.

8. Click on the **New** button again, and this time select **Queue** and click on **Next**.

9. Set **Name** to OC4JLocalQueue and **JNDI Name** to /jms/OC4JLocalQueue, and click on **Next**.

10. Click on the **Create a New Subdeployment** button accepting the default as **Subdeployment Name**, and click on **OK**.

11. Select a JMS server that is targeted to your OSB-managed server in the **JMS Servers** table, shown as follows:

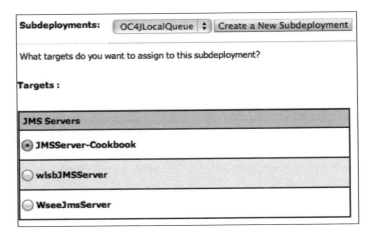

12. Click on **Finish** and you will be taken back to the summary of resources where you should see your queue and the connection factory you created before, as shown in the following screenshot:

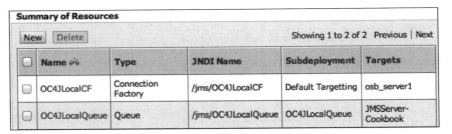

	Name △	Type	JNDI Name	Subdeployment	Targets
☐	OC4JLocalCF	Connection Factory	/jms/OC4JLocalCF	Default Targetting	osb_server1
☐	OC4JLocalQueue	Queue	/jms/OC4JLocalQueue	OC4JLocalQueue	JMSServer-Cookbook

13. From **Domain Structure** in the WLS console, expand the **Services** menu and the **Messaging** submenu followed by the **Bridges** submenu, shown as follows:

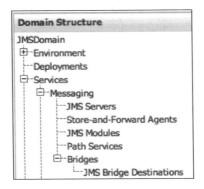

14. Click on the **JMS Bridge Destinations** menu item. This is where we configure the details of both ends of the bridge. Click on the **New** button, and you will be presented with the **Create a New JMS Bridge Destination** wizard. Enter the values detailed as follows, and when complete click on **OK**.

Property	Value
Name	OC4JLocalQueue
Adapter JNDI Name	eis.jms.WLSConnectionFactoryJNDINoTX
Connection URL	t3://[OSB Host Name]:[PORT]
Connection Factory JNDI Name	/jms/OC4JLocalCF
Destination JNDI Name	/jms/OC4JLocalQueue

15. Repeat the previous step for the remote JMS queue using the following values:

Property	Value
Name	OC4JRemoteQueue
Adapter JNDI Name	eis.jms.WLSConnectionFactoryJNDINoTX
Connection URL	opmn:ormi://[HOSTNAME]:[PORT]:[Container Name]
Connection Factory JNDI Name	The JNDI name of a connection factory on your OC4J server
Destination JNDI Name	The JNDI name of a queue on your OC4J server

16. You will now see your two **JMS Bridge Destinations** in the summary, shown as follows:

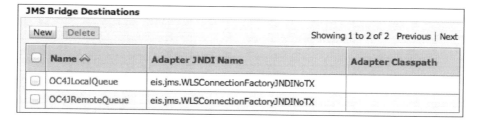

17. Click on the **OC4JRemoteQueue** destination you created and configure it, as shown in the following table, and then click on the **Save** button:

Property	Value
Initial Context Factory	oracle.j2ee.rmi.RMIInitialContextFactory
User Name	The username of the account on OC4J that you configured earlier.
User Password and **Confirm User Password**	The password for this account.

18. We can create the bridge now that we have created the destinations. Click on the **Bridges** item in the domain structure from WLS console and click on **New**. You will see the **Create a New Bridge** wizard. Enter `OC4JBridge` as **Name** and select the **Started** checkbox. Select **Duplicate-Okay** as **Quality of Service** and click on **Next**.

19. Select **OC4JLocalQueue** as **Existing Source Destination** and click on **Next**.

20. Select **WebLogic Server 7.0 or higher** as **Messaging Provider** and click on **Next**.

21. Select **OC4JRemoteQueue** as **Existing Target Destination** and click on **Next**.

22. Select **Other JMS** as **Messaging Provider** and click on **Next**.

23. Target the bridge of the managed server that your OSB services are running on and click on **Next**, followed by **Finish**.

24. Reboot your OSB-managed server(s) and your Admin server.

25. Once your OSB-managed server(s) has started, confirm that your bridge is functioning properly by selecting **Bridges** from the domain structure of the WLS console and clicking on the **Monitoring** tab. You should see your bridge is **Active** and **Forwarding messages**, shown as follows:

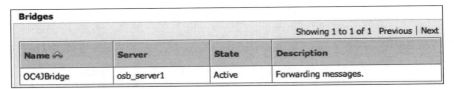

Bridges

Showing 1 to 1 of 1 Previous | Next

Name ⌂	Server	State	Description
OC4JBridge	osb_server1	Active	Forwarding messages.

26. Now we are ready to configure an OSB business server to publish messages to our local queue, and the message bridge forwards them to OC4J for us. Create a business service as you normally would, but make sure **Service Type** is **Messaging Service** (as shown in the following screenshot) and click on **Next**.

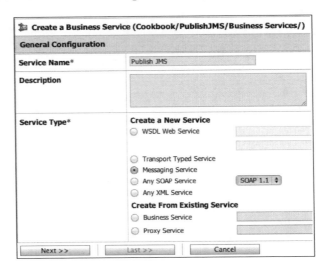

27. Configure **Request Message Type** to **Text** and **Response Message Type** to **None**, as shown in the following screenshot. Once complete, click on **Next**.

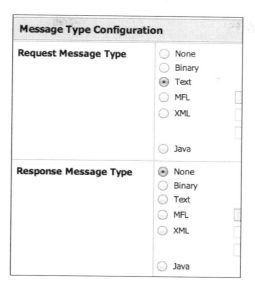

28. On the **Transport Configuration** screen (shown in the following screenshot); ensure that the **Protocol** is JMS and the **Endpoint URI** transport is constructed as follows, and then click on **Next**:

```
jms://[OSBHOST]:[PORT]/jms.OC4JLocalCF/jms.OC4JLocalQueue
```

29. Configure **Message Type** to **Text** for **JMS Transport Screen**, and then click on **Last** followed by **Save** and activate your session.

30. To create a simple proxy service, create one from the existing business service you defined previously. In the **Transport Configuration** screen, you should select **Protocol** as **HTTP** to make testing simple.

🖼 **Create a Proxy Service (Cookbook/PublishJMS/Proxy Services/)**		
General Configuration		
Service Name*	JMSWebFront	
Description		
Service Type*	**Create a New Service**	
	○ WSDL Web Service	Brc
		(port or b
	○ Transport Typed Service	
	○ Messaging Service	
	○ Any SOAP Service	SOAP 1.1 ⬦
	○ Any XML Service	
	Create From Existing Service	
	◉ Business Service	Cookbook/PublishJMS/Business Services/ · Brc

How it works...

This recipe publishes JMS messages to an OC4J server via a JMS message bridge. Our business service publishes messages to our local JMS queue, which is forwarded by the message bridge to the remote OC4J server. It is important to note (in the setup for this recipe) that the business service *returns* when the JMS message is accepted by the local JMS server and not when it gets to the OC4J server; this is handled by the bridge asynchronously.

There's more...

We could have used this method of a JMS bridge in our first recipe instead of the foreign JNDI provider, by having a remote OC4J queue as the source for the bridge and a local queue as the destination; so, the bridge would pull remote messages to our local OSB domain for the proxy service to pick up.

If you need a high message throughput, you will need to tune the message bridge as it defaults to only one thread per bridge. This can be done by either creating multiple bridges for the same JMS bridge destinations or (the preferred option) by creating a work manager for the JMS bridge. More information on this topic can be found in the *Performance and Tuning for Oracle WebLogic Server* documentation at `http://docs.oracle.com/cd/E23943_01/web.1111/e13814/bridgetuning.htm`.

This recipe would be simple to extend to other JMS providers by including different libraries on the classpath and adjusting the connection details appropriately.

In the recipe, we selected the quality of service as duplicate-okay, because some versions of OC4J do not offer true XA support and selecting anything other than the quality of service detailed previously will cause the bridge to fail (WebLogic server will try to perform a global transaction and the OC4J server will not have enrolled in it). If you're using an XA-compliant JMS provider (a late version of OC4J, another WLS domain, and so on), you may consider setting a higher quality of service if required.

Using WebLogic JMS Store-and-Forward for inter-domain messaging

It is getting increasingly common to require messages published to a WebLogic domain on which OSB is not running to trigger an OSB proxy service.

Store-and-Forward (**SAF**) allows you to get messages from a remote WebLogic domain to the OSB domain for processing, without the publisher being aware of OSB. Normally, without SAF you would have to configure the publisher to publish to a different location, which could cause problems if the network is slow or goes down, or it might not even be possible to configure your publisher.

This recipe shows how to use SAF to push JMS messages from a remote WebLogic domain to your OSB domain for consumption by an OSB proxy service.

Getting ready

For this recipe, you'll need access to your OSB domain, as well as another WebLogic Server domain (WebLogic 9.x or higher is required to use the Store-and-Forward feature).

You'll need to create a queue in your OSB domain to receive forwarded JMS messages. For this recipe, we'll assume a default JNDI name of /jms/remote.

How to do it...

1. First, we need to create the SAF sending agent on the WebLogic domain. Log in to the WebLogic console, then within the **Domain Structure** navigate to **Services | Messaging** and select **Store-and-Forward Agents**, as shown in the following screenshot:

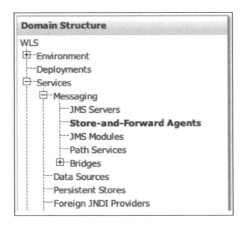

This will take you to the **Store-and-Forward Agents** window; click on **New** and give the agent an appropriate name (`CookbookSAFAgent` in our example), and set **Agent Type** to **Sending-only**. Click on **Next** and target the agent to an appropriate server or cluster in your WebLogic domain, and then click on **Finish**.

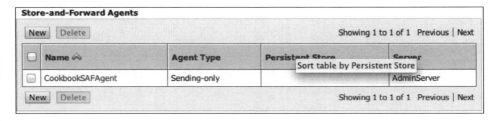

2. Next, we need to create a JMS module to collect together the configuration for the SAF sending agent. Within **Domain Structure**, navigate to **Services | Messaging** and select **JMS Modules**.

   This will take you to the **JMS Modules** window; click on the **New** button to launch the **Create JMS System Module** wizard. Give the module a name (we've assumed you use SAFAgent), and target it to the same WebLogic server or cluster as the SAF sending agent.

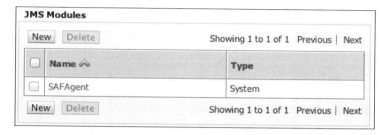

3. Next we need to create **SAF Remote Context**, which tells our WebLogic server how to connect to our remote OSB domain. Click on **JMS Module**, which we created in the previous step.

   Click on the **New** button and select the type of resource as **Remote SAF Context**, and configure as detailed in the following table:

Property	Value
Name	OSBDomain.
URL	The URL of the remote OSB server is in the format t3://[osbserver]:[port]. For example, t3://localhost:8011.
User Name	The username of an account with privileges to access the JMS queue you created before starting this recipe (/jms/remote). This could be weblogic, but do not use this for production.
Password	The password for the user.

The following screenshot shows the properties and their values:

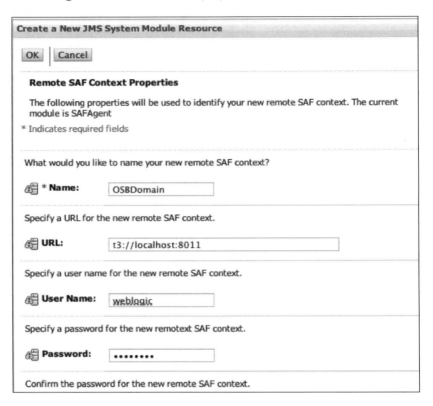

Once you have clicked on **OK**, you will see the newly created **SAF Remote Context** in **Summary of Resources** of your **JMS Module**.

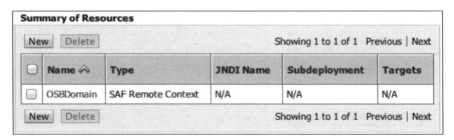

4. We now need to tell our WebLogic server how we're going to import our remote destination from our OSB server. From within the JMS module, click on **New** and select the type of resource as **SAF Imported Destination**, and click on **Next** and configure it, as detailed in the following table:

Property	Value
Name	OSB Imported Destinations
Remote SAF Context	**OSBDomain** (as created in the previous step)

SAF Imported Destinations Properties

Use this page to create a group of new SAF (store-and-forward) imported destinations. SAF imported destinations are collections of SAF queues and topics that locally represent JMS queues or topics on a remote server instance or cluster. Each collection of imported destinations is associated with a remote SAF context. They can also share the same JNDI prefix, time-to-live default (message expiration time), and SAF error handling policy.

* Indicates required fields

* **Name:** `OSB Imported Destina`

JNDI Prefix:

Remote SAF Context: OSBDomain ▼ | Create a New Remote Context

SAF Error Handling: None ▼ | Create a New Error Handling

SAF Default Time-To-Live: 0

☐ **Enable SAF Default Time-To-Live**

Click on **Finish**. You will now see your **SAF Imported Destination** in **Summary of Resources** of your JMS module.

Summary of Resources

New | Delete — Showing 1 to 2 of 2 Previous | Next

	Name	Type	JNDI Name	Subdeployment	Targets
☐	OSB Imported Destinations	SAF Imported Destination	N/A	Default Targetting	AdminServer
☐	OSBDomain	SAF Remote Context	N/A	N/A	N/A

5. We now need to import the remote destination from the OSB domain to our WebLogic domain. To do this, click on **SAF Imported Destination** that you created in the previous step, and click on the **Queues** tab.

6. Click on **New** to create a link to a queue on your OSB domain. Configure it, as detailed in the following table:

Property	Value
Name	Local name for the OSB queue that we wish to forward messages to
Remote JNDI Name	JNDI name for the JMS queue on the OSB server that we wish to forward messages to (`/jms/remote` in this example)

The following screenshot shows the properties and their values:

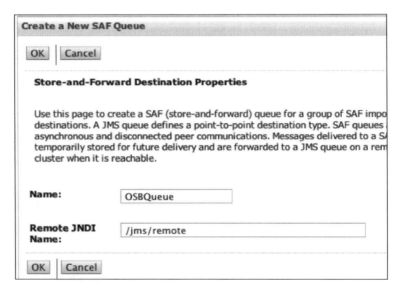

When you have clicked on **OK**, you will be presented with your imported queue in the **SAF Queues** summary.

7. Create a proxy service in the OSB console or Eclipse, as you usually would, but from the **Transport Configuration** screen in the wizard, select **JMS** as your **Protocol**, and **EndPoint URI** should be something like:

```
jms://[HOST]:[PORT]/weblogic.jms.ConnectionFactory/[QUEUE]
```

Where QUEUE is the JNDI name of the local queue that SAF is forwarding messages to, in our examples, /jms/remote is the queue.

Ensure the correct **Destination Type** is selected in the next screen and continue with the wizard as usual. For testing purposes, add a simple log or report action step to the pipeline to write out the content of the JMS message.

You can now deploy and test your OSB proxy service. Once you have validated that the proxy service is successfully consuming a message from the WebLogic domain, you can then implement the remainder of your proxy service, as required.

How it works...

The **SAF Sending Agent** on your remote **WebLogic Domain** forwards messages published to **Imported Destinations** to the **OSB Domain**. The OSB proxy then consumes these messages from the local queue as though they were published locally.

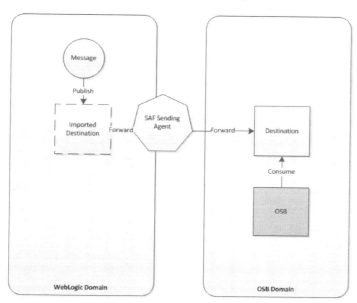

There's more...

This method could be used to forward messages from a remote domain, perhaps running an ERP, which publishes the messages you need to process. The advantage of the Store-and-Forward option is that it allows a JMS producer to produce to a remote destination without knowing it is a remote destination. This keeps the producer's configuration simple, or it might be required because the produce doesn't support remote JMS destinations.

You could also use this method to publish from OSB to a remote WebLogic server; you can do this by configuring the Store-and-Forward on the OSB server and the queue on the remote WebLogic server.

In step 4 of this recipe, we glossed over the error handling to simplify our configuration. Error handling is an important aspect of any JMS configuration and SAF is no different. The SAF error handling configuration allows you to specify an error handling policy to apply to all imported destinations, or a separate policy for each separate destination. It is common for such a policy to log and forward failed messages to an error-handling queue.

Configuring OSB to consume JMS messages from JBoss Application Server 5.1

In this recipe, we will configure Oracle Service Bus to consume messages published to JBoss Application Server (AS) 5.1.

Getting ready

This recipe assumes that you have access to your JBoss server, and that you have a working knowledge of JBoss Application Server and JBoss Messaging.

You need to ensure that Oracle Service Bus has access to the same Java client libraries as any normal JMS client would. For JBoss you need the following JAR files:

- `javassist.jar`
- `jboss-aop-client.jar`
- `jboss-common-core.jar`
- `jboss-logging-spi.jar`
- `jboss-mdr.jar`
- `jboss-messaging-client.jar`
- `jboss-remoting.jar`
- `jboss-serialization.jar`
- `jnp-client.jar`

- ► `log4j.jar`
- ► `concurrent.jar`
- ► `trove.jar`

These are located in your JBoss installation home (`JBOSS_HOME/client`).

How to do it...

1. First we need to create a JMS queue in JBoss and then connect to the JBoss admin console; the URL will be something like:

   `http://[hostname]:[port]/admin-console`

   The port normally defaults to `8080`.

   Use the side menu to go to **Resources | JMS Destinations | Queues**, as shown in the following screenshot:

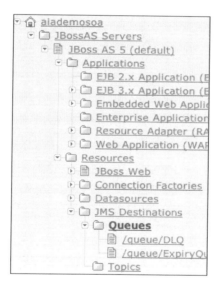

   Click on **Add New Resource** on the right-hand side of the web page, and follow the wizard to create a queue with the following details:

Property	Value
Resource template	`default (Queue)`
Name	`Cookbook Test Queue`
JNDI name	`/queue/cookbooktest`

Leave all the other fields blank or unset.

Once you have completed this, you should see your queue appear, as shown in the following screenshot:

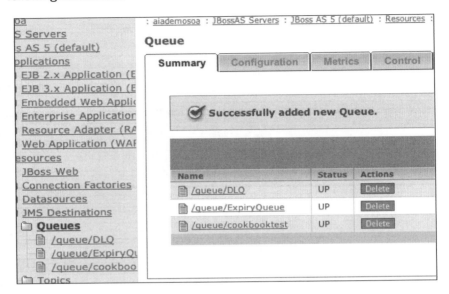

2. Copy the JBoss library files identified in the *Getting Started* section of this recipe to the `lib` directory of your OSB domain; it will be located here:

   `[ORACLE_HOME]/user_projects/domains/[OSB DOMAIN]/lib`

3. You must update your classpath for the OSB Admin server and your OSB server (if you've split them out during your domain's creation). To do this, you must edit your `setDomainEnv.sh` (or `.cmd` for Windows) file that is in the following location:

   `[ORACLE_HOME]/user_projects/domains/[OSB DOMAIN]/bin`

4. Add a line, like the following, to the end of your `setDomainEnv.sh` or `setDomainEnv.cmd` (all in one line) file:

   ```
   export CLASSPATH=$CLASSPATH${CLASSPATHSEP}${DOMAIN_HOME}/lib/
   optic.jar${CLASSPATHSEP}${DOMAIN_HOME}/lib/oc4j-internal.jar
   ```

   For Windows, edit `setDomainEnv.cmd`, with a line like the following:

   ```
   set CLASSPATH=%CLASSPATH%%CLASSPATHSEP%%DOMAIN_HOME%/lib/optic.
   jar%CLASSPATHSEP%%DOMAIN_HOME%/lib/oc4j-internal.jar
   ```

5. If your OSB domain is currently up, now would be a good time to restart; otherwise, start the domain up before continuing.

6. From the **Domain Structure** in the WLS console, expand the **Services** menu and select **Foreign JNDI Providers** from the **Administration** console of your OSB domain.

   Click on **New** and give it a descriptive name (for example, JBoss), and click on **Next** where you should target this to the OSB server or cluster and then click on **Finish**.

7. Next, we need to configure our foreign JNDI provider to point it to the JMS queue on JBoss. To do this, click on the provider you just created.

   This will take you to the **JNDI configuration** window; here we need to specify the JNDI client details of our JBoss JMS provider, as shown in the following table:

Property	Value
Initial Context Factory	org.jnp.interfaces. NamingContextFactory.
Provider URL	jnp://[HOSTNAME]:[PORT]. The port is normally 1099.
User	The username of an account with privileges to access these JMS resources on your JBoss server.
Password/Confirm Password	The password for this user.

8. Next, we need to configure a local JNDI link(s) for the JBoss queue that we wish to consume messages from.

   Click on the **Links** tab of the foreign JNDI provider that you created previously, and click on **New**. Give the link a descriptive name for the queue or topic you're going to link into your OSB's JNDI tree (CookBookQueue in the following example).

   For **Local JNDI Name**, enter a JNDI name for which this resource will appear as in OSB's JNDI tree. For **Remote JNDI Name**, enter the JNDI of the resource in your JMS provider's JNDI tree.

   For our example, we'll use the value specified in the following table; once this is done, click on **OK**.

Property	Value
Name	CookBookQueue
Local JNDI Name	jms/jboss/cookbooktest
Remote JNDI Name	/queue/cookbooktest

Repeat this process to create a link for the connection factory of the queue, using the values specified in the following table:

Property	Value
Name	ConnectionFactory
Local JNDI Name	jms/jboss/cookbookcf
Remote JNDI Name	ConnectionFactory

Once completed, our **Foreign JNDI Links** should look somewhat like the following screenshot:

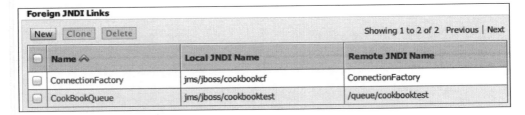

9. Create a proxy service in the OSB console or Eclipse, as you usually would, but from the **Transport Configuration** screen in the wizard, select **JMS** as your protocol, and the **EndPoint URI** should be something like:

```
jms://[OSBHOST]:[PORT]/[LINKCF]/[LINKQUEUE]
```

Where LINKCF and LINKQUEUE are the local JNDI names of the connection factory and queue respectively, which you defined in the previous step. In our example the **Endpoint URI** for this proxy service would be:

```
jms://[OSBHOST]:[PORT]/jms.jboss.cookbookcf/jms.jboss.cookbooktest
```

Ensure that the correct **Destination Type** is selected in the next screen and continue with the wizard as usual, making sure you add a step to the pipeline.

For testing purposes, a simple log or report action should suffice.

How it works...

This solution essentially would work in exactly the same way, even if the JMS destination was a local resource. OSB "thinks" it's accessing the JMS destination as a local resource. The important thing to note is that you need to include the classes normally required by this remote JMS provider to Oracle Service Bus, because even though it's locating the JNDI reference locally, it is still acting as a remote client to JBoss. It will connect JMS servers directly to JBoss via the connection factory you looked up locally.

There's more...

For those readers more experienced with the WebLogic server, you might note that we had to add the classes to the classpath and not just drop them into the domain's `lib` folder; this is because of the WebLogic server's (and Java's) class loading hierarchy. When the WebLogic server loads the JAR files in the `lib` directory, it loads them as a child to the system class loader for all J2EE applications. We need these classes loaded in the system class loader to be available for the server itself, and so we had to adjust the classpath.

You can easily extend this recipe to configure an OSB business service to publish messages to a JBoss queue, in a similar way as described in the *Creating an OSB business service to publish messages to OC4J* recipe in this chapter.

You might have realized that we used JBoss' default JMS connection factory. This was for simplicity, but it is recommended you create separate connection factories for JMS consumers or producers because this is a way of controlling JMS functionality without the need for code changes in remote clients.

13

Monitoring and Management

In this chapter we will cover:

- ▸ Capturing a composite completion status
- ▸ Monitoring message throughput in real time
- ▸ Deploy Monitor Express to BAM
- ▸ Configuring BAM Adapter
- ▸ Configuring a BPEL process to report the status to BAM Monitor Express

Introduction

In this chapter, we will look at how to monitor what is happening with our composites. We will look at how to check the completion status of composites from Enterprise Manager, as well as monitor their throughput and response characteristics.

We will also look at how some composite metrics can be quickly surfaced to the business user through **Business Activity Monitoring** (**BAM**).

Operational monitoring

Operational monitoring is performed by IT operations staff in order to ensure that the applications are running with acceptable performance and are available to end users. The SOA Suite tool for operational monitoring is the Enterprise Manager console. The focus of operational monitoring is things, such as:

- System availability
- CPU utilization
- Memory utilization
- Response time or composite duration

All of these can be monitored by Enterprise Manager. The core monitoring in Enterprise Manager is available out of the box and requires little or no additional configuration. SOA Management Pack extends the capabilities of Enterprise Manager, providing the ability to baseline configurations and establishing alerts when performance requirements are not met.

Business monitoring

Business monitoring is performed by business operations staff in order to ensure that applications are meeting the needs of the business. The SOA Suite tool for business monitoring is BAM. This can be used to monitor a number of things, such as:

- Order processing time
- Compliance to customer SLAs
- Value of orders with problems
- Hourly transaction values
- Load across different call centers

Unlike operational monitoring with Enterprise Manager, business monitoring with BAM requires work to be done to collect the necessary statistics and additional work to be done to create reports from those statistics. For statistics directly related to the performance of BPEL processes in a composite, this can be expedited by the use of the Monitor Express dashboard provided by SOA Suite, which allows for the monitoring of instrumented BPEL processes. Instrumentation of BPEL processes for Monitor Express is very quick and easy.

Capturing a composite completion status

By default, the SOA Suite configuration does not capture the final state of a composite, showing a question mark for **Instance State**, as shown in the following screenshot. In this recipe, we will enable capturing of the completion status so that when we list composite instances in Enterprise Manager, we will be able to see which ones have completed and which are still running.

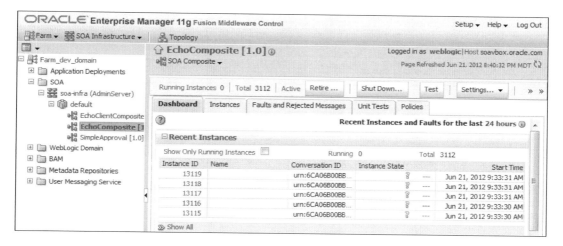

Getting ready

Log on to Enterprise Manager using `http://hostname:port/em`.

How to do it...

1. Right-click on the **soa-infra (AdminServer)** item in the EM navigation tree. Choose **SOA Administration** from the pop-up menu and then select **Common Properties**.

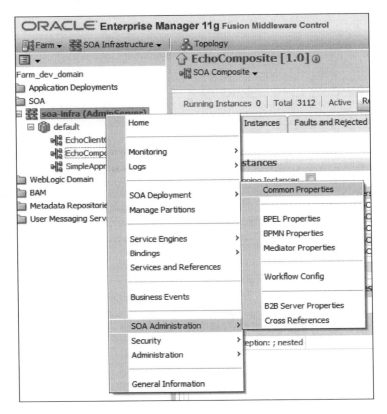

2. On the **SOA Infrastructure Common Properties** screen, select the **Capture Composite Instance State** checkbox and then click on **Apply**.

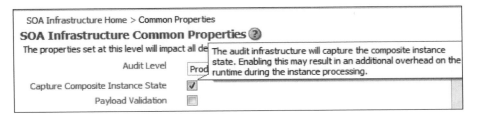

When prompted, confirm the action.

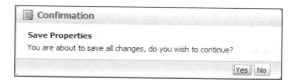

3. Execute a new composite, and then go to **Dashboard** for that composite and verify that rather than a question mark, the completed instance is now marked as **Completed**.

How it works...

Enabling **Capture Composite Instance State** causes SOA Suite to perform some extra work to track the completion status of the composites. This may have a small impact on performance, and the operations team will need to decide if the small overhead introduced by this monitoring is offset by the value of instantly being able to see the status of the composites in the dashboard.

Monitoring message throughput in real time

During execution, SOA Suite collects statistics on the number of messages received in a time period, the number of faults, and the execution time for the composites. These statistics are available through the EM console and provide a real-time updating view of the performance of SOA Suite. In this recipe, we will see how to monitor these statistics in real time by monitoring the number of messages processed by the SOA infrastructure over the last 5 minutes.

Getting ready

Log on to Enterprise Manager using `http://hostname:port/em`.

How to do it...

1. From Enterprise Manager, right-click on the **soa-infra** element in the tree and choose **Monitoring | Performance Summary** in the pop-up menu.

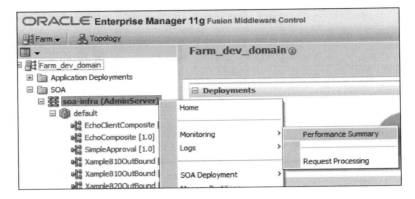

This brings up the **Performance Summary** screen that initially shows the total number of messages processed since the server startup.

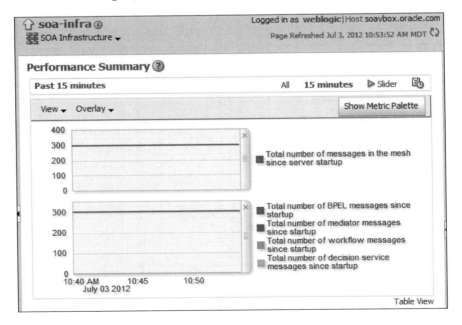

2. On the **Performance Summary** screen, click on the **Show Metric Palette** button in the upper-right corner to bring up a list of available metrics.

3. Navigate the tree to **SOA Infra Mesh | mesh** and select **Throughput of messages in the mesh in the last 5 minutes**. This will add a throughput chart to the **Performance Summary** screen. Throughput is measured by messages per second.

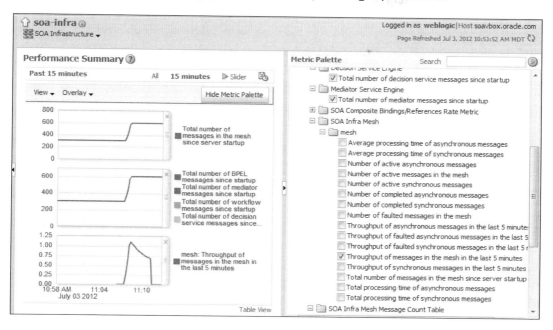

How it works...

The **Performance Summary** screen is continuously updated with the metrics requested by the observer. Unfortunately, it is not possible to save a list of metrics to monitor for later use; they must be added each time the user logs in to Enterprise Manager.

There's more...

The **Performance Summary** screen normally has a 15-minute window. However, it is possible to use the slider to zoom in on a smaller window within the last 15 minutes. To do this, click on the **Slider** link in the **Performance Summary** pane and adjust the slider to show the desired time range.

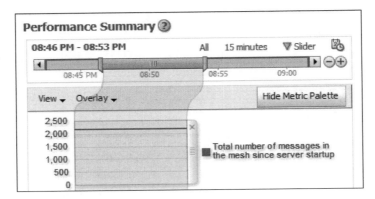

The time period can be set to 15 minutes by clicking on the **15 minutes** link, or it can be reset to all metrics since monitoring started by clicking on the **All** link.

Types of metrics

Metrics are split into different types, such as:

- Metrics that provide a number that starts when the SOA infrastructure is started, such as:
  - The total processing time of synchronous messages
  - The average processing time of asynchronous messages
  - The total number of mediator messages since startup

- Metrics that provide a point-in-time view, such as:
  - The number of active messages in the mesh
  - The number of active trading partners (a B2B metric)

- Metrics that cover the last 5 minutes, such as:
  - The throughput of asynchronous messages in the last 5 minutes
  - The throughput of faulted requests in the last 5 minutes

Sources of metrics

Metrics come from different sources, and the source is represented by its position in the metric tree. For example, B2B metrics can be found under the nodes in **Metric Palette** that start with B2B.

In addition to core SOA infrastructure (mesh) and service engines (BPEL, Mediator, rules, and so on), metrics are also collected for specific service and reference interfaces, allowing the monitoring of input requests and external calls.

Deploy Monitor Express to BAM

This recipe deploys Monitor Express to BAM so that the Monitor Express dashboard can be used to monitor the status of BPEL processes. This is an interface that can be given to a non-technical user, providing them with a view onto the current state of the BPEL processes. Before Monitor Express can be used, it must be deployed to the BAM server, and this recipe explains how to perform that deployment.

Getting ready

Open a command prompt (shell) on the machine where SOA Suite is installed. Log on to Oracle BAM at `http://hostname:port/OracleBAM` and launch **BAM Active Viewer**.

How to do it...

1. In the command shell, set the ORACLE_HOME environment variable to point to SOA Home.

   ❑ For Linux:

   ```
   $ ORACLE_HOME=/home/oracle/Middleware/OracleSOA1
   $ export ORACLE_HOME
   ```

   ❑ For Windows:

   ```
   C:\> set ORACLE_HOME=C:\Oracle\Middleware\OracleSOA1
   ```

2. Set the JAVA_HOME environment variable to point to the JDK.

   ❑ For Linux:

   ```
   $ JAVA_HOME=/home/oracle/jdk1.6.0_31
   $ export JAVA_HOME
   ```

   ❑ For Windows:

   ```
   C:\> set JAVA_HOME=C:\Oracle\jdk1.6.0_31
   ```

3. Edit the `$ORACLE_HOME/bam/config/BAMICommandConfig.xml` file and set the following:

   - `ServerName`: The name of the BAM server or localhost if the command is run on the same machine as the server
   - `ServerPort`: The listening port of the BAM server
   - `ICommand_Default_User_Name`: The administrative username
   - `ICommand_Default_Password`: The administrative user password

Sample settings are shown as follows:

```
<ServerName>soavbox</ServerName>
<ServerPort>7001</ServerPort>
<ICommand_Default_User_Name>weblogic</ICommand_Default_User_Name>
<ICommand_Default_Password>welcome1</ICommand_Default_Password>
```

4. Change the directory to `$ORACLE_HOME/bam/samples/bam/monitorexpress/bin` and run the setup command:

   - For Linux:

     ```
     $ ./setup.sh
     ```

   - For Windows:

     ```
     C:\> setup.cmd
     ```

A sample output is shown as follows:

```
BAM Home =/home/oracle/Middleware/Oracle_SOA1/bam

Using JAVA_HOME=/home/oracle/jdk1.6.0_31

Creating the Data Objects

Oracle BAM Command Utility [Build 16734, BAM Repository Version
2025] Copyright Â© 2002, 2011, Oracle and/or its affiliates. All
rights reserved.

Importing from file "/home/oracle/app/Middleware/Oracle_SOA1/
bam/samples/bam/monitorexpress/data_objects/MonitorExpress_
DataObjects.xml".

...

Reports successfully created

Setup ends successfully
```

5. Verify the Monitor Express report from **BAM Active Viewer** by pressing the **Select Report** button to bring up **Select a Report -- Webpage Dialog**.

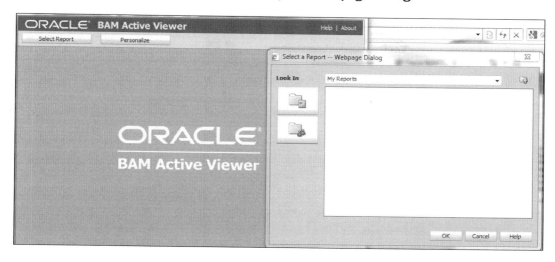

From the drop-down menu, choose **Shared Reports** and then double-click through the **Samples** and **Monitor Express** folders to reach the **Monitor Express Dashboard** report. Double-click on **Monitor Express Dashboard** to open the report and verify that it opens.

You have now successfully installed Monitor Express.

How it works...

Monitor Express is shipped as a sample set of reports by Oracle. Before use it must be deployed, and the setup script uses BAM ICommand to deploy the Monitor Express BAM objects and Monitor Express reports. After the reports are deployed, it is necessary to instrument your BPEL processes to feed data to the Monitor Express BAM objects.

Now that Monitor Express is deployed in your BAM server, you can start instrumenting your BPEL processes to be displayed in **Monitor Express Dashboard**.

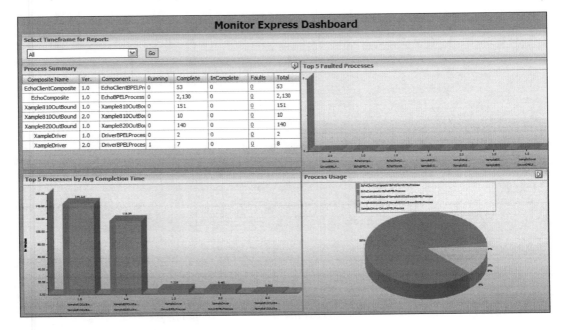

There's more...

It is possible to view the associated BAM data object used by Monitor Express using BAM Architect. It is also possible to view and edit the Monitor Express reports using BAM Active Studio.

See also

- ▶ The *Configuring BAM Adapter* recipe in this chapter
- ▶ The *Configuring a BPEL process to report status to BAM Monitor Express* recipe in this chapter

Configuring BAM Adapter

This recipe shows how to configure BAM Adapter, which is used by BAM-enabled composites. The adapter must be configured to point to the BAM server.

Getting ready

Log on to the WebLogic console `http://hostname:port/console`.

How to do it...

1. In **WebLogic Server Administration Console**, select **Deployments** from the **Domain Structure** pane.

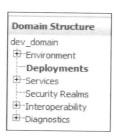

2. Locate **OracleBamAdapter** (**Resource Adapter**) and click on it.

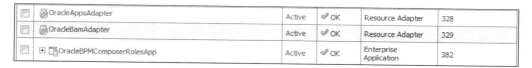

3. Navigate to the **Outbound Connection Pools** tab under the **Configuration** tab in the **Settings for OracleBamAdapter** screen.

4. Expand the **oracle.bam.adapter.adc.RMIConnectionFactory** section and click on the **eis/bam/rmi** link.

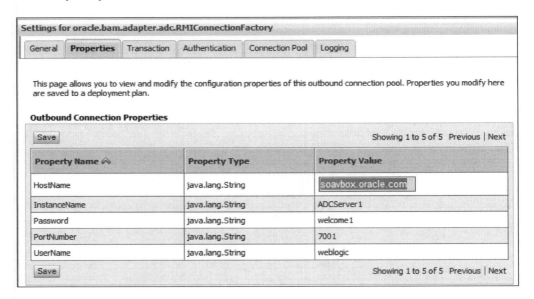

5. Set the properties to the correct values for your installation, and make sure that you press the *Enter* key after any changes.

6. When all the changes have been made, click on the **Save** button.

If prompted for a Deployment Plan location, make sure that the plan is saved in a location that is available to both the Admin server and all SOA-managed servers.

How it works...

The Monitor Express sensors in a BPEL process automatically make use of a BAM Adapter connection factory found at `eis/bam/rmi`. This provides an RMI route into the BAM server. Before this can be used, we need to configure it to point to the BAM server. Note, that there is only one BAM server in a BAM cluster because it is a singleton service. There may be multiple BAM web servers, but there is only one BAM server that hosts Active Data Cache.

See also

▶ The *Deploy Monitor Express to BAM* recipe in this chapter
▶ The *Configuring a BPEL process to report status to BAM Monitor Express* recipe in this chapter

Configuring a BPEL process to report the status to BAM Monitor Express

This recipe enables the monitoring of a BPEL process using the provided Monitor Express Dashboard. The BPEL process is instrumented so that it can populate the Monitor Express data object.

Getting ready

Open a BPEL process in JDeveloper.

How to do it...

1. In the JDeveloper BPEL editor, click on [Monitor] to switch to the monitor view.

2. In the monitor view click on the **Monitor Configuration** icon.

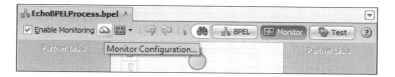

3. In the **Monitoring Configuration** dialog box, select the **Enable Activity Monitoring** checkbox. Leave the **Mode** as the default of **Scopes and Human Tasks Only**. Click on **OK** to apply the changes and enable activity monitoring for this process.

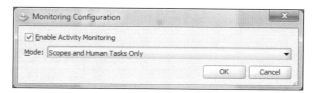

4. Using JDeveloper, deploy the modified composite to the SOA server. When deploying, make sure in the **Deploy Configuration** step that the **Ignore BPEL Monitor deployment errors** checkbox under the **BPEL Monitor** section is checked.

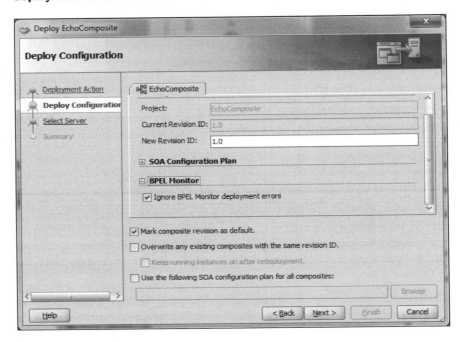

5. Execute at least one instance of the composite with the modified BPEL process and then navigate to **Monitor Express Dashboard** (see step 5 in the *Deploy Monitor Express to BAM* recipe). Verify that the modified composite and component are displayed in the **Process Summary** section of the dashboard.

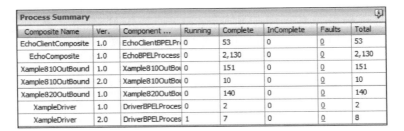

Composite Name	Ver.	Component ...	Running	Complete	InComplete	Faults	Total
EchoClientComposite	1.0	EchoClientBPELPr	0	53	0	0	53
EchoComposite	1.0	EchoBPELProcess	0	2,130	0	0	2,130
Xample810OutBound	1.0	Xample810OutBo	0	151	0	0	151
Xample810OutBound	2.0	Xample810OutBo	0	10	0	0	10
Xample820OutBound	1.0	Xample820OutBo	0	140	0	0	140
XampleDriver	1.0	DriverBPELProces	0	2	0	0	2
XampleDriver	2.0	DriverBPELProces	1	7	0	0	8

How it works...

The **Enable Activity Monitoring** checkbox allows the BPEL process to update the Monitor Express BAM object with information about what it is doing. This object is the same for all BPEL processes and collects information, such as the start and completion times for a process. The BAM data object is updated using a BAM connection factory found at `eis/bam/rmi`. This resource should be correctly configured for the BPEL process to update the BAM object. Similarly, the Monitor Express objects and reports should have been deployed before trying to deploy a BPEL process that collects the Monitor Express statistics.

There's more...

Monitor Express allows a BPEL process to be instrumented in multiple ways.

Capture points

The basic configuration of the BPEL process we did in this recipe captures the start and stop times for each scope and human workflow activity within the process. Other options are available to capture the start and stop times for all activities (**All Activities**), only human workflow (**Human Tasks Only**) or only the start and end of the BPEL process (**BPEL Process Only**).

Custom intervals

If we are interested in how long a process takes to execute between two arbitrary activities, then we can use the interval monitoring option to specify an interval name and the start and end activities. For each activity, we can specify the whereabouts of the activity, from where we wish to collect the data (at the start or the end usually).

Business indicators

Business indicators can be used to collect a business metric, such as the value of a transaction. They work by specifying the data to be collected as an XPath expression and then specifying the activities in the process from where the data should be collected.

Counters

Sometimes we just want to know how many times a given activity in a process was executed. We can do this by using a counter.

See also

- ▶ The *Deploy Monitor Express to BAM* recipe in this chapter
- ▶ The *Configure BAM Adapter* recipe in this chapter

Index

Thank you for buying
Oracle SOA Suite 11g Developer's Cookbook

About Packt Publishing

Packt, pronounced 'packed', published its first book "*Mastering phpMyAdmin for Effective MySQL Management*" in April 2004 and subsequently continued to specialize in publishing highly focused books on specific technologies and solutions.

Our books and publications share the experiences of your fellow IT professionals in adapting and customizing today's systems, applications, and frameworks. Our solution-based books give you the knowledge and power to customize the software and technologies you're using to get the job done. Packt books are more specific and less general than the IT books you have seen in the past. Our unique business model allows us to bring you more focused information, giving you more of what you need to know, and less of what you don't.

Packt is a modern, yet unique publishing company, which focuses on producing quality, cutting-edge books for communities of developers, administrators, and newbies alike. For more information, please visit our website: www.PacktPub.com.

About Packt Enterprise

In 2010, Packt launched two new brands, Packt Enterprise and Packt Open Source, in order to continue its focus on specialization. This book is part of the Packt Enterprise brand, home to books published on enterprise software – software created by major vendors, including (but not limited to) IBM, Microsoft and Oracle, often for use in other corporations. Its titles will offer information relevant to a range of users of this software, including administrators, developers, architects, and end users.

Writing for Packt

We welcome all inquiries from people who are interested in authoring. Book proposals should be sent to author@packtpub.com. If your book idea is still at an early stage and you would like to discuss it first before writing a formal book proposal, contact us; one of our commissioning editors will get in touch with you.

We're not just looking for published authors; if you have strong technical skills but no writing experience, our experienced editors can help you develop a writing career, or simply get some additional reward for your expertise.

Getting Started With Oracle SOA Suite 11g R1 – A Hands-On Tutorial

ISBN: 978-1-847199-78-2   Paperback: 482 pages

Fast track your SOA adoption – Build a Service-Oriented composite Application in just hours!

1. Offers an accelerated learning path for the much anticipated Oracle SOA Suite 11g release

2. Beginning with a discussion of the evolution of SOA, this book sets the stage for your SOA learning experience

3. Includes a comprehensive overview of the Oracle SOA Suite 11g Product Architecture

Oracle SOA Suite 11*g* R1 Developer's Guide

ISBN: 978-1-849680-18-9   Paperback: 720 pages

Develop Service-Oriented Architecture Solutions with the Oracle SOA Suite

1. A hands-on, best-practice guide to using and applying the Oracle SOA Suite in the delivery of real-world SOA applications

2. Detailed coverage of the Oracle Service Bus, BPEL PM, Rules, Human Workflow, Event Delivery Network, and Business Activity Monitoring

3. Master the best way to use and combine each of these different components in the implementation of a SOA solution

4. Illustrates key techniques and best practices using a working example of an online auction site (oBay)

Please check **www.PacktPub.com** for information on our titles

WS-BPEL 2.0 for SOA Composite Applications with Oracle SOA Suite 11g

Define, model, implement, and monitor real-world BPEL business processes with SOA-powered BPM

Foreword by
Clemens Utschig-Utschig, Sr. Principal Product Manager, Oracle SOA Suite
Harish Gaur, Director, Product Management, Oracle Fusion Middleware
Markus Zirn, VP Product Management, Oracle Fusion Middleware

Matjaz B. Juric   Marcel Krizevnik   [PACKT] enterprise

WS-BPEL 2.0 for SOA Composite Applications with Oracle SOA Suite 11g

ISBN: 978-1-847197-94-8   Paperback: 616 pages

Defi ne, model, implement, and monitor real-world BPELbusiness processes with SOA-powered BPM

1. Develop BPEL and SOA composite solutions with Oracle SOA Suite 11g

2. Efficiently automate business processes with WS-BPEL 2.0 and develop SOA composite applications.

3. Get familiar with basic and advanced BPEL 2.0.

Oracle BPM Suite 11g Developer's Cookbook

Over 80 advanced recipes to develop rich, interactive business processes using the Oracle Business Process Management Suite

Vivek Acharya   [PACKT] enterprise

Oracle BPM Suite 11g Developer's Cookbook

ISBN: 978-1-849684-22-4   Paperback: 512 pages

Over 80 advanced recipes to develop rich, interactive business processes using the Oracle Business Process Management Suite

1. Full of illustrations, diagrams, and tips with clear step-by-step instructions and real time examples to develop Industry Sample BPM Process and BPM interaction with SOA Components

2. Dive into lessons on Fault ,Performance and Rum Time Management

3. Explore User Interaction ,Deployment and Monitoring

4. Dive into BPM Process Implementation as process developer while conglomerating BPMN elements

Please check **www.PacktPub.com** for information on our titles

Printed in Great Britain
by Amazon.co.uk, Ltd.,
Marston Gate.